# PIRATES, JACK TAR, AND MEMORY

## NEW DIRECTIONS IN AMERICAN MARITIME HISTORY

# PIRATES, JACK TAR, AND MEMORY

## NEW DIRECTIONS IN AMERICAN MARITIME HISTORY

EDITED BY

Paul A. Gilje
William Pencak

MYSTIC
SEAPORT
THE MUSEUM
OF AMERICA
AND THE SEA

Printed in the United States of America

Library of Congress Cataloging in Publication Data

Gilje, Paul A., 1951-
Pirates, Jack Tar, and memory : new directions in American maritime history /
edited by Paul A. Gilje, William Pencak.
p. cm.
Includes index.
ISBN 0-939511-22-3
1. United States—History, Naval—To 1900.
2. United States—History, Naval—To 1900—Historiography.
3. Atlantic Coast (U.S.)—History, Naval.
4. Atlantic Coast (U.S.)—History, Naval—Historiography. 5. Seafaring life—United
States—History. 6. Seafaring life—United States—Historiography.
7. Sailors—United States—History. 8. Sailors—United States—Historiography.
9. Pirates—United States—History.
10. Pirates—United States—Historiography.
I. Pencak, William, 1951- II. Title.
E182.G554 2007
359'.0092—dc22
2007036488

# CONTENTS

# THE ELUSIVE JACK TAR

## PAUL A. GILJE

"Let any one trace a Cape Cod man" wrote sailor Nathaniel Ames, he "will find him performing one voyage from Boston and the next from New Orleans; today carrying plaster from Passamaquoddy to New York and tomorrow in a French whaler off the Falklands." Ames believed that following this capricious path across the high seas was a hopeless task. "It is as impossible to calculate his [the Cape Cod man's] movements as it would be to predict the direction and extent of the next skip of the most eccentric of all animals, the flea."[1] What made Jack Tar so elusive? It was more than the erratic movements and his willingness to sail under almost any flag. Jack Tar was also from the bottom of society. Generally young most sailors were under thirty— with little property, he is exactly the kind of person that is most difficult to trace. Sailors either perished at sea, or, more often, returned to land-based occupations and kept to their own anonymous life. Moreover, although by the nineteenth century most sailors could read and write, they remain relatively inarticulate for the historian who relies heavily upon diaries and records in archives that are ordinarily the product of the more affluent and successful.

Yet, since before the days of Samuel Eliot Morison intrepid scholars have sought to follow the eccentric and unpredictable lives of common seamen to tell stories that, despite the relative obscurity of the subject (and here Ames's metaphor of the flea is most apt), have had an impact on the course of history.[2] First, and most obviously, Jack Tar is an important part of Atlantic history. Over the last twenty years historians have raised a clarion for us to broaden our provincial horizons and realize that the United States, and the British American colonies that preceded it, were part of a larger Atlantic world. Ideas about race, slavery, and revolution followed the currents of the Atlantic Ocean, joining Europe, Africa, and the Americas in one interconnected whole. Manning the ships that brought goods and information over great expanses of salt water

[1]

were sailors who hailed from every part of the U. S. and many corners of the globe. A Jack Tar in 1800 might get a glimpse of Napoleon, and see the effects of racial genocide in Saint Domingue (Haiti). He might have pulled on an oar of a whaleboat in pursuit of a Leviathan, and suffered the stench of a packed slave ship delivering its human cargo to perpetual servitude. He could easily have served in a privateer—be it American, British, French, or of who knows what country—and have experienced impressment into His Majesty's Navy. He might have lived through shipwreck, or capture by pirates, or simply labored uneventfully aboard a merchant ship. Whatever his erratic course, he carried knowledge of one part of the Atlantic to another.

Second, as the brief survey of possible maritime experiences suggests, the lives of sailors made great stories. Tales of adventure on the high seas of strange lands and shipwreck reach back to Homer. Sailors themselves were famous for spinning yarns—telling their own stories—in an oral culture. But with the increased literacy of the American tar, and the rise of the democratic ideal that accompanied the age of revolution, more and more of these tales made it into print. In the first half of the nineteenth century a handful of articulate seamen helped to create an American literature of the sea. This movement began with the sea tales of James Fenimore Cooper who wrote largely from the perspective of the quarterdeck.[3] Richard Henry Dana Jr. provided the forecastle with its own special voice in *Two Years Before the Mast*.[4] The ultimate expression of this new American literature came in the sea novels of Herman Melville: not only in *Moby-Dick*, but also in *Omoo, Typee, Redburn, White Jacket, Israel Potter*, and *Billy Budd*.[5] If we are going to comprehend this American literature, we need to understand the culture from which it spawned.

But perhaps most importantly, sailors are significant because they provide us with some insight into the world of the common man. While there is no gainsaying the impact of great men on history, the whole thrust of social history since the 1960s has been to understand how regular people both affected and were affected by the larger course of historical events. Ever since Jesse Lemisch proclaimed the importance of this history "from the bottom up," sailors have been central to our understanding of the American working-class experience.[6] Seamen not only were the most Atlantic of denizens in the Atlantic world, they were often the important players in key events in the eighteenth and nineteenth centuries. In particular, sailors assumed a vital role in the rioting of the resistance movement that helped to drive the British North American colonies into rebellion against King George III. Atlantic sailors, too, were among the first workers to rely upon collective action as a form of labor negotiation. The term strike, some scholars believe, evolved from sailors striking the sails when they refused to labor for less than what they considered an appropriate wage.[7]

Some historians have emphasized the radical nature of this maritime work force. Lemisch believes that American seamen entered the American Revolution based on sincere convictions about defending their own life, liberty, and property connected to their experience in opposing British impressment and their participation in riots against imperial regulation. This commitment, Lemisch holds, led to a special patriotism that can be seen in the sailor's enthusiasm to fight in the revolution and his desire to escape imprisonment when captured by the British.[8] Marcus Rediker and Peter Linebaugh extend this analysis, adding an international dimension. Rediker's earlier work argues that the Anglo-American sailor rejected the capitalist ethos of the merchant class.[9] Together Rediker and Linebaugh wrote *The Many-Headed Hydra: Sailors, Slaves and Commoners and the Hidden History of the Atlantic* in which they claim that there was a persistent thread running through the course of Atlantic history that tied sailors, slaves, and laborers together in an ideal of communism, antinomianism, and equality in opposition to the forces of capital. Although they push shreds of evidence too hard and too fast, their vision of the Atlantic is breathtaking and highlights the significance of Jack Tar as a transmitter of information and ideas.[10]

Other scholars are less cosmic in their ambitions, but use the study of seamen to get at key issues of American history. Jeff Bolster's examination of the African-American sailor provides both a wonderful portrait of the broader maritime experience and the particular way life aboard ships could challenge traditional notions of race. In the wake of the emancipation of many slaves during the American Revolution, work at sea became one of the few viable employment opportunities for freed African Americans. Thousands of young African Americans signed aboard American vessels, serving cheek by jowl with white seamen, sharing the same forecastle and eating out of a common pot. Although racial tension could exist aboard ships and in ports, the shared work experience helped to transcend, if only for a few decades, the harsh boundaries of race. By the 1830s, after Southern states passed Negro Seamen Acts to limit the time a black sailor could stay in port, and after racism intensified in the North, African Americans became increasingly relegated to only two berths aboard ship: cook or steward.[11]

Margaret Creighton and Lisa Norling explore crucial shoreside attachments and deeper meanings of gender identity for nineteenth-century Americans. Creighton examines the world of whalemen, arguing that the boundary between shipboard life and life on land was not sharp and distinct. Despite a peculiar maritime culture and special male identity, whalemen remained connected to the shore through personal attachments, especially to women, work, and culture.[12] Norling traces important gender changes among the men and women who dominated whaling in the eighteenth and nineteenth century. Although living apart while the husband was at sea, men and women in the eighteenth century "shared a vision of the world as one unified place." By the early nineteenth century the notion of a separate sphere had developed where "new ideas about sexual difference . . . defined women and men as fundamentally different beings."[13]

Daniel Vickers offers us a complicated and variegated portrait of the social world of American seamen. Like Norling and Creighton, he emphasizes shoreside attachments. Indeed, in his most recent work Vickers demonstrates that for many sailors life at sea represented just one component of their working life. Most Jack Tars, in other words, went to sea for a few years in their late teens or early twenties and then found employment on land, sometimes in maritime trades, like the rigger Ashley Bowen, sometimes as farmers, and sometimes as day laborers. Those men who remained at sea longer, at least from the 2,000 individuals who sailed out of Salem, Massachusetts, that Vickers studied, became officers and captains as professional seamen. Vickers's publications also emphasize the differing experiences of seamen, depending on locality and time period. In other words, what it meant to be a whaleman from Nantucket, a fisherman from Marblehead, or a merchant seaman from Salem differed depending when you sailed, your social origins, and the town you came from.[14]

My own work focuses on the impact of the age of revolution on sailors and surveys the variety of conflicting and ambiguous meanings "liberty" had for the men who lived and worked on the waterfront. While I reject any monolithic portrait, I maintain that there were certain elements of consistency in American maritime culture that hold as true for the eighteenth as they do for the nineteenth century—sailors often behaved badly ashore, had relatively persistent ideas of gender emphasizing their male identity and right to exploit women, and, in turn worked hard and remained an abused labor force. I also trace Jack Tar's participation in the American Revolution and his emergence as a symbol of the nation during the early republic. *Liberty on the Waterfront* ends with a discussion of the efforts of middle-class reformers to reach sailors and an exploration of the failure and success of sailors to articulate their own grievances by the mid-nineteenth century.[15]

This new social history of the maritime world has allowed us to follow the movements of the sailor in much greater detail than many of us had imagined a quarter of a century ago. It has also pointed the way to sources that show Jack Tar may not have been as inarticulate as we first believed. But there is still more to do. Bill and I put this book together in an effort to further this endeavor. Our aim was to identify scholarship from all levels of the profession, and we therefore solicited essays from graduate students, newly minted PhDs, and senior scholars whose work has taken them to maritime subjects. The result is a collection of wide-ranging studies, some of which builds on previous work, but much of which represents previously unpublished research. We believe that all of the contributions to this book reflect the exciting new directions and ways to chase the elusive Jack Tar and to understand maritime history.

The first two essays deal with pirates. Rediker demonstrated the centrality of the pirate experience to the world of Jack Tar with a seminal article in 1981, in his *Between the Devil and the Deep Blue Sea,* and more recently *Villains of all Nations.*[16] In these works Rediker portrays pirates not as cutthroats, but as would-be proletarians rejecting a capitalist world order. Amy Bushnell does not take on Rediker directly. Instead she explores the complex relationship between legitimate and illegitimate trade in the borderlands of Spanish Florida. On the ambiguous fringes of empire, what made a pirate was less a specific action, and more the view of authorities. If authorities were willing to trade with ships from France or England, fine. If not, the same men who sailed on a merchant ship could turn to pillage and piracy. Crystal Williams addresses the Rediker thesis head on. Examining many of the same sources as Rediker, she comes to a very different conclusion. Admitting that "pirates exhibited some nascent yearnings for economic and social equality," she denies that there was any coherent ideology advocating "an egalitarian collectivist society." Instead, pirates were the "ultimate opportunists" who often violently sought individual gain.

Three essays are rooted in the eighteenth century. Michael Jarvis surveys the nature of the ship as an artifact, reminding us that we cannot truly understand the experience of Jack Tar without fully comprehending the physical surroundings of his work environment. The ship was a commodity whose form reflected its uses and the particular needs of the marketplace. It was also a social space that molded relationships. Jarvis instructs us that the ship itself, with its own history and life cycle, was important in the development of the Atlantic world.

Sarah Purcell and Frank Cogliano build on recent studies of memory and turn to the later recitals of Jack Tar's ordeal during the American Revolution. Purcell concentrates on the *Narrative and Captivity of John Blatchford*, published shortly after the war. She argues that this obscure sailor, who suffered imprisonment and served under six different flags during the course of the war, helped to define American nationality by publishing his woeful tale. Blatchford not only asserted an allegiance to the United States, but also claimed ownership of a new national identity by right of his sacrifice. Cogliano uses the reminiscences of the American Revolution by several sailors and compares them to pension applications in the nineteenth century. He finds that the pension applications hardly mentioned the prisoner-of-war experience while the published autobiographies dwelled upon it. Cogliano believes that sailors were willing to share the story of their imprisonment with family and friends, and even included them in their life stories, but were reluctant to go public officially with their saga of suffering as prisoners of war since that experience also represented a "whiff of failure." Cogliano thus reminds us that memory is often a consciously select process that depended heavily upon the use to which that memory was to be put.

The last four essays deal largely with the nineteenth century. Hester Blum, like Purcell and Cogliano, uses the literature of the sea as her starting point. Blum writes about James Fenimore Cooper's one foray into the genre of the common seaman's tale. She explores the peculiar interaction between Cooper the author and Ned Myers the yarn spinner in the production of a book that was both an economic and critical failure, yet remains a testament to the rising significance of the memory of the common man in the mid-nineteenth century. Dan Hicks offers us a multifaceted look at the naval experience of the War of 1812 centered on ship-to-ship combat. Sea battles were "affairs of honor" with an ethic of behavior similar to the dueling code that so consumed the officer corps and American "gentlemen"—like Aaron Burr and Alexander Hamilton—in the early republic. As such, these engagements loomed larger than their military significance to the war effort as symbols of American maritime prowess against the greatest naval power on the high seas, Great Britain. Hicks, however, extends his reading of the cultural experience of naval battles to their shoreside celebrations, which asserted American national identity and were used for partisan purposes. Inclusion of the common seamen in these celebrations, Hicks suggests, was packed with ambiguity since mainstream society did not quite trust Jack Tar always to behave himself when feted and treated with food and (especially) drink.

Both Amy Mitchell-Cook and Matthew Raffety address issues of authority and the relationship between officers and crews aboard ship. Mitchell-Cook studies shipwreck narratives to see what they have to say about the relationship between the quarterdeck and the forecastle. She finds that although there was an ideal of absolute authority of captain over crew, seamen often challenged and questioned that authority. Shipwrecks may have tested this relationship further, but shipwreck narratives, which were often authored by officers, were written to demonstrate the importance of maintaining the captain's authority in the face of adversity. Raffety traces key developments of discipline aboard ships in the first half of the nineteenth century. Pressure from the men at sea and reformers on land increasingly placed restrictions on the use of corporal punishment. Rather than abdicating discipline, captains sought a variety of means to sidestep these restrictions and maintain the discipline they believed necessary to control the ship.

All the essays add to our knowledge of Jack Tar. We see him as a pirate, learn something of the ships he sailed, and share his experience in the Revolutionary War and War of 1812. We also see him as a spinner of yarns—a great story teller—helping to mold his own and our national identity, while contributing to the development of a unique American literature. We see some Jacks seeking social mobility. We see others challenging authority aboard ships and during shipwrecks. If Jack in some ways remains elusive, and we still find it "impossible to calculate his movements," at least we will have traced further a part of his "eccentric" path as he is about to skip, like a flea, to his next unpredictable destination.

# NOTES

[1] Nathaniel Ames, *Nautical Reminiscences* (Providence: William Marshal, 1832), 36.

[2] Samuel Eliot Morison, *The Maritime History of Massachusetts, 1783-1860* (Boston: Houghton Mifflin Company, 1921; Boston: Northeastern University Press, 1979).

[3] For an evaluation of Cooper's sea literature, see Thomas Philbrick, *James Fenimore Cooper and the Development of American Sea Fiction* (Cambridge, Mass: Harvard University Press, 1961).

[4] Richard Henry Dana Jr., *Two Years Before the Mast: A Personal Narrative of Life at Sea*, ed. Thomas Philbrick (New York: Penguin Books, 1981).

[5] Herman Melville, *Moby-Dick, or the Whale* (1851; New York: The Modern Library, 1982); *Typee: A Peep at Polynesian Life During a Four Month's Residence in a Valley of the Marquesas* (1846; New York: New American Library, 1964); *Omoo: A Narrative of Adventures in the South Seas*, ed. Harrison Hayford (1847; Evanston: Northwestern University Press, 1968); *Redburn: His First Voyage. Being the Sailor-boy Confessions and Reminiscences of the Son-of-a Gentleman, in the Merchant Service*, ed. Harold Beaver (1849; New York: Penguin Books, 1976); *White Jacket: or the World in a Man-of-War* (1850; New York: New American Library, 1981); *Israel Potter: His Fifty Years of Exile*, ed. Harrison Hayford, et al. (1855; Evanston: Northwestern University Press, 1982), *Billy Budd and Other Stories*, ed. Harold Beaver (1924; New York: Penguin Books, 1967).

[6] Jesse Lemisch, "The American Revolution from the Bottom Up," in *Toward a New Past: Dissenting Essays in American History*, ed. Barton J. Bernstein (New York: Pantheon Books, 1968), 3-45.

[7] Peter Linebaugh and Marcus Rediker, "The Many-Headed Hydra: Sailors, Slaves and the Atlantic Working Class in the Eighteenth Century," in *Jack Tar in History: Essays in the History of Maritime Life and Labour*, ed. Colin Howell and Richard Twomey (Fredericton, New Brunswick: Acadiensis Press, 1991), 29-30.

[8] Jesse Lemisch, "Jack Tar in the Streets: Merchant Seamen in the Politics of Revolutionary America," *William and Mary Quarterly* 3rd ser., 25 (1968): 371-407; "'Listening to the Inarticulate:' William Widger's Dream and the Loyalties of American Revolutionary Seamen in British Prisons," *Journal of Social History* 3 (1969): 1-29; *Jack Tar vs. John Bull: The Role of New York's Seamen in Precipitating the Revolution* (New York: Garland Publishing, 1997).

[9] Marcus Rediker, *Between the Devil and the Deep Blue Sea: Merchant Seamen, Pirates, and the Anglo-American World, 1700-1750* (Cambridge: Cambridge University Press, 1987).

[10] Peter Linebaugh asnd Marcus Rediker, *The Many-Headed Hydra: Sailors, Slaves, Commoners, and the Hidden History of the Revolutionary Atlantic* (Boston: Beacon Press, 2000). See also Rediker, "A Motley Crew of Rebels: Sailors, Slaves, and the Coming of the American Revolution," in *The Transforming Hand of Revolution: Reconsidering the American Revolution as a Social Movement*, ed. Ronald Hoffman and Peter J. Albert (Charlottesville: University of Virginia Press, 1995), 155-98. .

[11] W. Jeffrey Bolster, *Black Jacks: African American Seamen in the Age of Sail* (Cambridge, Mass.: Harvard University Press, 1997).

[12] Margaret S. Creighton, *Rites and Passages: The Experience of American Whaling, 1830-1870* (Cambridge: Cambridge University Press, 1995), 151, 171; Creighton, *Dogwatch and Liberty Days: Seafaring Life in the Nineteenth Century* (Salem, Mass.: Peabody Museum of Salem, 1982).

[13] Lisa Norling, *Captain Ahab Had a Wife: New England Women and the Whalefishery, 1720-1870* (Chapel Hill: University of North Carolina Press, 2000), 7. For other discussions of gender in the maritime community see Margaret S. Creighton and Lisa Norling, eds., *Iron Men, Wooden Women: Gender and Seafaring in the Atlantic World, 1799-1920* (Baltimore: Johns Hopkins University Press, 1996); David Cordingly, *Women Sailors and Sailors' Women: An Untold Maritime History* (New York: Random House, 2001); Elaine Forman Crane, *Ebb Tide in New England: Women, Seaports, and Social Change, 1630-1800* (Boston: Northeastern University Press, 1998); Linda M. Maloney, "Women in Maritime America: The Nineteenth Century," in *Seamen in Society*, ed. Paul Adam (Bucharest: Commision Internationale d'Histoire Maritime, 1980), 3, 113-21; Suzanne J. Stark, *Female Tars: Women Aboard Ship in the Age of Sail* (Annapolis: Naval Institute Press, 1996).

[14] Daniel Vickers, "Nantucket Whalemen in the Deep Sea Fishery: The Changing Anatomy of the Early American Labor Force," *Journal of American History* 72 (1985): 277-97; *Farmers and Fishermen: Two Centuries of Work in Essex County, Massachusetts, 1630-1850* (Chapel Hill: University of North Carolina Press, 1994); "An Honest Tar: Ashley Bowen of Marblehead," *New England Quarterly* 69 (1996): 531-53; Daniel Vickers and Vince Walsh, "Young Men of the Sea: The Sociology of Seafaring in Eighteenth-Century Salem, Massachusetts," *Social History* 24 (1999): 17-38; Vickers and Walsh, *Young Men and the Sea: Yankee Seafarers in the Age of Sail* (New Haven: Yale University Press, 2005).

[15] Paul A. Gilje, *Liberty on the Waterfront: American Maritime Culture in the Age of Revolution* (Philadelphia: University of Pennsylvania Press, 2004).

[16] Marcus Rediker, "'Under the Banner of King Death': The Social World of Anglo-American Pirates, 1716 to 1726," *William and Mary Quarterly* 3rd ser., 38 (1981): 203-27; *Between the Devil and the Deep Blue Sea*, 254-87; *Villains of All Nations: Atlantic Pirates in the Golden Age* (Boston: Beacon Press, 2004)

# I

# HOW TO FIGHT A PIRATE

Provincials, Royalists,
and the Raiding of San Marcos de Apalache

AMY TURNER BUSHNELL

Foreign ships in Spanish waters stood in need of friendly ports, places where they could take refuge from storms, take on fuel, water, provisions, and naval stores, and possibly careen a vessel or turn over a cargo. Over the course of the sixteenth century, Spanish colonists desperate for markets and manufac tures allowed French, English, and Dutch corsairs to drop anchor in their ports. Trade with corsairs was called *rescate*, a word also used for barter, ran- som, and trade goods. Alarmed at the expansion of illicit trade and privateer- ing, the Spanish Crown ceased to classify sea rovers as legitimate combatants and began to punish them as pirates.[1] Fortifications arose and *naos* were con- verted into galleons in the major Spanish American ports, but in matters of defense as of supply, the inhabitants of the minor ports were on their own. When foreign sails appeared, they could only head for the hills. As late as 1639, the governor in Havana reported that the Cuban coast was unsafe for two or three leagues inland.[2]

In the seventeenth century, new enemies appeared: the Indies-based bucca- neers, self-licensed to commit acts of piracy. From their origins as hidehunters in northern Hispaniola, the "Brethren of the Coast" developed into logwood cutters, wreckers, and seaborne raiders who came ashore, Viking-like, to sack settlements, as Henry Morgan famously did at Maracaibo and Panama, Laurens de Graff at Campeche, and Michel, the Sieur de Grammont, at Caracas and Veracruz. Large raids could take years to organize. Meanwhile, the various bands of buccaneers kept themselves in condition by descending on the coastal towns of the Yucatan and the northern Gulf to raid storehouses and capture divers, guides, and hostages to trade for provisions and supplies.

It was in the buccaneers' interest to keep the minor ports in operation—to milk, not kill, the cow. They therefore came to an accommodation with local inhabitants in the stylized raid, by whose unwritten rules defense was limited, damage contained, and honor satisfied. From the standpoint of provincial Spaniards and Indians, paying off pirates was part of the cost of doing business in the peripheries of empire. From the Crown's point of view, the stylized raid, like the system of rescate before it, was flagrant collusion. Spain was beset by enemies, and her subjects were giving them aid and comfort.

For our purposes, Spain's subjects in America can be classified as either royalist or provincial, depending on whether their interests and the Crown's were in harmony or at odds. This essay, taking as an example the raiding of a minor Florida port and the ensuing dispute over how to fight a pirate, argues that royalist rules and provincial praxis may well have been irreconcilable.

San Marcos, nine miles up the St. Marks River from Apalachee Bay on the Gulf of Mexico, was the principal outlet for Apalache, a fertile province of some thirty Indian towns and villages set in the red hills of Florida. San Luís, the largest town, lay twenty miles north of San Marcos on the site of present Tallahassee. Smallest of Florida's three mission provinces, Apalache was also the newest, most populous, and farthest from the *presidio* of St. Augustine, the colony's one Spanish city, which lay tucked in the corner of a right angle formed by two lines of earlier missions, those of Guale reaching up the Atlantic coast and those of Timucua stretching across the peninsula to the marshes of the Gulf.

Spaniards had been prevented from expanding into those regions whose rivers debouched into the Gulf by Calusa, Pohoy, and Tocobaga naval power, but that power had been challenged by the swarming of treasure salvors and pirates around the 1622 wreck of the flagship *Maravilla* off Matecumbe Key.[3] Conversions began in Apalache in 1633 as an outreach of new missions in western Timucua. In 1637, Governor Luís de Horruytiner (1633-38) sent presidio pilots to chart and mark the channel of the St. Marks River, allowing the western missions to be supplied by sea from Havana instead of 200 miles overland from St. Augustine. The Indians were reportedly jubilant to see a ship in their ports, and "many asked for baptism." Two years later, Governor Damián de Vega Castro y Pardo (1638-45) opened a direct sea route between St. Augustine and San Marcos and began to provision the presidio with Apalache corn.[4]

Like other unguarded ports, San Marcos on occasion traded with corsairs. From the beginning, there were reports that "ships of enemies were entering there without anyone to report it." Informed that the *naturales* were trading with the enemy, Governor Diego de Rebolledo (1654-58) garrisoned San Luís. No sooner did the soldiers reach the province than a vessel of corsairs appeared at San Marcos and was "refreshed," in a classic case of *rescate*. Christian charity, explained the Franciscans, had moved them to succor "one little frigate in distress," "provisionless" and "defeated" by the sea.[5]

Everyone who counted had an interest in what passed through the western port. The governors commandeered a large share of Apalache's produce to provision the presidio. The friars, through their syndics, sold another portion to beautify their churches and pay off a loan. The *floridanos*, who had long since infiltrated the garrison and royal treasury, were the link to Cuban merchants and shipowners. The chiefs, "*señores naturales de la tierra*," controlled resources of land and labor and were middlemen in the trade with Indian groups to the north.[6] Unburdened by customs officials, San Marcos became an important outlet for deerskins, ranch products, and foodstuffs, which found a ready market in Cuba to sustain the growing population of Havana and provision the fleets of the Indies.[7]

Recognizing the ease with which a royally appointed official could be subverted by opportunities for profit, the Crown did not fully trust its own appointees. When, after the 1655 capture of Jamaica, Governor Alonso de Aranguíz y Cortes (1659-63) proposed to fortify San Marcos and preempt the English in the Gulf, the *Junta de Guerra* commented: "The governors of Florida, this one like his predecessors, for reasons of personal gain want to enlarge the military in order to enlarge their business ventures and be better placed to take advantage of the Indians. That this governor should offer to build a fort without cost to the royal treasury is proof of it."[8]

A port that generated no customs revenues could not expect to be fortified. Supporting the presidio and provinces was costing the Crown nearly fifty thousand ducats a year as it was, and as late as 1657, San Marcos had yet to produce a single *real*.[9]

In 1668 the privateer Robert Searles, with a license from the governor of Jamaica, attacked St. Augustine, shooting down women and children in the streets. As a result, the Crown granted the presidio an extra 10,000 ducats a year with which to start building a stone fort, the Castillo de San Marcos, which stands today in St. Augustine. At the request of Governor Pablo de Hita y Salazar, a smaller fort was authorized for San Marcos in Apalache, but not funded.[10] The need for it would soon become apparent.

In June 1677, a party of French and English buccaneers slipped up the St. Marks River and seized a frigate belonging to Havana merchant Diego de

Florencia. The vessel, lying at anchor near the warehouse at San Marcos Landing, was loaded with deerskins from Apalache and ranch products from Timucua, picked up at the port of San Martín on the Suwannee River, western outlet for the Province of Timucua.[11] In the attack, two Indian guards were killed and others injured. Shipmaster Juan de la Rosa escaped in his small-clothes, with bullets singing around him. In the warehouse the raiders found further deerskins, along with the kind of rescates used to buy them, mostly beads and iron tools, consigned to Juan Fernández de Florencia, local rancher, merchant, and acting *teniente*, or lieutenant governor, of Apalache Province.[12] In La Rosa's sea chest they found a valuable chunk of ambergris belonging to the Florencias and asked their captives how much they thought it was worth.

The pirates took three prisoners: Captain Antonio Francisco de Herrera, the officer-in-charge, Fray Francisco de Medina, and Fray Juan de Mercado. For their combined return the Franciscans of Apalache paid a ransom of thirty hogs. Exchanging captives for provisions was a common practice. Dutch corsair Cornelis Corneliszoon Jol, *Pié de Palo*, boasted to Cuban authorities in 1640 that he held for that purpose forty or fifty soldiers, civilians, and priests, and in Florida he could readily find more.[13]

On the lowlands between the marshes of the coast and the piedmont were several villages of outsiders who lived under Apalache protection. The Yamasees of Candelaria were tanners. The Chines of Asunción, "on the path to the sea," handled the traffic on the St. Marks river system and did some coastal navigation. The Tocobagas on the Wacissa River, which provided access by water to the large town of Ivitachuco, were coastal pilots and did the lightering across the bars of the Wacissa and the Suwannee.[14]

After the events of 1677, Governor Pablo de Hita Salazar (1675-80) advised the Tocobagas to close the Wacissa channel and withdraw from the coast so they could not be captured and used as guides. The governor's previous appointment as Corregidor of Vera Cruz had given him ample experience with pirates, and the advice was warranted. Indian mariners with a knowledge of local waters often fell into enemy hands when presidio ships were taken or coastal villages raided. Probably in response to a similar warning, the Chines moved farther from the coast. But the Tocobagas answered evasively that the Wacissa's main channel was already blocked by fallen trees and that they took their canoes out by a secret passage, and the governor did not press the matter. Experiments on the northern coast of Hispaniola had shown that, as a measure against rescate, resettlement was a mistake: it provided maroons and hidehunters with a place to live outside the rule of law, while the displaced settlers merely took their unruly habits elsewhere.[15]

After consulting with the treasury officials and Franciscans, Hita Salazar resolved to have the Indians start immediately on "some slight fort" to serve until the Crown should release funds for a more substantial one. He ordered military engineer Enrique Primo de Rivera to San Marcos, made arrangements with the chiefs for laborers and corn, and sent to Spain for a thousand pesos' worth of European manufactures of low unitary value and ready convertibility.[16] The Apalaches who did the construction, drawn from a provincial population of around 8,700, descended to San Marcos in weekly shifts. They drew a ration of two and a half pounds of corn a day and wages of one real, paid weekly in goods that they could exchange with neighboring tribes: hawksbells in two sizes, knives with black or white hafts, and scissors.[17]

The castillo of San Marcos de Apalache was erected on the point of land where the Wakulla River joins the upper St. Marks. As contemporaries knew the landscape, to the east were the bluffs and narrow beaches of the Tagabona; to the west, the snake-infested palmettos outlining the banks of the Guacara.[18] The castillo was a small, sixty-seven-foot-square stockade of palm logs whitewashed to look like plastered masonry, with a shallow moat flushed by river water. The four bastions were aimed in the four cardinal directions. In site plans the castillo appears to balance precariously on one corner.

The hamlet of San Marcos, a little over a mile north of the fort, contained a handful of palm-thatched huts, a circular Indian lodge called the *bujío*, and a warehouse, all of them probably built on pilings. There was also a landing place, which may or may not have had a wharf. Beyond San Marcos stretched a sea of sawgrass, with the narrow, elevated path to San Luís disappearing into a distant stand of pines. Placed on a site prone to flooding and short on firewood and fresh water, the post had attracted few inhabitants in its fifty years of existence. The castillo was manned by weekly detachments from the twenty-two-man garrison of San Luís, mostly younger men, and a similar detail of native auxiliaries guarded the warehouse. In 1682, the warden of the fort and perhaps the ensign were the only soldiers on permanent assignment at the "redoubt and river of San Marcos." There were, by contrast, seven soldiers assigned to the so-called "conquest of Apalachicola."[19]

The staunchly royalist Governor Juan Marquez Cabrera (1680-87), who succeeded Hita Salazar, believed that Spaniards were the only soldiers fit to occupy the 350 *plazas*, or man-spaces, in the Florida garrison. In the Crown's opinion, which he shared, floridanos and Indians should train in their respective militias and rise to the defense of their own homes and families unpaid. Since the 1660s, however, Spain had been unable to supply the presidio's demand for soldiers without resorting to Mexico City jails, filled with mestizos. To avoid putting Mexicans on the roster, Florida governors had given plazas to floridanos. Many of these were officers in the reserves, drawing the pay of a soldier without performing guard duty. One company showed a ratio of fifty-one officers to sixty-two soldiers. Furthermore, the governors had retained on the rolls officers and soldiers who had married into floridano families against regulations. Among those who had married without license was the former governor's son, Juan de Hita. By the time Marquez Cabrera arrived, at least half the garrison was Florida-born. Between 1680 and 1683 the governor discharged a total of twenty-four naturales, yet such was the shortage of Spaniards that he was left with 130 floridanos in the garrison, not counting fifteen plazas to widows and minors. If, like his successor, Diego de Quiroga y Losada (1687-93), Marquez Cabrera followed a policy of reserving posts in the provinces for *naturales*; probably well over half of the soldiers in Apalache were provincials.[20]

In the winter of 1681-82 a band of 400 French and English buccaneers under an unknown captain established themselves on Anclote Key near present Tarpon Springs to give their attention to the Keys and the Gulf.[21] Ships sailing outside of convoy, called *navíos de permiso*, were their natural prey: dispatch boats, fishing boats, supply frigates, and the pigs-and-chickens sloops that provisioned the fleets of the Indies. Within six months they had taken seven prizes, among them a St. Augustine supply frigate on her way home from Vera Cruz under the command of Salvador de Cigarroa, a lesser official in the treasury who enjoyed the rank of sergeant major in the reserves. In the Searles raid fourteen years before, Cigarroa had lost his wife and a baby daughter, and another daughter had been crippled for life. He surrendered the frigate without firing a shot.[22]

That was in January 1682. Two months later, a sail was reported in Apalache Bay. Pedro de los Arcos, warden of the castillo at San Marcos, was at San Luís making his Lenten confession.[23] As was the custom, Ensign Juan de Herrera, in charge during the warden's absence, notified Teniente Andrés Pérez at San Luís that a ship was coming into port. Crossing the bar of the St. Marks at high tide, the sloop came carefully up the channel between the oyster beds, made port, and anchored a stone's throw from the fort. She was out of Havana, property of the Cuban merchant Juan de Ayala.[24] Shipmaster Alonso Díaz Mejía had a packet of mail to deliver and two Franciscan passengers to disembark.

Late that night, the eighteenth of March, Arcos returned to San Marcos with three soldiers. If they were afoot or on horseback, they probably came in by the road from San Luís. An alternate, partly water route would have taken them by way of San Martín de Tomoli, a town overlooking the flatlands from Cody Scarp, where canoes were available for travel below the fall line of the Wakulla.[25] All was in order when Arcos arrived, and he sent his escort back to San Luís the next morning. During the day, a second party from San Luís arrived to welcome the passengers and receive the cargo: Teniente Pérez, two more Franciscans, one of them a lay brother, and merchant Juan Fernández de Florencia.

Apparently it did not occur to anyone—soldiers, friars, floridanos, Indians, or Cubans—that pirates too might have spotted the ship and be waiting for cover of darkness to follow her into port. San Marcos retired for the night. Pérez, Florencia, and one soldier put up in the bujío, along with six Indians from the guard of the warehouse. Warden Pedro de Arcos, his ensign, and five soldiers were quartered in the castillo. The crew of the sloop stayed on board, but shipmaster Díaz and the cabin boy slept in the castillo to escape mosquitos, as did the Franciscans.

Three years earlier, when the castillo was new, Hita Salazar had written out a set of instructions for its first warden, advising him to build a watchtower-beacon down on the Gulf and man it with two soldiers and two Indians during warm weather, the season of pirates, lest "a boatload of enemies" should "hide in the bay that the River of Wacissa makes at Cassina Point and from there introduce themselves by the River of San Marcos undetected."[26] But there were no watchers that evening, the nineteenth of March, when sixty-six French buccaneers left their frigate off Cassina Point and rowed into the St. Marks on the rising tide.

The pirates, in three fast, light *piraguas*, reached the confluence of the rivers before midnight. The moon came out as if on cue to reveal the white walls and menacing gun embrasures of the castillo. They drew back on their oars; then, seeing what was either a mast or a tree trunk, squatted down to view it in silhouette. It was the mast of the sloop.[27] They pulled the piraguas over to a point of land and stepped ashore, but the terrain was too swampy for walking. Daylight was approaching and their boats were knocking against each other in the falling tide. They returned to the piraguas and sat awhile in debate; then the captain came to a decision and they headed in their boats for the sloop.

[17]

Antonio de Benavides, the youngest soldier in the fort, was on watch. It was a cold night for the middle of March, and he went down to the kitchen to get warm. When he returned to his post at three or four o'clock in the morning and looked toward the water he saw a large, unidentified floating object. Antonio awoke corporal-of-the-guard Juan de Villalobos, who grabbed up a musket and ran to the wall. What he made out was not one large ghostly vessel but three small ones. Villalobos shouted, "Who goes there?" There was no answer. He raised his musket and fired.

One of the Franciscans awakened Arcos, who sent for the shipmaster. By the time Díaz got to the wall, voices were coming over the water. He shouted to warn first mate Francisco Romero and the others on the sloop: "To arms! To arms! The enemy is in the port!" As the first piragua drew up alongside the sloop, Romero and the crew jumped overboard. Díaz continued shouting to alert those in the bujío. The intruders responded with a shotgun blast in his direction. Yelling "Spaniards, to arms!" he went below, found a loaded musket leaning against the wall of the guardhouse, and rushed back to fire into the darkness in the sloop's direction.

The less excitable Villalobos thought he heard up to forty men wade ashore and divide into two parties, one of them heading toward the fort, the other toward the warehouse and bujío. Díaz continued to shout for ammunition, and when it came he managed to reload his musket and get off a second shot. His voice awakened Ensign Herrera, who ran with his weapons to the wall.

The real firepower in the castillo lay in the four iron cannon, two- and four-pounders. Díaz directed a soldier to aim one of the pieces toward the sloop and fire, but the gun carriage was caught and would not move. A second soldier refused to help the first and the two began to quarrel: "Pícaro!" and "Voto a Dios con armas!" Ensign Herrera, hurrying past to an embrasure overlooking the water, saw the carriage collapse. The gun knocked down Villalobos and fell on him, injuring his ribs.

By this time the enemy had encircled the castillo. Ensign Herrera repositioned himself at a landward embrasure, where he fought until daybreak, except for a brief pause to put on his clothes. As the castillo came into view in the light of dawn the attackers realized that the eighteen-foot walls were not stone but wood, a virtual stage set. The captain called down to the piraguas for grenades to set them on fire. This was too much for the listening friars. When Ensign Herrera returned to his post he found Fray Juan de León calling to the attackers through the porthole, asking for quarter. Turning to Herrera, Fray León urged him to go down and open the gate. Forgetting himself, the ensign swore, "No quarter! Voto a Cristo!" Another Franciscan, Fray Juan Ángel, opened his arms wide and prayed: "Lord, let them take me, not kill me!"

Soldiers heard Díaz protesting, "I'm not going to get involved, Padres!" and snatches of an argument between Warden Arcos and Ensign Herrera: "No, not the door," "our reputations," "burn to death," "friars be killed;" then Arcos again: "Padre, leave us," and "Padres, what are you doing? We shall die before we surrender!"—which the Franciscans told him was no solution at all. When they demanded, "Are you going to let us be burned alive?" Arcos threw his hands in the air and cried, "What are you waiting for, Padres? Speak!"

The French captain, surprised to see friars instead of soldiers show themselves on the wall to ask for quarter, asked them whether they spoke for everyone. As if in answer the gate swung open and the drawbridge started down. Arcos was standing on the curtain with the three friars "singing quarter" when the pirates strode in.

The warden found time to improve on this story, of course, before his court-martial. As he then told it, a friar had awakened him with news of the assault. He had ordered the men to their posts and had fought beside them for two hours, firing one of the guns until the very carriage had fallen to pieces. It was the friars, he said, who had taken it upon themselves to open the gate while he was down in the magazine getting ammunition, and the enemy were in the apron of the castillo before he knew it. If anyone was to blame, he said, it was Teniente Pérez, who could have come to his aid and did not.[28]

Those who were in the bujío at the time of the attack—the teniente, his party, and the crew of the sloop—had all headed for San Luís, but the pirates netted thirteen others: the two officers and five soldiers, Díaz, the cabin boy, and the four friars. Their lives were in no danger. Those who could raise ransom would be released immediately. The rest would work for the buccaneers for a year or two and then be let go. It was a form of indentured service doubling as a source of recruits for the brotherhood.[29]

In the San Marcos warehouse the pirates found a valuable prize, two to three hundred *arrobas* of corn, which the prisoners loaded onto the sloop while their captors gathered up the muskets and other weapons and broke them in pieces, dismounted the artillery, and put the guns and ammunition on board. They then demolished the bastion of the castillo facing the sea and retreated with their prize to the frigate at anchor in the channel down at Cassina Point. It had been a fine battle: nobody killed or badly hurt on either side and no pointless damage to property. San Marcos had been robbed but it would recover.

News of the attack reached San Luís around noon. Captain Antonio de Herrera, the officer who had been held for ransom in 1677, headed toward the port, accompanied by ranchers Marcos Delgado and Francisco de Florencia,[30] five soldiers, and around a hundred Indian auxiliaries. Teniente Pérez intercepted them and ordered Captain Herrera to head toward San Marcos Landing and post sentinels, avoiding an engagement until he, Pérez, could return with reinforcements, and to watch out for the ten or twelve Chines in the party, who might "try something rash." Half a league north of the landing, Captain Herrera's party ran into a sailor from the sloop, who reported that the enemy had finished sacking the port and was gone. It was true. The captain took possession of the empty castillo and set his men to repairing it.[31]

Meanwhile, at Cassina Point, the pirate captain was telling his prisoners that he would accept ransom in the form of provisions "as formerly." The group rate for ransoms was still, it seems, ten hogs. To handle the arrangements the pirates released six hostages in a launch: Fray Juan Ángel, Díaz, the cabin boy, and three soldiers, possibly those with injuries, as one of them was Villalobos. Captain Herrera sent all of them except his ensign on to San Luís. There, they learned that Teniente Pérez was under particular orders not to allow any payments of ransoms. Governor Marquez Cabrera, who followed royal instructions to the letter, had been charged not to negotiate with pirates.

When their demands brought no response, the pirates too sent off for reinforcements. Backed by a second frigate, they prepared to reoccupy San Marcos. On a date that no one bothered to record, three enemy vessels sailed into the port in broad daylight and trained their guns on the castillo. Captain Herrera prepared to abandon his post, but first, lest the enemy should make use of it, he demolished the castillo. The men who had been repairing the walls reversed themselves and razed them to the ground. They then set fire to the bujío, the warehouse, and the arbor where the soldiers cleaned their weapons. After posting sentries to watch the road, the landing, and the two river entrances, the captain retired as ordered, first half a league, then two leagues across the sawgrass and into the piney woods to El Pinal.

The enemy, in no hurry, allowed the Spanish ample time to reconsider the matter of ransom or launch a counterattack. Meanwhile, they made themselves at home. The larger ships left port; smaller vessels came and went to be careened and repaired. Perhaps this was when Samuel Johns, wrecker and turtle-hunter, brought his two frigates into port, along with four Apalache divers "given" him by the governor of Providence Island in the Bahamas. Local Indians killed two of Johns's men, whereupon, he said, "all those on the ships went ashore and burned the village."[32] The Spanish record notes only that the enemy came in two frigates and set fire to the *casas*.

The governor's interference with the stylized movements of attack and accommodation was exasperating pirates and provincials alike. Another vessel came into port and released two more soldiers with letters from the friars still in custody. If ransoms were not forthcoming immediately, the friars warned, the pirates meant to go up into the province and cut off everybody's head. Apalache was in danger of invasion.

By this time, reinforcements had reached San Luís, doubling the size of the garrison. Teniente Pérez, who knew better than to send a land force against a naval one, deployed his troops defensively to block the avenues of access to the interior: forty-five soldiers and over two hundred Indians in a series of defense lines. Sergeant Major Salvador de Cigarroa was back; the pirates had released him and kept the pilots and the ship.[33] He commanded the first line, a trench near San Marcos Landing from which his men could observe both of the river entrances plus the point. Captain Herrera dug in at El Pinal. The third line of defense and Pérez's base camp, complete with gun emplacements and artillery brought down from San Luis, was four leagues up the road from El Pinal, where a crossroad led to Tuscache Landing on the western side of the Tagabona.

After waiting a little while longer to give the governor one last chance to come up with ransom, the enemy released a third friar and began to show signs of coming ashore. The frigates reappeared in port with four piraguas and a launch which went back and forth importantly, sounding the harbor and inspecting the shore. Cigarroa, no ordinary officer, confided to his troops that they had no business being where they were; that what they needed to guard was the presidio's one last vessel, a ketch—"the whole salvation of the presidio and all the provinces"—which lay unloaded and camouflaged in Tuscache Creek.

On the morning of June 8 the pirates began to advance on the front line. When they were barely within arquebus range of Cigarroa's position, the defenders let off a ragged volley: half of the muskets misfired. Enemy landing craft could be seen going up the rivers on either side. If the pirates should land and meet in a pincerlike movement behind them, Cigarroa's troops would be cut off. The Apalaches in the front line saw no virtue in being captured and set to diving wrecks or rowing galleys.[34] Having scarcely loosed an arrow or fired a shot, they rose up in a body and ran.

Crying, "The Indians have gone off and left us!" the soldiers leaped up to follow, Cigarroa at their head. They overran El Pinal and Captain Herrera's men joined them. When the captain tried to stop the rout, somebody gave him a shove and he fell in the river. Soldiers and Indians ran past together, Cigarroa yelling over his shoulder that they were on their way to Tuscache Landing with a hundred Frenchmen behind them. The men at the third line heard them coming. They too jumped up, abandoning the guns, and all three groups ran on together, not toward the landing at Tuscache but to Tomoli. For those from the front lines it was a genuine twenty-one-mile marathon, corroborating the Franciscan claim that soldiers were good for nothing except to "ask enemies into the house."[35] At Tomoli, where he could look out across the lowlands, Cigarroa made a stand to face his pursuers. There were none. There were no Frenchmen at Tuscache, either, where Captain Herrera was tromping around in mudholes looking for the ketch, which he was supposed to scuttle. By the time Cigarroa marched back into San Marcos four days later the enemy had left, taking with them the last two prisoners: Warden Pedro de Arcos and the soldier Francisco Hernández.

On their way back to Anclote Key the pirates forced one of the two to guide a party of thirty-five Frenchmen up the San Martín River to the ranch houses of La Chua, which they surprised and set on fire at two o'clock in the morning. For the release of owner Thomás Menéndez Marquez, his son-in-law Juan de Hita, and four servants they demanded a purse of money and 150 head of cattle. According to Governor Marquez Cabrera, who missed no opportunity to discredit provincials, not one of the five reserve captains in the vicinity of La Chua went to don Thomás's rescue. Instead, the chiefs of three Timucuan towns, with sixteen of their vassals, ambushed the French retreat and freed the captives in a skirmish that left one Indian dead.[36]

When news of the second occupation of San Marcos and the attack on La Chua reached St. Augustine, Marquez Cabrera sent Captain Francisco Fuentes to Apalache to investigate. Fuentes and the Franciscans were antagonists of long standing; his path across the province can be traced by the angry letters from both sides, copied for the governor's file on the abuses of the friars.[37] From one of the letters we learn that the Indians of Ivitachuco were starting on some defenses of their own.

Arcos and Hernández added details to the story of the first occupation when they arrived in St. Augustine in August, the pirates having dropped them off along the coast of Cuba. In captivity they had learned that five English and

French pirate captains, including the feared Lorencillo (Laurens de Graff), had met that summer in the Keys and shaken hands on a plan to join forces under Monsieur Agramón (the Sieur de Grammont) and attack St. Augustine.[38] The attacks on San Marcos had been small stuff, keeping one band of buccaneers busy and in provisions while they waited for their leaders to unite against a larger prize.

During Warden Arcos's absence, his companions-at-arms had convinced the governor that he alone was responsible for the loss of the castillo. No sooner had Arcos returned than he was arrested, court-martialled, given a dishonorable discharge, and sent into exile. The Junta de Guerra, reviewing the case two years later, inquired why the governor had made a scapegoat of the warden when others were equally responsible. The next time Marquez Cabrera had soldiers to punish, he would be sure to err on the side of severity.[39] About the less-than-heroic role of the friars, the record is pointedly silent. Of the Spanish eyewitnesses, they alone were not asked for testimony, and only two of the four were identified, but there are signs that their role in the fracas was not forgotten. When Fray Juan de Ángel was appointed visitor to the provinces some time later, the governor objected that he was incompetent, and a fellow Franciscan volunteered that Fray Ángel was "illiterate" and "a public scandal."[40]

Marquez Cabrera returned to a policy of closing rivers and moving villages. He did not exactly close San Marcos, but he placed obstacles in the way of those who wished to go there and began collecting customs with an efficiency that Cuban authorities thought unwarranted. Floridanos and Franciscans spoke nostalgically of Governor Hita Salazar, who had "let people make a living any way they pleased," and of the good old days when "everybody was free to buy and sell what he needed, licitly, without being hindered or disturbed."[41]

For the next five years, no pirate season was complete without a fresh attempt on the Atlantic coast. Bands of buccaneers began to refit and revictual their ships along the inland waterway in the minor ports of Guale—exposed settlements which the Indians soon abandoned. The Gulf remained a useful staging area. In 1684, for instance, Captain Thomas Jingle (Hinckley) of New England, with a letter-of-marque from the governor of New Providence in the Bahamas, went out with five other captains to cruise the Keys, where they captured the St. Augustine frigate *La Plantanera* on her way to Vera Cruz. Hinckley sent a raiding party inland, guided by Indians, in an unsuccessful effort to surprise an unidentified "Spanish city" on the Gulf Coast. In Apalachee Bay he joined forces with five more ships, and only then did the fleet head for St. Augustine.[42]

Marquez Cabrera was not the only Spanish governor to refuse to negotiate with pirates. When Laurens de Graff and the Sieur de Grammont took Campeche in 1685, and Grammont offered to exchange all of its inhabitants for a few of his men who had fallen into Spanish hands, the governor in Mérida responded haughtily that "Spain was rich enough in men and in treasure to rebuild and repeople Campeche."[43]

No one, however, was rebuilding the defenses at San Marcos, nor would they for another thirty years.[44] All that Hita Salazar had accomplished by putting a castillo in the port was to accumulate a cache of artillery, ammunition, and provisions for the enemy to carry away. Attention turned to Apalachicola, Apalache's trading partner to the north, where provincials and royalists agreed not to give ground to English traders. In 1689 Governor Diego de Quiroga y Losada ordered Primo de Rivera into Apalachicola to build a blockhouse trading post, which he did near the town of Coweta with twenty-four soldiers and a hundred Apalaches. But Spain was not equipped to win a trade war. In 1691 the Apalachicolas left the Spanish sphere of influence to move closer to the traders of Charleston, entering Anglo history as the Lower Creeks.[45]

In 1695 the Apalaches started on a third fort, this time in San Luís. When Queen Anne's War broke out in 1702, and Colonel James Moore besieged St. Augustine, they hurriedly finished the stockade, completing it just as Moore entered Apalache with a second army of Carolinians and Creeks. The strongholds at San Luís and Ivitachuco withstood the attack in opposite ways. True to royalist form, Teniente Jacinto Roque Pérez, in the blockhouse at San Luís, refused to ransom either Spanish soldiers or Indian auxiliaries, who went to the stake side by side. True to provincial form, the "King of the Attachookas," don Patricio de Hinachuba, did not put his 130 armed men and "strong and well-made Fort" to the test, but compounded with the enemy and ransomed his town with church plate, horses, and provisions.[46]

On the peripheries of empire, Spaniards and Indians survived by circumventing the mandates of a distant Crown. Their exposed situation obliged them to come to terms with enemies who could move into minor ports and isolated outposts whenever they chose. Like the earlier system of rescate, the stylized pirate raid, combining limited defense with limited damage, was as reasonable to provincials as it was offensive to royalists. The rampant smuggling of the eighteenth century would be equally divisive, as "Spanish governors attributed contraband to a combination of the foreigner's greed . . . and the creole's inherent degeneracy."[47] Three centuries of pressure would not be enough to make

[24]

the minor ports surrender their freedoms, however tacit, to a state without the power to protect them; royalist efforts to bring the provincials into line would only confirm them in the certainty that they were doubly victimized: by the king's enemies and by the king's friends.

# NOTES

[1] Irene Wright, "Rescates: With Special Reference to Cuba, 1599-1610," *Hispanic American Historical Review* 3, no. 3 (August 1920): 335.

[2] Paul E. Hoffman, *The Spanish Crown and the Defense of the Caribbean, 1535-1585: Precedent, Patrimonialism, and Royal Parsimony* (Baton Rouge: Louisiana State University Press, 1980), 224-36; I. A. Wright, "The Dutch and Cuba, 1609-1643," *Hispanic American Historical Review* 4, no. 4 (November 1921): 628.

[3] Gov. Juan Fernández de Olivera, October 13, 1612 [in this and the documentary references that follow, place of origin is St. Augustine and addressee is the Crown unless otherwise indicated], Archivo General de Indias, *ramo* Gobierno: Santo Domingo, *legajo* 229, document 74 [hereafter SD 229/74]; Oliver Dunn, "Trouble at Sea: The Return Voyage of the Fleet of New Spain and Honduras in 1622," *Terrae Incognitae* 11 (1979): 29; Wright, "The Dutch and Cuba," 610.

[4] Gov. Luís Horruytiner, June 24, 1637, SD 225; Gov. Damián de Vega Castro y Pardo, August 22, 1639, SD 225.

[5] Junta de Guerra, [Spain], July 14, 1660, SD 839/10; Friars in chapter, September 10, 1657, SD 235.

[6] Friars in chapter, September 10, 1657, SD 235; Amy Turner Bushnell, *Situado and Sabana: Spain's Support System for the Presidio and Mission Provinces of Florida*, Anthropological Papers of the American Museum of Natural History 74 (New York: American Museum of Natural History, 1994); Bushnell, *The King's Coffer: The Proprietors of the Spanish Florida Treasury, 1565-1702* (Gainesville: University Presses of Florida, 1981); Bushnell, "Ruling the Republic of Indians in Seventeenth-Century Florida," in Gregory A. Waselkov, Peter Wood, and M. Thomas Hatley, eds., *Powhatan's Mantle: Ethnohistory of Indians in the Colonial Southeast* (Lincoln: University of Nebraska Press, 1989), 195-213. A *real* was one-eighth of a *peso*, one-eleventh of a ducat. An *arroba* was a weight of 25 pounds.

[7] I. Wright, "Rescates," 341-42; John H. Hann, *Apalachee: The Land Between the Rivers* (Gainesville: University Presses of Florida, 1988), 126-59.

[8] Junta de Guerra, [Spain], July 14, 1660, SD 839.

[9] Bushnell, *The King's Coffer*, 64-65, 90-91; Friars in chapter, September 10, 1657, SD 235.

[10] Luís Rafael Arana and Albert Manucy, *The Building of Castillo de San Marcos* (Eastern National Park and Monument Assoc., 1977); Dorris LaVanture Olds, "History and Archaeology of Fort Saint Marks in Apalache" (Master's thesis, Florida State University, 1962), 6-15.

[11] Testimonies of Juan de la Rosa, Antonio de Herrera, and Juan Fernández de Florencia, San

Luís, December 24, 1677, fols. 584-86 in the Domingo de Leturiondo Visita of Apalache and Timucua, 1677-1678, Archivo de Indias, ramo Escribanía de Cámara, legajo 156 [hereafter EC 156]; Amy Turner Bushnell, "The Menéndez Marquez Cattle Barony at La Chua and the Determinants of Economic Expansion in Seventeenth-Century Florida," *Florida Historical Quarterly* 56, no. 4 (April 1978): 415-17, 424, 428.

[12] On the Florencias, see Amy Turner Bushnell, "Patricio de Hinachuba: Defender of the Word of God, the Crown of the King, and the Little Children of Ivitachuco," *American Indian Culture and Research Journal* 3, no. 3 (July 1979): 1-21; Bushnell, *The King's Coffer*, 6, 14, 34, 135, 145-48.

[13] Robert S. Weddle, *Wilderness Manhunt: The Spanish Search for La Salle* (Austin: University of Texas Press, 1973), 44; Gov. Pablo de Hita Salazar, September 6, 1677, SD 839/46; Hann, *Apalachee*, 136-39; I. Wright, "The Dutch and Cuba," 625-29.

[14] Hann, *Apalachee*, 33-45, 68, 153-54; "Don Patricio, Cacique of Ivitachuco, and Don Andrés, Cacique of San Luís, to the King," San Luís, February 12, 1699, in Mark F. Boyd, Hale G. Smith, and John W. Griffin, *Here They Once Stood: The Tragic End of the Apalachee Missions* (Gainesville: University of Florida Press, 1951), 25; Bushnell, "The Menéndez Marquez Cattle Barony," 416, 424.

[15] Presidio in Common, [June 4, 1681], in the Hita Salazar Residencia, EC 156-G; Robert S. Weddle, *Spanish Sea: The Gulf of Mexico in North American Discovery, 1500-1685* (College Station: Texas A&M University Press, 1985), 391-97, 401-2, 411; Weddle, Wilderness Manhunt, 71; Gov. Juan Marquez Cabrera, July 16, 1682, SD 839/71; Hann, *Apalachee*, 40-45, 153-54; Wright, "Rescates," 348, 353-59.

[16] Gov. Hita Salazar, September 6, 1677, SD 839/46; Hita Salazar, Order for the Trade Goods, April 26, 1678, SD 839/50; Weddle, *Spanish Sea*, 396-98; Luís Rafael Arana, "Enrique Primo de Rivera (1621-1707): A Spanish Florida Soldier," *El Escribano* 5 (July 1968): 17-26.

[17] Ex-Gov. Hita Salazar, May 15, 1683, and Francisco de la Rocha, May 20, 1683, testimonies in Auto on the Trade Goods, June 3, 1683, SD 229/159. An Apalache whom the Spanish sent to spy on the English in Apalachicola in 1675 they outfitted to pass as a deerskin trader with a supply of beads, hatchets, and hawksbells. See Juan Fernández de Florencia, May 25, 1675, SD 839/32-28.

The figure of 8,700, taken from a 1675 census, represented four-fifths of the population of the three provinces combined. See Amy Turner Bushnell, "'That Demonic Game': The Campaign to Stop Indian *Pelota* Playing in Spanish Florida, 1675-1684," *The Americas* 35, no. 1 (July 1978): 4-5; Hann, *Apalachee*, 160-80.

[18] Descriptions of the topography and the 1679 fort are taken from Olds, "Fort Saint Marks"; Mark F. Boyd, "The Fortifications at San Marcos de Apalache," *Florida Historical Quarterly* 15, no. 1 (July 1936): 3-34; Boyd, Smith, and Griffin, *Here They Once Stood*, 101-2; Lucy L. Wenhold, "The First Fort of San Marcos de Apalache," *Florida Historical Quarterly* 34, no. 4 (April 1956): 301-14; Hann, *Apalachee*; Clifton Paisley, *The Red Hills of Florida, 1528-1865* (Tuscaloosa: University of Alabama Press, 1989), 1-43.

Bernard Romans mistakenly identified the western river as the Tagabona in his 1774 "two whole sheet maps" reproduced in P. Lee Phillips, *Notes on the Life and Works of Bernard Romans* [1924], facs. ed. with intro by John D. Ware (Gainesville: University Presses of Florida, 1975), 19.

[19] Gov. Marquez Cabrera, June 14, 1681, SD 839/67.

[20] *Fiscal* of the Council of the Indies, May 12, 1682, comment on Gov. Marquez Cabrera, June 14, 1681, SD 839/67; Bushnell, *The King's Coffer*, 64-65; Nicolás Ponce de León II, February 19, 1664, SD 225, and August 4, 1690, SD 234/113; Joseph de Prado and Juan Menéndez Marquez, June 30, 1668, SD 229/134; Gov. Marquez Cabrera, June 28, 1683, SD 229/160.

[21] Weddle, *Spanish Sea*, 398. For a broader view of the French presence see Weddle, *Wilderness Manhunt*, and William Edward Dunn, *Spanish and French Rivalry in the Gulf Region of the United States, 1678-1702: The Beginnings of Texas and Pensacola* (Austin, Tex.: The University, [1917]).

[22] Gov. Marquez Cabrera, July 16, 1682, SD 839/71; Marquez Cabrera, Muster, [early December 1680], with Marquez Cabrera, June 28, 1683, SD 229/160; Bushnell, *The King's Coffer*, 115, 147-48; Salvador de Cigarroa, March 11, 1678, SD 229/147; Ex-Gov. Hita Salazar, May 20, 1683, SD 226, and February 8, 1684, SD 839/84.

[23] This narrative of the first 1682 occupation of San Marcos is pieced together from testimonies taken in St. Augustine from Juan González and Antonio de Benavides on May 25, 1682; in San Luís, from Juan de Herrera on July 20, 1682, Juan de Villalobos on July 21, 1682, Antonio Francisco de Herrera on July 22, 1682, and Juan Jiménez on July 24, 1682; and again in St. Augustine, from Alonso Díaz Mejía on August 6, 1682, Francisco Hernández on August 20, 1682, and the Pedro de Arcos's confession on August 25, 1682, all with Gov. Marquez Cabrera, July 16, 1682, SD 839/71.

[24] His career is summarized in William R. Gillaspie, "Sergeant Major Ayala y Escobar and the Threatened St. Augustine Mutiny," *Florida Historical Quarterly* 47, no. 2 (October 1968): 151-64, and detailed in Gillaspie, "Juan de Ayala y Escobar, *Procurador* and Entrepreneur: A Case Study of the Provisioning of Florida, 1683-1716" (PhD diss., University. of Florida, 1961), 29-30.

[25] Paisley, *The Red Hills of Florida*, 4, 25, follows Boyd in calling this a "secret canoe route." It has since disappeared. See Boyd, Smith, and Griffin, *Here They Once Stood*, n. 77, 101-2.

[26] Gov. Hita Salazar, Instructions for the Fort of San Marcos de Apalache, April 7, 1679, with Hita Salazar, March 6, 1680, SD 839/62-60.

[27] Shipmaster Alonso Díaz Mejía reported the pirates' side of the story. He was in their hands only one night, being in the first group released.

[28] Pedro de Arcos confession, August 25, 1682, filed with Gov. Marquez Cabrera, July 16, 1682, SD 839/71.

[29] Francisco Ruíz, Declaration on the pirates, October 15, 1685, SD 839/82; Declarations on Martín de Goyas, Martín Fernández, and Pablos Delgado, all on May 9, 1683, in Auto on the Corsair Abraha, May 8, 1683, with Gov. Marquez Cabrera, June 28, 1683, SD 226/104.

30 On these two individuals see Bushnell, "Patricio de Hinachuba," 3-4, 14-16; Mark F. Boyd, trans. and ed., "The Expedition of Marcos Delgado from Apalache to the Upper Creek Country in 1686," *Florida Historical Quarterly* 16, no. 1 (July 1937): 2-32; Weddle, *Wilderness Manhunt*, 75-86; Hann, *Apalachee*, 53-60.

31 This account of the post-raid period and the second occupation of San Marcos is reconstructed from Gov. Marquez Cabrera, July 16, 1682, SD 839/71, and the aforementioned testimonies of Juan de Herrera, Juan de Villalobos, Antonio Francisco de Herrera, and Juan Jiménez, plus testimonies taken in San Luís from Francisco de Florencia on July 21, 1682, Salvador de los Santos and Carlos Pérez, both on July 22, 1682, and Lorenzo Guerrero on July 24, 1682, all of them filed with the governor's report.

32 Weddle, *Spanish Sea*, 401-2, 411. The Johns statement is on 402.

33 Gov. Marquez Cabrera, July 16, 1682, SD 839/71; Ex-Gov. Hita Salazar, May 20, 1683, SD 226.

34 Gov. Marquez Cabrera, July 16, 1682, SD 839/71; Auto on the Corsair Abraha, May 8, 1683, with Marquez Cabrera, June 28, 1683, SD 226/104; Declarations of Glodo Satre and Elmo Mermique, runaway servants, January 11, 1686, in Marquez Cabrera, March 19, 1686, SD 839/82; Weddle, *Spanish Sea*, 408.

35 Friars in chapter, September 10, 1657, SD 235.

36 Bushnell, "The Menéndez Marquez Cattle Barony," 428; Gov. Marquez Cabrera, July 16, 1682, SD 839/71.

37 With other anticlerical materials, they went to the Crown in Gov. Marquez Cabrera's mail packet of June 28, 1683, SD 226/105.

38 Francisco Hernández testimony, August 20, 1682, and Pedro de Arcos confession, August 25, 1682, filed with Gov. Marquez Cabrera, July 16, 1682, SD 839/71; Weddle, *Spanish Sea*, 399-400.

39 Gov. Marquez Cabrera, Sentencing of Pedro de los Arcos, St. Augustine, September 22, 1682; Fiscal of the Junta de Guerra, Madrid, October 20, 1684, appended to Marquez Cabrera, July 16, 1682, SD 839; Appeal of the Five Sentries, April 15, 1688, SD 234/9.

40 Maynard Geiger, O.F.M., *Biographical Dictionary of the Franciscans in Spanish Florida and Cuba (1528-1841)*, Franciscan Studies 21 (Paterson, N.J.: St. Anthony Guild Press, 1940), 25; see also Hann, *Apalachee*, 120-21.

41 Gov. Marquez Cabrera, July 16, 1682, SD 839/71; Auto on Resettling the Guales, August 21, 1684, with Marquez Cabrera, August 26, 1684, SD 226/118; Gov. Joseph de Córdoba Ponce de León, Havana, October 6, 1683, SD 234/55; Franciscans of the Province of Santa Elena, June 4, 1681, and Presidio in Common, [June 4, 1681], in the Hita Salazar Residencia, [EC] 156-G.

42 Auto on the Corsair Abraha, May 8, 1683, with Gov. Marquez Cabrera, June 28, 1683, SD

226/104; Gov. Marquez Cabrera, October 6, 1687 [sic], SD 839/113; Ex-Gov. Hita Salazar, Report on the Pirates, May 20, 1683, with idem, May 24, 1683, SD 226; Auto on Resettling the Guales, August 21, 1684, with Gov. Marquez Cabrera, August 26, 1684, SD 226/118; Auto on the Pirates, November 11, 1684, in the Marquez Cabrera Residencia, EC 156-C-3, fol. 17; Thomás Menéndez Marquez and Francisco de la Rocha, September 30, 1686, SD 234/65; Gov. Diego de Quiroga y Losada to Gov. James Colleton of Carolina, November 12, 1687, SD 839/116; J. Leitch Wright, Jr., "Andrew Ranson: Seventeenth Century Pirate?" *Florida Historical Quarterly* 39, no. 2 (October 1960): 136-38.

[43] Quoted by Jean Bassford von Winning in "Forgotten Bastions Along the Spanish Main: Campeche," *The Americas* 6, no. 4 (April 1950): 424-25.

[44] When he was acting governor, shipowner Juan de Ayala built a blockhouse to use as a Yuchi and Yamasee trading post. See Olds, "Fort Saint Marks," 21-25, 28-35; Gillaspie, "Sergeant Major Ayala y Escobar," 163-64.

[45] Fred Lamar Pearson Jr., "Anglo Spanish Rivalry in the Georgia Country, 1670-1691," in Eugene R. Huck and Edward H. Moseley, eds., *Militarists, Merchants and Missionaries: United States Expansion in Middle America* (Tuscaloosa: University of Alabama Press, 1970), 14-16.

[46] Hann, *Apalachee*, 210-12, 393; Bushnell, "Patricio de Hinachuba," 9.

[47] G. Early Sanders, "Counter-Contraband in Spanish America: Handicaps of the Governors in the Indies," *The Americas* 34, no. 1 (July 1977): 75.

# II

## NASCENT SOCIALISTS OR RESOURCEFUL CRIMINALS?
### A Reconsideration of Transatlantic Piracy, 1690-1726

### CRYSTAL WILLIAMS

Bartholomew Roberts was one of the most successful pirates ever, if one counts success by the number of ships taken. However, like so many others, he had begun his maritime career on a merchant ship, and had been forced to join the pirates when his ship was captured. Roberts, sometimes known as Black Bart, attempted to justify his own choices and comfort the newly forced men aboard his vessels with these words: "In an honest service, there is thin commons, low wages, and hard labour. In this, plenty and satiety, pleasure and ease, liberty and power; and who would not balance creditor on this side, when all the hazard that is run for it, at worst, is only a sour look or two at choking. No, a merry life and a short one shall be my motto."[1]

Any roseate pirate could have easily expressed the same sentiments. Unfortunately, the reality of a pirate's life was often much more grim. Statements such as Roberts's, as well as trial depositions, journals, and execution remarks can provide valuable insight into the experiences of pirates, the social relations aboard pirate ships, and the culture the pirates created. Using these sources, this essay will explore the social context of piracy, the reasons men became pirates, the relationships they formed on board, and how this pirate culture compared to the culture of seamen in general, as well as to all of Anglo-American society.

Both popular and scholarly historians have long been fascinated with the adventures of the pirates. As so often happens, the criminal lives of the pirates were romanticized after they were no longer a threat to society. Notorious captains such as Blackbeard and Captain Kidd gained mythical status, and books about pirates were extremely popular in England from the 1720s, continuing through the nineteenth century. In the last few decades, social historians have begun to explore the lives of common working-class people. Accordingly, they have found the history of seamen, including pirates, particularly enlightening.

Because pirates had at least some greater measure of freedom than did men in the navy, their behavior can reveal the sentiments of a large group of mariners taken to the extreme.[2]

While many authors have studied and written about pirates, Marcus Rediker's interpretations have dominated the field for over twenty years and have influenced nearly every work written since. Other scholars may offer a unique narrative, focus on a specific aspect of piracy, or devote their inquiry to a particular period or region, but they often accept and use Rediker's analysis as near fact. Rediker's work on pirates is a model of comprehensive and insightful research, yet is still an interpretation that should not go unquestioned. Marcus Rediker argues that pirates formed a social order characterized by egalitarianism, with power in the hands of the crew. Rediker contends that men became pirates in order to rebel against the social and economic oppression they experienced in the hierarchical, capitalist world and that in certain periods the continuation of their collective lifestyle became more important than the pursuit of prizes.[3] However, Rediker obscures the truth by insisting on finding noble motivations behind the activities of pirates. While pirate crews may have exhibited some collective tendencies, they were generally not organized on a basis of egalitarianism, nor were they anticapitalist. In fact, they simply used whatever means necessary, including crime, to further their individual interests. In order to construct an accurate interpretation, it is important to examine closely pirates in this period without looking for a social consciousness that did not exist.

The men who became pirates in the late seventeenth and early eighteenth century did not possess an awareness of class that would have allowed them to organize collectively to resist capitalism. While they established a unique world of their own and often expressed resentment toward the world they had left behind, the society they created was characterized by greed and barbarity, not egalitarianism. Piracy could take many different forms, and it could hold very different meanings for the various men who pursued it. Some were drawn by the lure of instant wealth. Others had an inexplicable thirst for adventure and violence. Conversely, there were those men who felt wronged by society and saw piracy as a way to exact revenge. However, there was no common ethos, no lofty goal that drove pirates to resist the oppression that society had dispensed them. They simply tried to make their way in the world in the manner that suited them most at the time.[4]

Becoming a pirate could appear very lucrative to a seaman of the late seventeenth or early eighteenth century. When compared to life in the navy or aboard a merchant vessel, the life of a pirate might seem inviting. The life of a sailor in the British Navy was far from pleasant. Navy ships were often under-staffed, so the workload was excessive. The meager pay and rations were usual-ly even more onerous than the work, and diseases such as scurvy were often rampant. Working on a merchant vessel or a privateer could be better, as there was usually more food of a higher quality. However, merchant captains were often harsh, and discipline could be as strict on these ships as in the navy.[5] Joining the pirates almost certainly offered the opportunity for making more money. One captured pirate stated that it was possible to make twenty-five shillings a month on a merchant vessel, but on a pirate ship you could make seven or eight pounds.[6] Furthermore, honest employment was often hard to find in times of peace. The navy needed fewer men, employment as a privateer practically disappeared, and wages on merchantmen dropped. John Evans explained that he became a pirate captain because, by 1722, wages were not as good as they had formerly been, and berths were scarce because of the great number of seamen.[7] If the life of a pirate truly offered "plenty and satiety, pleasure and ease," then it would seem logical that men were jumping at the chance to join the pirates. However, potential pirates seldom exhibited this enthusiasm for "going on the account."

Force, more than lucre, brought many men to piracy. This point has been frequently overlooked or diminished. Some evidence indicates that pirate ships normally would take no married man.[8] In addition, pirates often claimed that they would "force no prisoners, but those that remained with them were vol-unteers."[9] Historians have picked up on these assertions and have argued that nearly all men who became pirates did so by choice. Rediker asserts that pirates only began to relax their policy against forcing men when the number of will-ing volunteers dwindled in the 1720s.[10] However, upon closer examination, it seems that willingness was not always the deciding factor and that pirate crews were often very concerned with increasing their numbers, even in earlier peri-ods. Although certainly not every man was forced (as they liked to claim when faced with execution), force was one of the primary methods of obtaining men.[11] Men were usually taken when their vessel, often a merchant ship, was captured. Any man with skills was especially at risk, as pirates were often in need of carpenters, doctors, boatswains, and musicians. For example, Captain Fly forced William Atkinson because he was a skilled navigator.[12] Thomas Davis testified at his trial that Captain Bellamy had forced him because he was a sin-gle man and a carpenter.[13] When Captain Roberts was captured and brought to trial, the court discovered that four of his men were forced musicians. These men had been treated very poorly, "having sometimes their fiddles, and often their heads broke, only for excusing themselves, or saying they were tired."[14] However, it was not necessary to have skills in order to be forced into pirate service. Captain Spriggs forced nearly all of the men he captured to join him. Those men who would not sign the articles he and the crew "beat and cut in a barbarous manner."[15] After their ship had been captured by Spriggs, two sailors reported that Spriggs and his crew whipped men on their ship, including a twelve-year-old boy, to compel them to turn pirate.[16] The strength of a pirate crew lay in its numbers, especially when capturing other armed ships.

Even those men who were captured and agreed to sign the pirates' articles often exhibited sincere reluctance. Many of those the pirates claimed as volunteers were only volunteers in the sense that they chose pirating over marooning or death. For example, Stede Bonnet captured Rowland Sharp, who at first refused to sign the articles. He finally did, after Bonnet threatened to shoot him several times.[17] In another instance, John Houghling, a pirate taken from the captured *Pennsylvania Merchant*, also claimed in 1700 the pirates had forced him. He testified that he had been stranded on an island with nothing to eat. When the pirates came back later to pick him up, the captain caned and drubbed him with a sword, and then threatened to maroon him if he did not join.[18] Matthew Barry said the pirates who captured his ship compelled him to sign their articles by making him eat lighted candles. He also testified that he had seen the pirates torture other men by sticking needles in their fingers.[19]

Although some of these claims can be discounted as attempts to protect one's reputation or life, in at least some instances there was enough evidence to cause a court to agree men were forced. Admiralty courts were generally very harsh towards pirates, but they acquitted the navigator, William Atkinson, along with two other men captured at the same time because the court believed they were coerced into piracy. Some men who were acquitted had even been accepting shares of captured loot. Generally, the key to this leniency was the ability to prove that they had practiced some form of resistance to piracy.[20] Nicholas Simonds claimed that he had shot a pirate through the body when his ship was being captured, and that later on he had tried very hard to get away.[21] Thomas South claimed he had been forced by Captain Bellamy, who had threatened to maroon him if he did not join. South testified that he had repeatedly tried to escape from the pirate ship, and he was acquitted as the court agreed he had been pressed into service.[22] In another case, Joseph Swetser was found not guilty when he and other pirates testified that he had begged to go ashore, but had been tied to the mast and threatened with whipping instead.[23] Similarly, the court acquitted the master of prisoners aboard Captain Roberts's ship, Harry Glasby, because he had tried to escape twice and had generally treated the prisoners well.[24] Out of Roberts's entire crew, seventy-four men were acquitted, as opposed to only fifty-two who were executed, indicating that the court was convinced that the crew contained a high proportion of genuinely forced men.

Another way in which men became pirates was to stage a mutiny on their own privateering vessel. This method accounted for a fairly small percentage of pirates, but descriptions of how mutinies occurred provide insight into the motives of those who wished to become pirates and those who did not. Oftentimes men would refuse to join their own crewmates who designed to overthrow their captain. In other cases, the captain of a merchantman or privateer wished to turn pirate and his crew would not join him. Howel Davis eventually became a successful pirate, but his men resisted the first time he proposed piracy. Davis was chief mate of the *Cadogan*, commanded by Captain Skinner. The *Cadogan* was captured by the pirate ship of Captain England, who barbarously murdered Skinner by pelting him with glass bottles, whipping him, and shooting him through the head.[25] England then asked Davis to join him, to which Davis, showing his opposition to piracy, replied that he "would sooner be shot to death than sign the pirate's articles."[26] However, England was so impressed with Davis's bravery that he gave Davis command of the *Cadogan* and released him. He then gave Davis written orders to take the rest of the cargo and dispose of it in Brazil to his best advantage. The crew, however, did not even want to have this slight connection to piracy. The crew took over the *Cadogan* and steered toward Barbados, where the merchants who were the rightful owners of the cargo were located. They then turned Davis over to the authorities, who imprisoned him for three months.[27] These refusals of captured men to join the pirates show that at least some men did not find the life of a pirate that attractive and felt they were better off in their current station of life.

On the other hand, those who did mutiny and became pirates often stated that they did so because they had been treated badly by their captains. William Fly overthrew the captain and mate of the privateer on which he was employed. However, before his execution for numerous acts of piracy, he refused to admit that murdering them had been a sin. He felt he was justified because the master and mate had used the crew badly. One of Fly's crew members warned shipmasters "against severity and barbarity to their men, which they were persuaded is the reason of so many turning pirates."[28]

This reasoning suggests that, at least for some, piracy may have been a way to retaliate against bad treatment and usage by harsh captains. However, there are other instances in which the crew mutinied for more base economic reasons, and they were not consistently violent toward authority figures. In one mutiny the crew aboard a merchant vessel simply wished to pursue a course that would bring them more money, and therefore deposed the captain and stole the ship along with its cargo. Significantly, after this mutiny, many of the ship's crew did not want to, nor did they become pirates. Furthermore, the new captain, George Cusack, later abandoned several of his crew in order to have fewer men with whom to share his plunder.[29] Avery, one of the most celebrated pirates, began his career when he convinced most of his shipmates aboard a merchant vessel, the *Duke*, to assist him in overthrowing their captain so that they could seek wealth upon the coasts of India. Neither Avery nor the other men held any ill will toward their captain, as they invited him to join them. The captain did not wish to become a pirate, and Avery allowed him and several other men to take a boat and go ashore.[30] When William Buttler's ship was captured by pirates, they forced two of his "honest young men" to join them, stole the rum and sugar, and then allowed Buttler to go free.[31]

As a consequence of practicing force, pirate captains often had to contend with the prospect of their men running away. The presence of so many unwilling men, eager to desert, raises serious questions about the collective goals and aspirations of pirate crews. Discontented men usually tried to escape when the ship stopped to provision or careen. Sometimes they would ask to be allowed to join a privateer or a merchant ship that had been plundered and was being released. This willingness to leave illustrates the unhappiness many men felt with the pirate lifestyle. Isaac Sun, captured by Bartholomew Roberts, testified that he had repeatedly refused to sign the articles, and had been cut and beaten for doing so. Later, he tried to escape, was recaptured, and a drunken jury of pirates sentenced him to be shot.[32] On another occasion, some forced men escaped from Roberts on two of his ships.[33] Peter Hooff, who had been pressed into service by Captain Bellamy, was whipped for attempting to run away.[35] Some men would even resort to a kind of reverse mutiny to end their careers as pirates. In one instance, a group of seamen had taken off with their vessel and turned pirate when their captain had gone ashore. Soon thereafter, however, the forced men on this ship staged an uprising against the pirates and were able to overcome them and bring the ship into port.[36]

It is not surprising that forced pirates might at some point run away, perhaps in an effort to try to return to their former, calmer lifestyles. Not all deserters, however, had joined the pirates against their will. Many had readily volunteered but had realized that being a pirate was not so much better than working on any other ship. Just before Captain Kidd's capture, several of his men had attempted to go ashore, and were whipped for doing so when they were recaptured. A few days earlier, several other crew members deserted when the ship stopped for wood and water.[37] Harry Glasby, who was the master of prisoners on the ship, had tried to escape Captain Roberts in the West Indies. However, Roberts caught Glasby and two accomplices, and shot the other two.[38] Fern, the carpenter of Captain Phillips, attempted to escape, and Phillips shot him. The next day, Phillips shot another man for the same offense. These incidents terrorized the rest of the crew and convinced them not to attempt an escape.[39]

More frequently than not, these pirate ships were characterized by a lack of unity in purpose. In addition to those who wished to escape, there were also plenty of men who desired to end their piratical careers through legal means. This acceptance of submission to authority certainly illustrates that many pirates were not entirely satisfied with their life, nor committed to pursuing an egalitarian lifestyle no matter the cost. Neither did they necessarily feel an intense loyalty to their crew, since they were completely willing to separate and do what was best for themselves. In 1699 the King issued a proclamation declaring that if pirates would surrender themselves immediately they would be pardoned for all piracies committed before a certain date. One of Captain Kidd's men stated that he and the rest of the crew rejoiced when they heard about the proclamation.[40] Entire crews began to seek pardons, and many men whose crews were not surrendering begged to be let go so that they might surrender individually. Yeats, a man Captain Vane had trusted with command of one of his ships, had often attempted to quit the piratical life and finally was able to take advantage of an opportunity to escape from Vane and surrender to the King's pardon.[41] The British government sent the former privateer, Woodes Rogers, to take over the island of Providence, which had become a haven for pirates. Most of the pirates quickly accepted the certificates of pardons offered to them. In fact, over 400 pirates in the area—all but those under Captain Vane—surrendered.[42] When Vane's crew was finally captured, they were convicted and hanged in front of all the other former pirates. The convicted men railed at the others, accusing them of cowardice, stating that they never thought they would see the day that "ten such men as they should be tied up and hanged like dogs, and 400 of their sworn friends and companions quietly standing by to behold the spectacle."[43] The camaraderie of pirates only extended so far; in the end they all looked out for themselves.

This camaraderie was also very weak between the various pirate crews. Although Rediker argues that pirates "showed a recurrent willingness to join forces in sea and in port," it appears that these alliances were often not honored.[44] When two or more captains joined, their union could be disrupted if any of the parties felt things were not going the way they would like, or if one felt they were strong enough to stand alone and thus would gain more in fending for themselves rather than sharing. Captain Avery entered into an alliance with the captains of two other ships with significant cargoes and convinced them to place their valuables on his ship, under three seals, because his ship was the most strongly armed and was the most able to protect the treasure of gold dust. During the night, Avery enticed his men with tales of wealth, and they accordingly slipped away from the others and felt no "qualms of honor" rising within them.[45] Captain Spriggs separated from Low by stealing a ship with eighteen men in the night, because they had been quarreling.[46] In fact, Captain Johnson believed that it was an excellent idea to put "some of the pirates into authority," and to give "all the effects taken aboard a pirate vessel to the captors; for in the case of plunder and gain, they like it as well from friends as enemies."[47] Indeed, there was no honor among thieves.

When men chose to become pirates their aim was to maximize profits rather than simply to sustain an egalitarian society. They stole those items that were worth the most and could be sold easily and without detection. Captain Roberts captured a long string of ships, which kept his company well stocked with provisions. However, the crew began to think "of something worthier of their aim, for these robberies that only supplied what was in constant expenditure by no means answered their intentions; and accordingly they proceeded again for the coast of Guinea, where they thought to buy gold dust very cheap."[48]

If pirates went "on account" for a variety of reasons and had little loyalty to one another, they were also not particularly egalitarian in organization. One of the most important elements in Rediker's argument that pirates formed a collective, egalitarian culture is the fact that nearly all pirate crews signed articles.[49] These articles were agreements between all of the crew members and their captain, which set up rules of conduct for the ship as well as delineating the way in which plunder was to be apportioned. Rediker is right that these articles tended to be relatively egalitarian. On most pirate ships the captain usually received one and a half to two shares, while the boatswain, carpenter, and gunner would receive one and a quarter to one and a half. Every other man received one share.[50] Pirate articles may have been more egalitarian than some, but by no means was this sharing of profit new or radical. Fishing vessels in particular had similar shares doled out to captains and crews. Furthermore, the primary focus of the articles was always the division of loot. The goal of a pirate ship was to make money, not to provide a floating welfare state. While some attempts at leveling social distinction and providing for the collective good appear, there is also evidence that these articles were sometimes bent, if not broken. Several pirate captains, most notably Blackbeard, bullied and intimidated their crews to sustain their hierarchical command, regardless of supposedly egalitarian articles.

Land-based pirate communities also had inegalitarian elements. Rediker argues that pirates wished to continue their egalitarian lifestyle on land, even after their days at sea had ended.[51] The most notable of these communities were formed at Port Royal, Jamaica, and Madagascar. However, the motivation for the formation and operation of these communities may have a much simpler explanation. Because pirates had been flagrantly breaking the law, they could not return to the communities they had left behind, or any other part of civilized society, without facing almost certain hanging. When the only other option was death, their creation of remote societies does not necessarily indicate that they were trying to create an alternative egalitarian world, or that they disagreed with the hierarchical nature of the society they had left behind. In fact, at least on Madagascar, life was far from tranquil, communal, or egalitarian. Johnson noted that the pirates living in the community they had formed on Madagascar "began to divide from one another, each living with his own wives, slaves and dependants, like a separate prince; and as power and plenty naturally beget contention, they sometimes quarreled with one another, and attacked each other at the head of their several armies."[52] This behavior indicates that these men did not see each other as equals and were more concerned with their own gain than the collective good. Johnson went on to say "if power and command be the thing which distinguish a prince, these ruffians had all the marks of royalty about them, nay more, they had the very fears which commonly disturb tyrants, as may be seen by the extreme caution they took in fortifying the places in which they dwelt."[53] These pirates quickly set about establishing positions of authority for themselves individually with few attempts to live in harmony or equality with their comrades.

Furthermore, many captains were not beyond deserting their men in order to save everything for themselves. Both Stede Bonnet and Blackbeard marooned at least part of their crew. On one occasion, Blackbeard abandoned most of his crew, which at that time included Bonnet, and took off with the ship they had just captured.[54] At one point Captain Avery and his crew had decided that they would try to slip back into society at the new settlement of Providence and live off their plunder. However, when Avery was parceling out the dividends, he hid a large stock of diamonds from the crew. The men did not approach Avery about this because they had not realized the value of the stones when they had first taken them from a prize ship.[55] These examples indicate that not all captains were interested in what was best for their men, and many crew members must have often been suspicious of their masters. At the least, captains and crews were willing to take advantage of each other. Captain Roberts had a pirate ship as well as a sloop, which was fast and agile. Upon spying a brigantine, which he thought had a large cargo, he took the sloop and forty men to pursue the prize, and left Kennedy in charge. However, in his haste, Roberts had forgotten to take sufficient provisions and had to land. When he finally received news from the main ship, he learned that Kennedy had taken off with the ship as well as a prize ship they had captured earlier. The ease with which Kennedy betrayed Roberts reveals his lack of any binding sentiments.[56]

There were also possibilities for dissension among crew members, who often had a difficult time agreeing on which ships to take, or whether to overthrow their captain. Rather than representing some nascent democracy, this lack of unity often resulted from personal pique, a lack of communal identity, and even an acceptance of social distinctions. Stede Bonnet's crew could not agree among themselves or with him on which course to sail. Bonnet threatened and punished them, and narrowly avoided mutiny.[57] When Captain Phillips captured some small fishing vessels, he found John Rose Archer aboard one of them. Archer joined the pirates and "was immediately preferred over other people's heads, to be quartermaster to the company; which sudden promotion so disgusted some of the older standers; especially Fern, the carpenter, that it occasioned some mischief."[58] This preferential treatment was due to the fact that Archer had been a crew member of Blackbeard, which greatly impressed Phillips. Phillips's crew again experienced dissension later when they had forced many men into service. Several of the new pirates wished to try to get away. However, they were unable to do so because, "the old pirates were always jealous of the newcomers, and consequently observant of their behavior; this was done with the utmost caution, chiefly when they were lying down together, as though asleep, and, at other times, when they were playing at cards; both which they feigned often do for that purpose."[59]

Pirate crews were far from harmonious and united; they constantly formed factions based on their differences. The crew aboard Captain Lowther's ship felt "commotions and intestine disturbances, by the divisions of its members," which nearly ended in their destruction.[60] One of the men, Massey, caused this commotion because he wished to attack some French settlements on land rather than continue their piracy at sea. Eventually, the crew broke up into separate groups and Massey turned himself over to the governor of Jamaica.[61] Kennedy, who took off with Captain Roberts's pirate ship and prize, could not bring his company to any kind of agreement. Most of them wished to give up pirating altogether and go home.[62] Later, Captain Roberts formed another crew, and they were very successful. However, "being almost always mad or drunk, their behavior produced infinite disorders, every man being in his own imagination a captain, a prince, or a king."[63] Roberts saw there was no easy way to control the crew, and so took on a more "magisterial carriage toward them."[64] It seems logical that class distinctions, whether pre-existing or created, may have played a role in who won these types of battles.

While many captains dominated their crews with harsh discipline, there is, as Rediker points out, also significant evidence that pirates resented hierarchy. Crews voted out a captain when he did not follow the wishes of the majority. For example, Captain Hornigold refused to take English sloops so the crew voted to replace him with Captain Bellamy.[65] In addition, pirates exhibited a hatred for the captains of captured ships and would often inquire of their men on whether their captain had treated them well. If a captain had mistreated the crew, the pirates often punished him in varying degrees of barbarity. A good and fair captain was usually allowed the choice of either joining the pirates or being released.[66]

This practice might appear the result of a sense of injustice and reflect an egalitarian impulse, but these incidents can be misconstrued and need to be seen in the context of a generic violence that permeated the pirates' world. Pirates were cruel to nearly everyone they encountered, often regardless of social status or occupation. They were frequently particularly violent to their prisoners. Sometimes prisoners were killed for a purpose; primarily to keep them from talking should the pirate vessel be captured. However, there are many instances in which pirates killed or tortured people purely for pleasure. Spriggs and his men seized a Portuguese ship, which was very valuable to them.

Not satisfied with great quantities of loot, the crew decided to play a game with the men for their own diversion. They chose a practice called a "sweat" in which they lit candles and placed them in a circle around a mast and forced the prisoners to run around the candles while the pirates stood in an outer circle holding sharp instruments such as penknives and forks.[67] On another occasion, the pirates sent a dish of candles down to one of the prisoners, and forced him to eat them while they held a sword and pistol to his breast. Spriggs' crew committed countless episodes of extreme violence. They sweated another man and crippled several others by breaking all their bones, purely for amusement.[68] Captain Low's crew rivaled that of Spriggs in their capacity for savagery. They captured a French vessel, and after plundering the ship they decided to burn it. Low's men took "all of the crew out of her, but the cook, who, they said, being a greasy fellow would fry well in the fire; so the poor man was bound to the main-mast, and burnt in the ship, to the no small diversion of Low and his mermidons."[69] Later, Low and his crew captured a ship whose men did not surrender quickly and attempted to defend themselves. For this effrontery, the pirates barbarously cut them. They were especially violent toward two Portuguese friars, whom they tortured for sport.[70] After they took another ship, Low ordered his men to place lighted matches between the fingers of the ship's crew, which "burnt all the flesh off their bones; then cut them in several parts of their bodies with knives and cutlasses; afterwards took all their provisions away, and set some of them ashore in an uninhabited part of the country."[71] In perhaps the most horrifying incident, Low and his men ripped up the body of the master of a whaling ship and took his entrails out. They then cut off the ears of another master they had captured and forced him to eat them with pepper and salt.[72] Most pirates did not treat women with any more regard than they did men. Captain Anstis's crew took a woman they had captured, and "twenty-one of them forced the poor creature successively, afterwards broke her back and flung her into the sea."[73] While some of this behavior could be interpreted as backlash against numerous years of economic and social oppression that nearly all seamen of this period faced, the widespread and indiscriminate use of violence practiced by many pirates indicates aberrant, criminal personalities more than simple dissatisfaction with the social order.[74]

Such brutality denies the equality of men. Pirates were not particularly concerned with racial equality either. Black men may have been treated more equitably at sea than on land. In many cases, more occupations were available to black men on ships, and they were often judged by their abilities as sailors as well as by their color.[75] However, there is little evidence to indicate that blacks were treated much better by pirates than by other seamen. Free and slave blacks were present on many pirate vessels, and slave ships were often taken as plunder.[76] One captain stated that when his ship was captured by Spriggs, the pirates took his ship and all of his men but had given him his liberty and "25 negroes."[77] This incident indicates that Spriggs most likely had slaves in his possession which he possibly plundered from a slave ship.

Black men were often assigned the most menial jobs on pirate ships, and some captains actually held slaves. Rowland Sharp testified at his trial about how he was treated when taken by the pirates. Sharp stated "I was but like a Negro, and they made slaves of all of that colour."[78] Once, when Captain Bellamy stopped to careen, the slaves on board were put to work building huts. Johnson states that Bellamy treated these slaves in the same manner as West India planters.[79] The pirates under Captain Martel, when heavily pursued by a man-of-war, left their ship and set it on fire, with twenty Africans aboard who were all burnt.[80] In a similar incident, Captain Roberts burnt a ship with eighty Africans on board, because "unshackling them cost much time and labour."[81] Sharks ate those who jumped overboard to avoid being burnt.[82] Some pirate accounts also mention American Indians on board. They too were often treated as inferior, near the level of servants. Thomas Mumford, an Indian employed by Captain Low, was acquitted of piracy charges, because he acted "as a servant on board."[83]

There are still many unanswered questions about pirates. Those pirates who never went to court, most of whom were probably illiterate, have completely disappeared from history. Also, it is extremely difficult to interpret the last words of a man about to be executed. A great deal of the sources available to historians come from captains, or from officials who came into contact with pirates. Therefore, we still may not know the true story of life on a pirate ship. Many generalizations that hold true for pirates of English origin, operating in large crews in the short time frame prior to 1726, are less valid for non-English pirates, or for pirates who worked on a more individual basis or in smaller crews. Perhaps pirates would be better compared with other criminals because the fact that they stole on a regular basis seems to be as important a defining characteristic as was their association with the general seafaring population.

Pirates exhibited some nascent yearnings for economic and social equality. However, the evidence does not entirely support the idea that they possessed a coherent ideology or philosophy based on those yearnings. We cannot say that pirates consciously formed an egalitarian collectivistic society. By imbuing them with characteristics that some scholars regard as noble, such as a desire to level economic and social distinctions, we obscure the reality of their brutal and selfish lifestyle. In many ways, pirates were the ultimate opportunists, taking advantage of the crossroads of a multitude of economic and political events at precisely the right moment. For men in the navy or merchant service, or even more so the unemployed seaman, the line between privateer and pirate was simply too thin to raise concern about crossing it. There is no doubt that the rise of piracy was closely tied to mercantilism and the emergence of a capitalist economy. Furthermore, piracy did not flourish during times of war, when adequate employment could be found aboard legitimate privateering vessels. Large amounts of capital changing hands and an excess of seamen converged at precisely the right moment with the absence of a visible, coercive government, a consequence of the colonial situation. In a barren new land where money meant everything, there was no legal or social apparatus to coerce men into abiding by the laws and rules of civilization. The fact that many men chose to take advantage of this situation does not necessarily imply that they were somehow unhappy with this new world of capital. Rather, they saw an opportunity; they were attempting to take part in capitalist enterprise through the easiest method they saw as available to them—crime. They chose to become criminals—pirates—not because they were anticapitalist, but precisely because they wanted to take advantage of capitalism.

# NOTES

[1] Charles Johnson, *A General History of the Robberies and Murders of the Most Notorious Pirates*, ed. Arthur Hayward (London: Routledge & Kegan Paul, Ltd., 1926), 212. Scholars have debated the identity of Charles Johnson, and some claim definitively that Johnson was a pseudonym for Daniel Defoe. However, more recently, this theory has been seriously undermined and discarded by many. In any case, the works of Johnson are generally considered to be accurate sources and are accepted as mostly factual by historians of piracy. Roberts, how he became a pirate, and his crew are also discussed in the *Boston News-Letter*, August 15-22, 1720.

[2] These historians include Robert Ritchie, *Captain Kidd and the War Against the Pirates* (Cambridge, Mass.: Harvard University Press, 1986); Jesse Lemisch, "Jack Tar in the Streets: Merchant Seamen in the Politics of Revolutionary America," *William and Mary Quarterly* 3rd Ser., 25 (1968): 371-407; David Cordingly, *Under the Black Flag; The Romance and the Reality of Life Among the Pirates*, (New York: Random House, 1996); and Marcus Rediker, *Between the Devil and the Deep Blue Sea: Merchant Seamen, Pirates, and the Anglo-American Maritime World, 1700-1750*, (New York: Cambridge University Press, 1987), and *Villains of All Nations: Atlantic Pirates in the Golden Age* (Boston: Beacon Press, 2004.).

[3] Rediker, *Villains of All Nations*, 26, 37, 61; Rediker, *Between the Devil and the Deep Blue Sea*, 255-56.

[4] While large-scale piracy is usually the topic of discussion, there are also a significant number of instances of robbery on a smaller scale that should technically be considered piracy. For example, Captain Worley left New York in a small boat with only eight other men and few provisions. In another case, three men and one woman attempted to steal a ship out of Chesapeake Bay, as they desired to become permanent pirates. Studying these types of incidents could lead to very different conclusions about piracy than have thus far been offered. They do help to demonstrate that choosing to become a pirate was more an act of a desperate criminal seeking easy money than that of a downtrodden laborer seeking revenge. See Captain Charles Johnson, *A General History of the Robberies and Murders of the Most Notorious Pirates*, ed. David Cordingly (New York: Lyons Press, 1998), 270-73; High Court of Admiralty papers (HCA), 49/104; Great Britain, Public Record Office, Colonial Office, London (PRO).

[5] Rediker, *Villians of All Nations*, 44-45.

[6] Trial of John Houghling, Cornelius Franc, and Francois Delaunee, Colonial Office Papers (CO) 5/1411, (May 13, 1700), PRO.

[7] Johnson, *A General History*, 1998 ed., 308.

[8] *The Trial of Eight Persons Indited for Piracy* (Boston: Green for Edwards, 1718), 34. This close-proximity, single-sex environment has prompted B. R. Burg to argue that nearly all pirates were homosexual. While this is an interesting argument, I have found little evidence to support it. B. R. Burg, *Sodomy and the Perception of Evil: English Sea Rovers in the Seventeenth Century Caribbean* (New York: New York University Press, 1983).

[9] John Franklin Jameson, *Privateering and Piracy in the Colonial Period: Illustrative Documents* (New York: Macmillan, 1923), 308; *The Tryals of Major Stede Bonnet* (London: B. Cowse, 1719), 37.

[10] Rediker, *Villians of All Nations*, 48-49.

[11] Nearly every pirate claimed force when faced with certain death. However, this does not deny the substantial evidence that many of them actually were forced. *Trials of Eight Persons Indited for Piracy*, 10; *The Tryals of Thirty-Six Persons for Piracy* (Boston: Kneeland, 1723), 6.

[12] *The Tryals of Sixteen Persons for Piracy* (Boston: Edwards, 1726); Cotton Mather, *The Vial Poured Out Upon the Sea: A Remarkable Relation of Certain Pirates Brought unto a Tragical and Untimely End, Some Conferences with them after their Condemnation, their Behavior at their Execution, and a Sermon Preached on that Occasion,* (Boston: T. Fleet, 1726), 3; the *Boston News-Letter*, June 30-July 7, 1726.

[13] *Tryals of Eight Persons*, 35; There are numerous examples of this practice. Cornelius Franc was taken because he spoke several languages, see CO 5/1411.

[14] Johnson, *A General History*, 1998 ed., 232-33.

[15] Ibid., 326-27.

[16] *Boston News-Letter*, July 16-23, 1724.

[17] *Tryals of Bonnet*, 29. Captain Bunce told William Cunningham he would be "put on a maroon key" if he did not join, Johnson, *A General History*, 1926 ed., 584.

[18] CO 5/1411.

[19] HCA 49/104.

[20] *Tryals of Sixteen Persons; Tryals of Eight Persons.*

[21] HCA 49/104.

[22] *Tryals of Eight Persons.*

[23] *Tryals of Thirty-Six Persons,* 19.

[24] HCA 1/99; Johnson, *A General History,* 1998 ed., 236-39.

[25] Johnson, *A General History,* 1998 ed., 81, 132.

[26] Ibid., 132.

[27] Ibid., 132-33.

[28] Mather, *The Vial Poured Out Upon the Sea,* 21; Benjamin Colman, *It is a Fearful Thing to Fall into the Hands of the Living God: A Sermon Preached to Some Miserable Pirates, July 10, 1726, on the Lord's Day Before their Execution* (Boston: Edwards, 1726), 39; *Boston News-Letter,* June 30-July 7, 1726.

[29] Johnson, *A General History,* 1926 ed., 144; *The Grand Pyrate, or, the Life and Death of Captain George Cusack, the Great Sea-Robber: With an Account of all his Notorious Robberies both at Sea and Land: Together with his Trial Condemnation and Execution* (London: Jonathan Edwin, 1676) is another instance of mutiny.

[30] Johnson, *A General History,* 1926 ed., 25-26.

[31] *Boston News-Letter,* July 29-August 5, 1725.

[32] Ibid., 235.

[33] W. Noel Sainsbury et al., eds., *Calendar of State Papers, Colonial Series, America and the West Indies,* 34 (London: His Majesty's Stationery Office, 1860- ), 161.

[34] *Tryals of Eight Persons,* 24.

[35] *Boston News-Letter,* April 29--May 6, 1725. In a similar case, Nicholas Simons and Jonathan Barlow, two forced men, staged a successful mutiny against the pirates who had captured them, described in the *Boston News-Letter,* February 4-11, 1725.

[36] Graham Brooks, ed., *Trial of Captain Kidd* (Edinburgh and London: William Hodge & Company, Ltd.,1930), 143-44.

[37] Johnson, *A General History,* 1998 ed., 237.

[38] Ibid., 317.

[39] Brooks, *Trial of Captain Kidd*, 141.

[40] Johnson, *A General History*, 1998 ed., 69.

[41] Ibid., 103.

[42] Ibid., 17.

[43] Rediker, "'Under the Banner of King Death': The Social World of Anglo-American Pirates, 1716 to 1726," *William and Mary Quarterly* 3rd Ser., 38 (1981): 219-20.

[44] Johnson, *A General History*, 1998 ed., 30.

[45] Ibid., 325.

[46] Ibid., 41.

[47] Ibid., 193.

[48] Rediker, *Villains of All Nations*, 73-75.

[49] All men, that is, except servants, slaves, or forced men who had not signed the articles. Johnson, *A General History*, 1926 ed., 182-84; *Tryals of Thirty-Six Persons*, 13.

[50] Johnson, *A General History*, 1926 ed., 184. For another example, see Johnson, *A General History*, 1998 ed., 278.

[51] Rediker, *Villains of All Nations*, 31; Rediker, *Between the Devil and the Deep Blue Sea*, 276.

[52] Johnson, *A General History*, 1998 ed., 36-37. This community was formed by Captain Avery, but grew to include men who had served under many different captains.

[53] Ibid.

[54] Charles Ellms, ed., *The Pirates Own Book: Authentic Narratives of the Most Celebrated Sea Robbers* (1837; Salem, Mass.: Marine Research Society, 1924), 211.

[55] Johnson, *A General History*, 1998 ed., 31. Avery never really profited much from these diamonds, as he was unable to reveal his possession of them without arousing suspicion.

[56] Ibid., 174-5.

[57] Jack Leland, "Stede Bonnet Captured at Cape Fear."

[58] Johnson, *A General History*, 1998 ed., 215.

[59] Ibid., 318-19.

[60] Ibid., 279.

[61] Ibid., 280.

[62] Ibid., 171.

[63] Ibid., 194.

[64] Ibid.

[65] *Tryals of Eight Persons*, 25.

[66] Johnson, *A General History*, 1998 ed., 220.

[67] Ibid., 326.

[68] Ibid., 328-9.

[69] Ibid., 295.

[70] Ibid.

[71] Ibid., 300.

[72] Ibid., 306. The list of Low's brutalities is virtually endless; in another case, his crew whipped the master of a whaler and tortured him for sport, See Ibid., 305.

[73] Ibid., 261.

[74] Marcus Rediker believes this extreme violence is a product of what he identifies as the final period in the golden age of piracy, 1722-26, and was a response to increased pressure and violence from government officials capturing and executing pirates, see Rediker, *Villians of All Nations*, 170-72.

[75] For more discussion of these issues see W. Jeffrey Bolster, *Black Jacks: African American Seamen in the Age of Sail* (Cambridge, Mass.: Harvard University Press, 1997).

[76] Tryals of Bonnet, 29; Johnson, *A General History*, 1926 ed., 239.

[77] *Boston News-Letter*, January 21-28, 1725.

[78] *Tryals of Bonnet*, 30.

[79] Johnson, *A General History*, 1926 ed., 484.

[80] Johnson, *A General History*, 1998 ed., 45.

[81] Ibid., 204.

[82] Ibid.

[83] *Tryals of Thirty-Six Persons*, 6.

# III

## ON THE MATERIAL CULTURE OF SHIPS
## IN THE AGE OF SAIL

### MICHAEL J. JARVIS

Fundamental to the global expansion of Europe from the fifteenth century onward were the regular voyages of countless ships between ports scattered throughout the world. Within the seventeenth- and eighteenth century Atlantic, vessels carried the myriad free and coerced migrants who planted and expanded new settlements, the supplies they required, and the wide array of commodities they produced. When we credit the role of mariners and ships in connecting homelands and far-flung settlements, metropolitan markets and colonial ventures, core and periphery, it becomes apparent that much of Atlantic world history rests firmly upon maritime history, as the very term "Atlantic" ought to imply.[1]

Denizens of the Atlantic world were intimately acquainted with sailing vessels. Most—black and white—made transoceanic passages to reach the Americas, and many also traveled by water regionally or locally in coastal vessels to avoid slow and tedious overland journeys. Ships carried the commodities that settlers labored long and hard to produce, ferrying them to regional entrepôts and markets abroad. Maritime transportation linked mother country with colony and colonies with each other, promoting during the century before the American Revolution economic specialization in staples in some areas (the Caribbean sugar islands), diversification in others (the middle colonies), and the development of maritime services and supplies in yet others (New England, Bermuda, North Carolina). Ships were vital even to the backwoodsman on the frontier, who sold livestock and timber often destined for Caribbean plantations in exchange for tools and goods manufactured in England and tropical luxuries such as rum, sugar, and molasses. News, letters, and information traveled along with cargoes on board ships, part of a larger, international cultural exchange linking and integrating emergent American creole societies. The eighteenth-century ship combined the modern-day services of Greyhound, Roadway, and

[51]

A.T.&T., and was the principal—often the sole—vehicle on a colonial "information highway."[2]

Despite its ubiquity and undeniable significance in shaping world history, the sailing vessel remains among the most under-studied objects of early America and the early modern Atlantic. Although its services and cumulative contribution in circulating commodities have long been credited by economic historians, and individual ships such as Columbus's *Santa Maria*, Drake's *Golden Hind*, the Pilgrims' *Mayflower*, Cook's *Endeavour*, the whaleship *Essex*, and the slave-bearing *Amistad* have been studied in detail verging on fetishism, the ship as a physical entity has barely been explored. Advocating a more conceptually complex understanding of ships by borrowing from theoretical and methodological developments in the fields of material culture studies and historical architecture, this essay considers the sailing ship as an artifact and focuses principally on four linked elements: the evolution, circulation, and diffusion of ship form and design; the ship's role as a commodity and an embodiment of its owners' capitalistic goals; the ship's function as a physical setting or stage that influenced social interactions among its crew and passengers; and the ship's propensity to assume a discrete cultural and social identity of its own to become an animate object in more than a physical sense of the term. For this essay I draw mainly upon examples from the seventeenth- and eighteenth-century North Atlantic and Caribbean generally and the workings of Bermuda's merchant fleet in particular, but the issues raised and variations in practice that emerge from this initial exploration of the subject can be geographically and temporally extended far beyond these areas.

Ships are first and foremost physical objects and artifacts belonging to particular times, places, and cultures. Although they were arguably the most complex machines of the early modern world, ships can be reduced descriptively to Aristotle's basic elements of form and matter and situated individually within a comparative and comprehensive taxonomic assemblage. Efforts at formal classification immediately reveal the vast array of rigging arrangements, sizes, and hull designs of vessels sailing the world's seventeenth- and eighteenth-century oceans, as well as considerable regional and ethnic variation in contemporary terms used to describe a given vessel and its constituent parts. A ship (generically an oceangoing vessel) was not always a ship (technically a three- or more masted vessel carrying square-rigged sails on all masts); rather it was a protean form exhibiting many permutations in numbers of masts and yards supporting configurations of square and fore-and-aft sails best suited to the vessel's purpose and the oceanic geography where it operated. The British employed the measure of "ton" to assess a vessel's size or capacity and computed it in at least three usually unequal figures: measured tons (size as built), laden tons (internal volume of cargo space), and registered tons (legally recorded size for imperial and colonial tax assessment purposes). Using the variables of keel length, beam width, and hold depth, formulas for computing measured tons could yield the same tonnage figure for hulls with quite different proportions. To further complicate matters, the British ton differed from Spanish *toneladas*, Dutch *lasten*, and French *tonneaux*, all of which also varied in the attributes they measured and computationally changed over time.[4]

Part of the confusion over assessing tonnage stemmed from the fact that the physical size of oceangoing vessels varied considerably across time and space. Vessels ranged from tiny coastal craft involved in intraregional and inter-island trades (the Dutch Caribbean *kleine vaart*, for example) to enormous first-rate battleships and long-distance European merchantmen trading with Asia. Larger vessels have received more scholarly attention than "coasting" vessels involved in local trade, which remain particularly understudied in Anglo-America. Their small size and their frequent omission from most naval office shipping lists renders them nearly invisible to historical inquiry. But small size did not automatically render a vessel a coaster or preclude it from long-distance trade: sloops as small as four and five registered tons made 2,500-mile round-trip voyages between Bermuda and Jamaica in the 1680s. New England colonies had similarly small vessels engaged in long-distance trade.[5]

Hull shape also varied considerably. Assessed by modern marine architects in terms of a ship's block coefficient, the carrying capacity of a vessel varied according to how full or sharp were a vessel's lines, which was intimately connected with sailing performance. Designed to maximize cargo volume yet operate with a smaller crew by reducing sail area, Dutch flyboats, for instance, revolutionized European trade because they slowly but cheaply carried vast quantities of low value, bulky commodities between ports. Because of their commercial efficiency, they became increasingly emulated elsewhere in Europe over time. At the other extreme of hull shape, sharp-lined and fast-sailing Bermuda and Jamaica sloops specialized in quickly moving smaller cargoes through dangerous Caribbean waters. Privateers and pirates also eagerly sought them as useful commerce raiders. These vessels sacrificed greater carrying capacity for speed. Other elements of the fabric of sailing vessels—timber, cordage, metal fittings, and canvas—perhaps varied less than form, although the various constituent woods used in construction significantly affected a vessel's sailing characteristics, upper size limits, cargo capacity in weight and volume, and longevity, and thus deserve careful consideration as well.[6]

Function fundamentally shaped form and influenced choices among fabrics. The wide range of sailing craft launched by European and American shipyards can be read or situated within a sort of evolutionary scheme that responded to other developments within the Atlantic world over time. Different types of vessels were designed, built, and refined over time to fill traditional and newly emerging economic niches within the Atlantic world commercial system. The forms and fabrics of Gloucester fishing schooners, Jamaican sugar droghers, and European slavers working the West African coast vary because they were built to facilitate very different maritime activities in different oceanic settings. The desire for speed and maneuverability was common to all three, but the exigencies of harvesting fish in cold northern waters, shuttling plantation goods to local markets in the warm, teredo-infested Caribbean, and procuring slaves in a succession of African coastal settlements and then racing to get as many as possible alive to American markets produced important differences in ship design and construction. Over time, typical or optimal vessel attributes emerged for each of these maritime sectors, in equilibrium with prevailing environmental and market conditions. Although the *Trans-Atlantic Slave Trade Database* documents a wide variety of ship sizes and rigging types (ranging from the 1,667-ton, ninety-man French ship *Comte de Forcalquier* in 1787 and 1790 to the ten-ton schooner *Hesketh* of Liverpool in 1761 or the twelve-ton sloop *Abigail* of Newport, Rhode Island, in 1758), ships in the 150- to 250-ton range emerged among British, French, and Dutch slavers as the rig and size best suited to the Upper and Lower Guinea slave trade in the eighteenth century. Although more than a few regional shipbuilders steadfastly adhered to traditional forms and resisted innovation, the wide range of Atlantic vessel forms demonstrates that others were open to experimentation with new materials and designs.[7]

The diversity of ships within the early modern Atlantic is directly (although not exclusively) linked to the emergence and increasing integration of regional colonial trade networks, the rise of specialist navies concurrent with the escalation of European imperial rivalries, and greater exploitation of coastal and pelagic natural and cultural resources—various Atlantic fisheries, shipwreck salvage, pearl-diving, and salt-raking, to name a few. A particular Marblehead schooner might over the course of its career sail as a Grand Banks fishing vessel, a merchantman freighting provisions between North American and

Caribbean ports, and a privateer preying on French or Spanish shipping, effectively circulating in three different Atlantic maritime sectors. Whether such a pattern of diversified usage was typical or exceptional remains unclear, however, since we know little about degrees of specialization within and between maritime sectors. The form, fabric, and function of a given vessel are thus arrays of characteristics that can be situated on a spectrum ranging between specific, highly specialized attributes that suit it to a particular maritime use and generally utilitarian qualities that make it flexibly suited to multiple uses. Ships were readily modified, however, and structurally enhanced (rerigged, hold configurations altered, physically expanded vertically and laterally) as needs arose to fit better, new, or different maritime uses. They were also subject to wear and natural deterioration that entailed periodic refitting or rebuilding. Form and fabric were thus changeable, and descriptions must be situated in time for a given vessel. Far from static entities, ships were organically and often repeatedly altered over the course of their life spans.[8]

A considerable volume of past scholarship devoted to the evolution of ships and shipbuilding within different national and cultural traditions has made considerable inroads in creating a taxonomy for the early modern world's array of vessels. Still, the task of closely studying (or even surveying) the thousands of vessels plying the waters of the North Atlantic alone in any given year is daunting. Major groupings for vessels have been established according to maritime sectors of activity (naval, merchant, fishing and whaling, etc.), broad square-sail and fore-and-aft rigging differentiation, and size ranges according to tonnage and number of crew. These approximate taxonomic biological family and genus designations. Nevertheless, local evolutionary patterns and particularity in terms of material choices and design elements still need considerably more study in many regions and periods in order to reach the finer level of species. The fossil record, as it were, still remains substantially incomplete. Fortunately, maritime historians can share this considerable task with a broad coalition of other scholars, ranging from art historians, marine artists, and model builders keenly attentive to architectural detail, to museum curators researching and conserving surviving sailing craft or their constituent parts, to underwater archaeologists excavating, recording, and sometimes raising the physical remains of lost vessels.[9]

A further challenge to mapping out the broad evolution of early modern vessels stems from the inherently mobile nature of sailing ships and the propensity for individual design elements to become spatially diffused as shipbuilders elsewhere appropriated them. Take, for example, the Bermuda sloop, which emerged as a distinctive vessel type in the late seventeenth century. Its constituent strands of design and construction material have their origins in the 1619 shipwreck of Dutch shipwright Jacob Jacobson in Bermuda. Choosing to remain in the English colony, Jacobson trained a generation of Bermuda-born boatbuilders in the 1630s. The boats he and his students produced to accommodate intra-island transport, fishing, and wreck salvage sprang from the design of Dutch craft used to navigate the Zuider Zee but were constructed with the island's unique, rot-resistant cedar. These early vessels used fore-and-aft loose-footed triangular "Bermuda" sails to enable sailors to navigate through the island's maze-like reefs and reach windward locations despite the island's prevailing southwesterly winds. Additional design elements reached the island as various English and Dutch privateers and Spanish prizes called there in the 1630s and 1640s. The island's first oceangoing craft put to sea in the 1650s and 1660s. Many were only slightly larger and more complex than local boats. Although they grew in size and added booms and various headsails to their sloop rig in the eighteenth century, the island's sloops had a finite upper size limit, since the cedar trees that local shipbuilders favored rarely grew to heights of more than forty feet. Shipbuilding in Bermuda was also limited by the island's small size of only twenty-one square miles; even though eighty to ninety percent of the island was deliberately reforested to supply the shipbuilding industry, the timber available in any given year was limited. Sailing principally to Caribbean destinations through pirate- and privateer-infested waters during the wartime years of 1689 to 1714, the early Bermuda sloops underwent a natural selection of sorts as slower, less-maneuverable sloops were captured and faster hull and sail configurations prevailed and were replicated in future sloops built to replace those lost or captured. The product of fifty years of seventeenth-century experimentation and adaptation in local waters, the indigenous Bermuda sloop was thus further refined in the crucible of contested Caribbean trade before emerging as a famous fast carrier in the eighteenth century. Its small size, shallow draft, speed, decay-resistant hull, and maneuverability made the Bermuda sloop ideally suited for trading at smaller, sometimes difficult to access colonial ports in the Caribbean and along the southern North American coast.[10]

Bermudian shipwrights had not long achieved their ideal vessel form before their counterparts in other colonies began to incorporate these elements in their own shipbuilding efforts. Direct diffusion occurred as Bermudian craftsmen emigrated to Jamaica, the Bahamas, the Chesapeake, and the Carolinas from the 1660s onward. Indirect diffusion through study and emulation took place as well. Ships are nothing if not migratory, assuring that their form and characteristics were observed, critiqued, and selectively copied by a wide potential audience in ports around the world. Diffusion of elements of the Bermuda sloop such as its sharp hull lines, signature raked-back mast, and raised stem and bowsprit, took a variety of paths into the Chesapeake. Several dozen Bermudians emigrated to the fledgling port town of Norfolk in the 1680s and 1690s, taking with them Bermuda-built vessels, building techniques, and slaves trained in sloop construction. John and Robert Tucker, Nathaniel Tatem, Daniel Hutchings, Richard Joell, and other Bermudians in Norfolk continued to build and operate sloops in Virginia using local water-resistant timbers from the nearby Great Dismal Swamp. Virginia and Maryland shipwrights also had many opportunities to examine Bermuda sloops, since dozens called annually at Chesapeake ports to sell the salt that Bermudians raked in the Turks Islands. When Bermudian vessels underwent repairs in Chesapeake yards, local shipwrights had even greater opportunities for detailed study. By 1761, a *Maryland Gazette* advertisement boasted that a newly launched hull was "built . . . very much after the Bermudas mould" as a selling point.[11]

A third path of technological diffusion emerged during the Seven Years War as North American shipwrights sent slaves they owned to Bermuda to apprentice in the island's yards. They returned to their home colonies in 1764 with practical experience and firsthand knowledge of Bermuda sloops built "by the eye," without using drafts. Although Bermudian shipwrights did not follow drafts, the Royal Navy recorded the hull lines of at least one Bermuda sloop in the 1740s. A broad international audience became familiar with its sail plan and design after Swedish naval architect Fredrik af Chapman included it in his magnum opus *Architectura Navalis Mercatoria*, published in 1768. Lloyd's insurance registers for the years 1764 and 1776 reveal an Atlantic-wide circulation of Bermuda-built vessels trading in the Mediterranean, Baltic, and Caribbean Seas, and along the African coast.[12]

At the dawn of the eighteenth century, the Bermuda sloop was a unique sailing craft, the product of a locally specific shipbuilding tradition. By the onset of the American Revolution, it had become just one among many sleek and speedy colonial vessels. It lost its primacy in the age of sail, thanks in large degree to its own successful operation, wide circulation, and consequent diffusion. The schooner followed a similarly broad and expansive dissemination;

although earlier pictorial evidence has dispelled the long-held myth of the schooner's invention in Gloucester, Massachusetts, in 1713, the Atlantic diffusion of both this significant rig and its name warrant further research. Dozens of other discrete local shipbuilding traditions similarly blended nautical architectural elements together within a network of mutual influence extending throughout Europe and her colonies. Each of these deserves closer study.[13]

Drafts of hull lines abstract and record the form of individual vessels to create a virtual ship on paper for easier circulation and potential duplication. Vessels also assumed the functionally abstract role of commodity, given the right set of economic circumstances. The relevance of conceptualizing a ship as a commodity (or as Arjun Appadurai elaborates, the commodity context or potential "moment" within the social life of any "thing") varied widely and was often determined by the degree of separation between the builder and owners of any given ship and the uses to which that ship was put. Due to the initial cost of procuring materials and paying various necessary craftsmen, most vessels were built under contract. Smaller craft requiring less capital outlay and favorable market conditions (especially for fast ships during wartime) encouraged some speculative construction, however. Some New Jersey farmers, for instance, seasonally built small vessels during slack winter months and sold them to augment household incomes. Professional shipwrights across the Delaware and throughout the Chesapeake turned out better quality ships to supply the needs of indigenous colonial merchant fleets. New England shipwrights produced vessels for multiple markets from the mid-seventeenth century onward, serving the needs of local carrying, fishing, and whaling fleets. But they also built under contract and on speculation for English and other colonial buyers. Vessel sales to overseas customers went a long way toward meeting New England's considerable trade deficit with Great Britain before 1775. By 1773, nearly a third of Great Britain's merchant fleet of 7,694 vessels had been built in the colonies, with New England figuring most prominently in production. Vessels built to be sold abroad were thus born as commodities but thereafter functioned as platforms for transportation or harvesting various marine resources. They rarely resumed commodity status unless they were resold. Naval vessels built in state dockyards never experienced a commodity moment of exchange, since builder and owner were both the state.[14]

Some Bermudian and other American colonial vessels also bypassed an initial commodity moment because their builders, owners, and operators were the same individuals, usually consortia of interrelated families who contributed timber,

construction skills and labor (their own and their slaves'), and necessary import-
ed materials to keep construction costs low (in Bermuda's case, between £1
and £2 local currency per ton in the early eighteenth century). Such informal-
ly built and owned vessels were more akin to family workshops or farms elsewhere in their ownership and operation. Because there was no separation
between builders and owners, Bermudian shipbuilders were particularly concerned with the quality of the sloops they partly owned and on which their
friends and kinsmen would sail. Bermudian vessels were at least potential commodities all the time, however, since ship captains were usually empowered to
accept a compelling sale offer while the vessel was trading abroad. Between a
third and half of Bermuda's annual shipbuilding production was commissioned by merchants in other colonies or speculatively built for sale abroad.
Due to their reputation for high quality, performance, and longevity,
Bermuda's sloops were themselves staples in the island's trade, fetching
between £10 and £12 sterling per ton in the 1750s. Some Bermudian yards
even shipped prefabricated sloop frames to Caribbean buyers in the 1760s for
assembly there. St. Eustatius was a particularly lucrative market for older
Bermuda sloops, where French, Spanish, and Dutch buyers acquired not only
fine vessels, but usually also their British registries as well, which were useful
in facilitating interisland smuggling efforts. As commodities, ships circulated in
Atlantic business markets much like the cargoes they carried. Turnover in ownership due to sale, capture, or legal seizure was generally much less frequent
than cargoes, however.[15]

In its most abstract form, a ship was reduced to a financial instrument or a
risk assessment. Ownership in larger vessels was often fractionally divided
among large numbers of investors to spread risk. Unlike merchant investors,
smaller shareholders came from a broad spectrum of professional backgrounds
and often had no connection to the building or operation of the vessels they
owned. Much like investors in joint-stock trading companies, they transferred
their shares, received dividends on successful voyages, and realized gains or
losses when their vessels were sold or went missing. To them, a ship was ideally a money-making machine whose operation was left in the hands of experts,
a potential for gain rather than a tangible object. Marine insurers further
abstracted ships into statistical probabilities of loss, considering ships and their
cargoes as perishable entities that more or less successfully negotiated natural,
navigational, and man-made hazards in peace and war. Insurance underwriters
gambled on a specific ship's survival on a given voyage or period. To better set

the odds, they scientifically assessed a ship's quality. Lloyd's of London, for instance, assigned to the eighteenth-century vessels it insured letter ratings (A to E) with numbered subclasses to establish the rates offered to policyholders. Underwriters minutely examined the physical form of a ship to determine its age, condition, and potential flaws, but once insured and set in motion, the ship became a bet.[16]

Ships were more than mere objects or commodities, however, since they took on important social dimensions and, more than most objects, directly and profoundly touched the lives of large numbers of people. They called into being various and frequently overlapping communities of individuals who came together to build, own, and operate them. Building a ship required the specialist skills of a diverse coterie of craftsmen, including shipwrights, carpenters, caulkers, block-makers, sailmakers, blacksmiths, joiners, and painters. These professionals were variously organized in guilds, employed individually, or retained in state-run dockyards, depending on time period, nationality, and location. The raw materials from which ships were fashioned further extended the constellation of contacts to include ship chandlers, rope-makers, weavers, coopers, lumberjacks and sawyers, naval stores producers, iron-founders, various metal-smiths, and manufacturers, each of them constituting links in local, regional, and global commodities chains. In the many places where necessary shipbuilding materials were locally unavailable, the very act of ship construction spurred the expansion of shipping. Provisioning a ship added a host of additional agricultural and processing contacts. Building a ship thus created a temporary community involving the coordinated and collective labors of dozens, if not hundreds, of men to convert masses of timber, iron, hemp, and canvas into a complex and valuable object. Individual ships also transformed the sites of their construction, since sustained shipbuilding fostered economic development and professional diversification in the ports and regions where they were built.[17]

Once launched and fitted out, ships belonged to another generally smaller and more durable social community of owners and investors. Merchants composed a third community connected to ships that sometimes overlapped with the pool of owners, but in other cases were only transiently linked by their rental of cargo space or the whole vessel for a particular voyage or passage leg between ports. A fourth community—the ship's company—had the most intimate and sustained contact with a given vessel, which was both their residence and their workplace. The composition of this group was also often fragile and highly fluid. Captains and mates frequently made repeat voyages in the same vessel and were therefore most inclined to feelings of attachment. Far less is known about how durable were the combinations of ordinary seamen that formed the vessel's crew over its career. Did the typical forecastle have a stable core of repeat voyagers, or were the relationships between individual foremast jacks rarely sustained beyond a voyage or two? Desertion mid-voyage and crew turnover when a vessel paid off upon completing a trading circuit could indicate disaffection with a particular ship or her captain, a disinclination to revisit noisome destinations, the appeal of more lucrative berths, or better employment opportunities on land. Immediate employment in another ship while their present vessel unloaded or refitted also prompted seamen to shift. Persistence in crew composition might reflect social ties to shipowners or officers (a trend especially prevalent in Bermuda, where the same families owned and manned sloops, and white fathers, sons, and brothers, and family slaves, often went to sea together), or individuals' pursuit of promotion through repeated service, or strong personal friendships with fellow shipmates all attached to a particular ship. How durable or ephemeral were the social relations within most individual shipboard communities? Given our overwhelming ignorance about personnel turnover and desertion rates in seventeenth- and eighteenth-century merchant ships, our current conflicting scholarly assessments—ranging from strong attachment to extreme transience—are speculative at best. The many ships that carried passengers (be they free emigrants singly and in families, indentured servants, or African slaves) temporarily hosted a fifth community of migrants who were bound by their shared ordeal of crossing the ocean and who interacted in multifarious ways with ships' crews.[19]

Ships were also social spaces, divided by custom into discrete, role- or class-inflected zones. The social distance between aft cabin and forecastle has long been noticed, but the exclusivity and gradations of social spaces within ships varied considerably according to their size and purpose. A naval ship of the line, for instance, had a wide array of specialized social and vocational spaces for its commander, commissioned officers and midshipmen, surgeon, various warrant officers, and general crew. The mass of seamen within the general crew were further sorted into watches, stations, and messes with proprietarial physical spaces where they worked (parts of the ship, specific [often named] guns) and ate together. Part of the training of any seafaring newcomer was to learn the complex social geography of his ship. Ships often had racialized space established by custom and formal orders. Although the messes and sleeping quarters among large and often interracial crews in most naval vessels were integrated, practices varied on merchant ships. On the ill-fated whaleship *Essex*, for instance, black crewmen occupied the forecastle while white sailors slept aft in steerage. Bermudian sloops and many coasting colonial vessels were often physically so small that white and black crew members shared quarters in the steerage adjoining the master's tiny cabin. A gendering of social space also occurred. Although spartan conditions and a vigorous work regimen imparted an overtly masculine cast to most shipboard space, sites of traditionally femi- nine tasks such as cooking and washing, and areas actually occupied by women, remained exceptional. Space also reflected social hierarchies. The quarterdeck on naval and many merchant ships was the exclusive domain of captains and privileged officers, whose social space was further demarcated into windward and leeward sides. One's visible "residence" within the ship was also closely tied to his occupational and social ranking. Work was publicly and collectively performed under the scrutiny of watch officers and peers. Well- or poorly exe- cuted tasks, especially while in sight of land, produced pride or shame among the officers and crew as a whole, while the constant assessment and consensus of the watch with whom one worked established a sailor's social worth over the course of a voyage.[19]

A ship's deck was furthermore a social stage upon which various seafaring rituals and ceremonies were performed: Sunday divine services, burials at sea, formal floggings at the grating, and King Neptune's initiation of new sailors upon crossing the equator, to name a few. Larger Spanish ships often had shrines to the Virgin Mary or other saints on their quarterdecks, sacred spaces to anchor religious rituals. Swedish and Dutch vessels like the warship *Vasa* and the East Indiaman *Batavia* had hundreds of human and animal carvings throughout whose contemporary significance and social meaning are unfortu- nately lost to us. Anthropologist Greg Dening argues that deeper, but often historically elusive, social "plays" were also continuously enacted on vessels while underway between and among officers and crew members, making ships profoundly social--and often socially contested—places. Underscoring the importance of physical space, Dening suggests that Sir Joseph Banks's appro- priation of much of the HM Armed Ship *Bounty*'s limited area below deck for a botanical nursery significantly contributed to that ship's famous mutiny through crowding and by disrupting traditional shipboard social geographies. Although the plots of the daily dramas played out on countless ships were sel- dom as explosive as that of the *Bounty*, they were all shaped by the physical form and state of the ship/stage on which their individual actors assumed traditional roles and negotiated shipboard life and the exigencies of their individual voyages.[20]

The physical spaces of ships were clearly invested with many social meanings, but ships themselves also assumed a character and meaning that most objects never acquired. Within the vast array of material culture, some objects are more socially "alive" than others. Since time immemorial, merchants and seafarers invested ships with particular identities and formed emotional connections with individual vessels. The life of a ship "quickened" on the stocks as it took shape, personified by construction terms like head, ribs, bottom, and planked skin. Local builders also often adhered to regionally and culturally relevant customs, conventions, and ceremonies in selecting shipbuilding sites and in building and launching their vessels to instill good fortune. When launched, vessels were ritually christened with various liquids (holy water, rum, champagne) and named in culturally significant and conventional ways. The naming of vessels is highly significant. Within Bermuda's colonial merchant fleet of 1716, nearly half (45 of 91) the vessels bore Christian names associated with the families that owned them (27 female and 13 male names or pairs of names, 4 couples, and the *Three Brothers*), reflecting the substantially kin-based organization of the island's trade. A further 13 vessels were named for birds and beasts, while others invoked virtues like *Amity, Blessing, Industry* and *Success*. Elsewhere, British vessels commemorated famous battles, events, and persons, boasted martial spirit or threats (*Revenge*), or took their names from local locations, classical or contemporary literature, insects, and other sources. Quaker religious affiliation is suggested by vessels bearing "friend" in their name, or in the French *Le Trembleur*, while Spanish vessels frequently bore the names of the Virgin Mary and other saints. Naval vessels possessed a slightly different set of naming conventions that varied by national tradition. On larger ships, figureheads of men, women, and various animals further personified or made animate the ship in the eyes of its owners and crew.[21]

Despite the gender of the vessel's name, the ship itself was considered feminine and referred to as "she" by at least the mid-eighteenth century in Anglo-American circles. (The historical moment when this occurred particularly clamors for refinement and further investigation into ethnic and cultural variations.) Over the course of her life, "she" accrued a biography of her own, reflecting her sailing characteristics, events that happened over her career, and the judgments, observations, and sentiments of the men who commanded and sailed her. Reputations attached themselves to vessels much as they did to people, formed, modified, and maintained according to the concensus of her change-able shipboard community. Speedy passages and profitable voyages led sailors to pronounce their ships "good" or lucky, while deaths, accidents, and bad omens observed under way cast a pall on an "ill-fated" ship. Because ships had names and personalities all their own, few seamen felt neutrally about them; attitudes ranged from fondness and sentimental attachment to antipathy, but were generally felt more intensely and immediately than landsmen might toward a house, workshop, or factory.

If ships took on the semblance of life and followed their own life-cycles, then they also endured deaths. Retirement and a peaceful end might come at the hands of wreckers when old, worn out, or obsolete vessels were dismantled after a productive life or through natural decay after being beached or abandoned on a remote shore. But ships also perished violently in storms, battles, and ship-wrecks, and were destroyed by elemental forces, burned to the waterline, or crushed by ice floes. Popular impressions of the overwhelming dangers of the sea suggest that such violent losses were common, but our current knowledge of how ships variously ended their lives is woefully inadequate to establish how typical this was. Like human burials, ships leave physical remains that vary widely in degrees of completeness and preservation due to the nature of their "death" and environmental factors. Nautical archaeologists assume the role of coroners or forensic scientists as their "autopsies" record surviving material traces of a given wreck and hopefully (with enough diagnostic physical evi-dence and documentary research) identify the "body" by name. (Treasure hunters might be alternatively likened to self-interested bounty hunters in search of a particular, wealthy missing person). In assessing post-depositional deterioration and modifications, nautical archaeologists engage in a taphono-my of sorts, identifying environmental factors (n-transforms) that shaped the state of preservation, as well as cultural transformations (c-transforms), such as contemporary wrecking activities and recent salvage attempts by amateur and professional divers. Cargo evidence (if it survives) can be likened to a forensic identification of a "last meal," potentially useful in confirming identi-ty. Close examination of the frame and planking might facilitate an assessment of the geographic origins, age, and state of "health" of a vessel at the moment of death, while evidence of trauma such as gouges in surrounding reefs, charred timbers, and shattered sections of the hull can help to establish a cause of death. Like Egyptian mummies, some wrecks are exhumed, preserved, and

[64]

put on public display for educational purposes, but the expense of conservation and the large size of most vessels result in most being re-interred or left in situ in their watery graves.

As agents of exploration, cultural and economic expansion, and global interaction and integration, sailing ships played a seminal role in the overlapping histories of early America, Europe, the Atlantic world, and of globalism in general. This essay hints at the multidimensional facets of identity and meaning embedded in ships as artifacts and physical objects. In their numbers and diversity of forms they mirrored the prolific expansion in volume, growing mobility, and occupational specialization of the world's early modern population as a whole. Experimentation with, and technical diffusion of, elements of marine architecture can be likened to the widespread cultural creolization that occurred, especially in the Americas as European settlers, African slaves, and Native Americans came to inhabit the same spaces. With names and personalities of their own, ships were also distinct inhabitants of the Atlantic World worthy in their own right of biography. They at once reflected the national and ethnic backgrounds of their creators and crews and took on taxonomic ethnicities of their own through their specific attributes of size, rig, and purpose within a wider array of possible forms.

Perhaps the best way to conceptualize the multiple levels of considering ships is to liken them to houses. Most social historians use the household as a basic unit of study and recognize that the physical size, location, and condition of the house say much about its occupants' place within their local community. The size, layout, and modification over time of houses also shaped and were shaped by intrafamily social interaction. Architectural historians and archaeologists have charted evolutions in seventeenth- and eighteenth-century North America from early, simple, and often impermanent single-story hall or hall-and-parlor houses to larger, more substantial vernacular buildings that exhibited considerable regional variation and greater specialization in room use, to the widespread mid-eighteenth-century adoption of symmetrically arranged Georgian houses, reflecting an emphasis on privacy, individualism, and subscription to a pan-imperial cultural aesthetic. Concurrent with this evolution in many regions was the physical distancing of social inferiors—servants and slaves—by relocating them to nearby outbuildings or more distant quarters. Like the ship, the early modern house was both residence and workplace for most of its inhabitants. Houses too had racialized and gendered spaces, but varying degrees of patriarchal authority and

[65]

intrafamilial, often intergenerational negotiations chiefly determined the social geography imposed upon each household's configuration of rooms. As both malleable artifacts and social stages, investigations of specific construction techniques and materials, dissemination of architectural elements, the social and economic uses of rooms, and the cultural meanings embedded in building and furnishing houses are all relevant to fully comprehending the house as an object. Although sailors were more constrained in modifying their seagoing home, they similarly shaped and were shaped by the ships in which they lived and labored.[22]

Maritime historians can benefit greatly from expanding our conceptual understanding of ships and borrowing ideas and approaches developed in the fields of material culture studies, historical archaeology, and terrestrial social history community studies. By sharing more common ground, maritime history can also shed its traditional association with romantic, technical, and antiquarian topics and broaden its relevance to a larger segment of the historical profession as a whole. We may learn from patterns of uneven coverage in these other fields as well. Institutional buildings, stately mansions, and the houses of the well-to-do more often survive and attract study than the much greater number of physically smaller, more modest, and more vernacularly variable homes in which most denizens of the Atlantic world dwelt. Within maritime studies, large three-masted ships have received similarly disproportional attention, despite the multitude of smaller but more historically elusive vessels engaged in regional and interregional trades.

For most historians, the lives and activities of the people who inhabited terrestrial and maritime spaces are the real focus of our attention. Ideally, we strive to situate them within the larger social context of their surrounding communities. But like houses, the physical arrangement of ships established influential parameters on the social stage upon which our subjects interacted and worked. Generalizations developed around particular types of vessels at specific historical moments, when extended to seafaring culture as a whole, distort our understanding of maritime social history and mask the extraordinary variety of maritime experiences that paying close attention to ships will help us to recover. As one of the primary agents and sites of global integration, ships great and small, famous, notorious, and anonymous, deserve their own biographies as important and ubiquitous denizens of the Atlantic world.

## NOTES

[1] The origins of this essay lie in conversations with fellows at the John Carter Brown Library and my own research on Bermuda's maritime history. The author would like to thank Chandos Michael Brown, Norman Fiering, Paul Gilje, and Daniel Vickers for their helpful comments on earlier drafts.

[2] For an overview of colonial British American economic development, see James Shepherd and Gary Walton, *Shipping, Maritime Trade, and the Economic Development of Colonial North America* (Cambridge: Cambridge University Press, 1972); John McCusker and Russell Menard, *The Economy of British America, 1607–1789* (Chapel Hill: University of North Carolina Press, 1985), esp. 71–208, 277–330; and Stanley Engerman and Robert Gallman, eds., *The Cambridge Economic History of the United States, vol. I: The Colonial Era* (New York: Cambridge University Press, 1996).

[3] Material Culture studies emerged in the 1980s as a distinct interdisciplinary field with practitioners drawn from social history, archaeology, cultural and economic anthropology, art history, and museum and decorative arts studies. Publication has chiefly taken the form of edited volumes rather than monographs: Simon Bronner, ed., *American Material Culture and Folklife: A Prologue and Dialogue* (Ann Arbor: University of Michigan Research Press, 1985); Arjun Appadurai, ed., *The Social Life of Things: Commodities in Cultural Perspective* (New York: Cambridge University Press, 1986); Barrie Reynolds and Margaret Stott, eds., *Material Anthropology: Contemporary Approaches to Material Culture* (Lanham, Maryland: University Press of America, 1987); Robert Blair St. George, ed., *Material Life in America, 1600–1860* (Boston: Northeastern University Press, 1988); Mary Douglas and Baron Isherwood, *The World of Goods: Towards an Anthropology of Consumption* (London: Routledge, 1996); Ann Smart Martin and J. Ritchie Garrison, eds., *American Material Culture: The Shape of the Field* (Winterthur, Del.: Henry Francis duPont Winterthur Museum; Knoxville, Tennessee; distributed by University of Tennessee Press, 1997); Tim Dant, *Material Culture in the Social World: Values, Activities, Lifestyles* (Philadelphia: Open University Press, 1999); Jules David Prown and Kenneth Haltman, eds., *American Artifacts: Essays in Material Culture* (East Lansing: Michigan State University Press, 2000); P. M. Graves-Brown, ed., *Matter, Materiality and Modern Culture* (London: Routledge, 2000); Fred Myers, ed., *The Empire of Things: Regimes of Value and Material Culture* (Sante Fe, New Mexico: School of American Research Press, 2001); Alison Wylie, *Thinking from Things: Essays in the Philosophy of Archaeology* (Berkeley: University of California Press, 2002). See also the articles in the *Journal of Material Culture*, launched in 1995. For a rare attempt to blend recent material culture theory with shipwreck archaeology see Richard Gould, *Archaeology and the Social History of Ships* (Cambridge: Cambridge University Press, 2000).

[4] Robert Freidel, "Some Matters of Substance," in Steven Lubar and W. David Kingery, eds., *History from Things: Essays on Material Culture* (Washington: Smithsonian Institution Press, 1993), 41–50; Frederic Lane, "Tonnages, Medieval and Modern," *Economic History Review* 2nd ser., 17 (1964): 213–33; Gary Walton, "Colonial Tonnage Measurements: A Comment," *Journal of Economic History* 27 (1967): 392–97; Christopher French, "Eighteenth-Century Shipping Tonnage Measurements," *Journal of Economic History* 33 (1973): 434–43; John McCusker, "The Tonnage of Ships Engaged in British Colonial Trade during the Eighteenth Century," *Research in Economic History* 6 (1981): 73–105. On Spanish, Dutch, and French tonnage, see Carla Rahn Phillips, *Six Galleons for the King of Spain: Imperial Defense in the Early Seventeenth Century* (Baltimore: Johns Hopkins University Press, 1986), 60–61; R. De Bock, "Tonnen, Tonnenmaat, en Lasten," MAB 12 (1960): 117–33; A. van Driel, *Tonnage Measurement: Historical and Critical Essay* (The Hague: Government Printing Office, 1925), 6–34; Richard Unger, *The Ship in the Medieval Economy*, 600–1600 (London: Croom Helm, 1980), 29–32, 203–50.

[5] Jamaica Naval Office Shipping List, PRO CO 142/13; *Hannah and Rebecca* (5 tons), arrived July 23, 1688; *Dove* (4 tons), arr. Aug. 6, 1688; *Thomas's Adventure* (5 tons), arr. Dec. 21, 1688. Bernard and Lotte Bailyn found that thirteen percent (24 of 180) of the vessels in New England's 1698 merchant fleet were less than twenty tons, Bailyn and Bailyn, *Massachusetts Shipping, 1697–1714* (Cambridge. Harvard University Press, 1959), 78, 81.

[6] David Cordingly, *Under the Black Flag: The Romance and the Reality of Life among the Pirates* (New York: Random House, 1996), 158, 163–164; Ralph Davis, *The Rise of the English Shipping Industry in the Seventeenth and Eighteenth Centuries* (London: Macmillan, 1962), 44–46, 48–50, 61–62, 74–80; Robert Albion, *Forests and Sea Power: The Timber Problem of the Royal Navy, 1652–1862* (Cambridge, Mass.: Harvard University Press, 1926), esp. 3–38; Virginia Wood, *Live Oaking: Southern Timber for Tall Ships* (Boston: Northeastern University Press, 1981). Hull surface also varied regionally; Scandinavian and other Northern European shipbuilders favored clinker-built hulls with overlapping planking while French and Iberian craftsmen built flush- or caravel-planked hulls.

[7] Beth Preston, "The Function of Things: A Philosophical Perspective on Material Culture," in Graves-Brown, ed., *Matter, Materiality, and Modern Culture*, 22–49; Mihaly Csikszentmihalyi, "Why We Need Things," in Lubar and Kingery, eds., *History from Things*, 21–22; *Trans-Atlantic Slave Trade Database*, data query of tonnage; Herbert Klein, *The Atlantic Slave Trade* (New York: Cambridge University Press, 1999), 90–93, 142–49. In the age of exploration, ships further functioned as platforms for scientific inquiry and mobile laboratories, Richard Sorrenson, "The Ship as a Scientific Instrument in the Eighteenth Century," *Osiris* 2nd ser., 11 (1996): 221–36.

8 For assertion of the flexible use of colonial fishing schooners, see Daniel Vickers, *Farmers and Fishermen: Two Centuries of Work in Essex County, Massachusetts, 1630–1850* (Chapel Hill: University of North Carolina Press, 1994), 145–49. On the evolution of European navies, see especially Jan Glete, *Navies and Nations: Warships, Navies, and State-building in Europe and America, 1500–1860* (Stockholm: Almqvist and Wiksell International, 1993); Jaap Bruijn, *The Dutch Navy of the Seventeenth and Eighteenth Centuries* (Columbia, S. C.: University of South Carolina Press, 1990).

9 For exemplary surveys of vessel forms and evolution, see Howard I. Chapelle, *History of American Sailing Ships* (New York, W. W. Norton & Company, 1935); Unger, *The Ship in the Medieval Economy*, esp. 6–31, 203–50; J. H. Parry, *The Age of Reconnaissance* (New York: The New American Library, 1964), 67–84; Joseph Goldenberg, *Shipbuilding in Colonial America* (Charlottesville: University Press of Virginia, 1976), 10–30, 77–95. William Baker's *Sloops and Shallops* (Columbia: University of South Carolina Press, 1966) provides a good example of a focused study of a particular vessel type. Although limited by their short temporal scope, see also Harold M. Hahn, *The Colonial Schooner, 1763–1775* (Annapolis: Naval Institute Press, 1981), and James Handerson, *Sloops and Brigs: An Account of the Smallest Vessels of the Royal Navy during the Great Wars, 1793–1815* (London: Coles, 1972).

10 Howard I. Chapelle, *The Search for Speed Under Sail, 1700–1855* (New York: W.W. Norton, 1967), 67–68; Michael Jarvis, "Cedars, Sloops and Slaves: The Development of the Bermuda Shipbuilding Industry, 1680–1750," (Master's Thesis, College of William and Mary, 1992), 10–11, 16–31, 34–36; Jarvis, "'In the Eye of All Trade': Maritime Revolution and the Transformation of Bermudian Society, 1612–1800," (PhD diss., College of William and Mary, 1998), 353–72. The Bermuda sloop grew from an average of 19.5 registered tons for the thirty-two sloops built in 1715 to 23.33 registered tons in 1733 and 32.2 tons in 1749, PRO CO 41/6 7.

11 Bermuda Naval Office Shipping List, January 1–December 31, 1716, Public Record Office, CO 41/6–7 database; *Maryland Gazette*, September 3, 1761; Arthur Middleton, *Tobacco Coast: A Maritime History of the Chesapeake Bay in the Colonial Era* (Newport News: Mariners' Museum, 1953), 220–25. In 1716, for instance, a fifth of all vessels entering Bermuda (35 of 156) arrived from the Chesapeake; two decades later, 25 of the 38 sloops mentioned in the *Virginia Gazette* between early September the end of December 1737 came from Bermuda. On Bermudian emigration to Norfolk, see Michael Jarvis, "Commercial Colonization: Norfolk, Bermuda, and the Creation of Atlantic Families, 1680–1750," paper presented at the Society of Early Americanists Conference, Norfolk, Virginia, March 9, 2001.

12 *Lloyd's Register of Shipping*, 26 vols. (London, 1764, 1776; reprint, London: Gregg Press, 1963) database; Fredrik af Chapman, *Architectura Navalis Mercatoria* (Stockholm, 1768; reprint London: Coles, 1971), plate LVII; Howard I. Chapelle, *The History of*

*American Sailing Ships* (New York: Bonanza Books, 1935), 296–99; Chapelle, *Search for Speed Under Sail*, 65–66; William A. Baker, *Sloops and Shallops* (Barre, Mass.: Barre Pulications, 1966), 118–25; John Millar, *American Ships of the Colonial and Revolutionary Periods* (New York: W. W. Norton, 1978), 343; Henry Wilkinson, *Bermuda in the Old Empire* (Oxford: Oxford University Press, 1953), 341–42; Jarvis, "In the Eye of All Trade," 402–406.

[13] Edward Morris, *The Fore-and Aft Rig in America, A Sketch* (New Haven: Yale University Press, 1927), 174–82; Chapelle, *History of American Sailing Ships*, 12–13.

[14] Appadurai, "Introduction: Commodities and the Politics of Value," in Appadurai, *The Social Life of Things*, 13–16: Shepherd and Walton, *Shipping, Maritime Trade, and the Economic Development of Colonial North America*, 241–45; Richard Champion, *Considerations on the Present Situation of Great Britain and the United States of North America, with a View to their Future Commercial Connections* (London: J. Stockdale, 1784), 14; Goldenberg, *Shipbuilding in Colonial America*, 17–19,72, 80–98; James Levitt, *For Want of Trade: Shipping and the New Jersey Ports, 1680–1783* (Newark: New Jersey Historical Society, 1981), 88–93; Simeon Crowther, "The Shipbuilding Industry and the Economic Development of the Delaware Valley, 1681–1776," (PhD diss., University of Pennsylvania, 1970), 28–29, 127–28; Jacob Price, "A Note on the Value of Colonial Exports of Shipping," *Journal of Economic History* 36 (1976): 704–24; McCusker and Menard, *Economy of British America*, 75–80, 85, 97–99, 318–21.

[15] Jarvis, "In the Eye of All Trade," 384–90, 396–402; Ralph Davis, *Rise of the English Shipping Industry*, 159–74; Alured Popple, Answers to Board of Trade, 1740; William Popple to Board of Trade, March 3, 1749, PRO CO 37/13, ff. 184–85; 16, ff. 85, 90–92. In 1758, for instance, the Dutch Nieuw Westindische Compagnie in St. Eustatius collected sale duties of two percent on 21 Bermuda vessels sold there for more than 27,000 pieces of eight and £750 St. Christopher currency, equivalent to more than £4,000 sterling; St. Eustatius Journael, 1758, Nieuw Westindische Compagnie Papers, vol. 624, fol. 184, Algemeen Rijksarchief, The Hague.

[16] Davis, *The Rise of the English Shipping Industry*, 82–84, 87–89, 106, 162–63, 374–77; Crowther, "Shipbuilding Industry and the Economic Development of the Delaware Valley," 28–29, 170–71. Extensive division of ownership of vessels was less common in smaller vessels and in the colonies. Marine insurance was also less widely available in the British colonies than in England; Harold Gillingham, *Marine Insurance in Philadelphia, 1721–1800* (Philadelphia: Patterson and White, 1933), 18–19, 31–102.

[17] Eyup Ozveren, "The Shipbuilding Commodity Chain, 1590–1790," in Gary Gereffi and Miguel Korzeniewicz, eds., *Commodity Chains and Global Capitalism* (Westport, Conn.: Greenwood Press, 1994); Jacob Price, "The Economic Function and the Growth of American Port Towns in the Eighteenth Century," *Perspectives in American*

*History* 8 (1974): 133–60; Gary Nash, *The Urban Crucible: Social Change, Political Consciousness, and the Origins of the American Revolution* (Cambridge, Mass.: Harvard University Press, 1979), ch. 3; McCusker and Menard, *Economy of British America*, 320–22.

[18] N. A. M. Rodger asserts that at least in the 1750s and 1760s, most British sailors were strongly attached to their ships and officers. He claims that some of the desertion that did occur was from one naval vessel to another as sailors sought reunions with former shipmates, *The Wooden World: An Anatomy of the Georgian Navy* (London: Collins, 1986), 119–24, 137–44, 192–204. Marcus Rediker counters that eighteenth-century merchant sailors readily deserted ships for better pay and to escape harsh officers, and that ship companies had a high degree of turnover, Rediker, *Between the Devil and the Deep Blue Sea: Merchants Seamen, Pirates, and the Anglo-American Maritime World, 1700–1750* (Cambridge: Cambridge University Press, 1986), 101–105, 113. On migrants bound by common shipboard experiences, see Virginia DeJohn Anderson, *New England's Generation: The Great Migration and the Formation of Society and Culture in the Seventeenth Century* (Cambridge: Cambridge University Press, 1991), ch. 2; Alison Games, *Migration and the Origins of the English Atlantic World* (Cambridge, Mass.: Harvard University Press, 1999), 69-71.

[19] Rodger, *Wooden World*, 16–29; Rediker, *Between the Devil and the Deep Blue Sea*, 83–89, 95–96; Nathaniel Philbrick, *In the Heart of the Sea: The Tragedy of the Whaleship Essex* (New York: Viking, 2000), 34–35; Haskell Springer, "The Captain's Wife at Sea," and Margaret Creighton, "Davy Jones' Locker Room," in *Iron Men, Wooden Women: Gender and Seafaring in the Atlantic World, 1700–1920*, eds. Margaret Creighton and Lisa Norling (Baltimore: Johns Hopkins University Press, 1996), 93–95, 103–04, 118–37. W. Jeffrey Bolster found that on most eighteenth- and early nineteenth-century merchant and naval vessels in which black sailors served, living quarters were racially integrated, *Black Jacks: African American Seamen in the Age of Sail* (Cambridge, Mass.: Harvard University Press, 1997) 78-84, 88–93. For interracial Bermudian crews, see Michael Jarvis, "Maritime Masters and Seafaring Slaves in Bermuda, 1680–1783," *William and Mary Quarterly* 3rd ser., 59 (2002): 596–602, 604–05.

[20] Henning Henningsen, *Crossing the Equator: Sailors' Baptism and Other Initiation Rites* (Copenhagen: Munksgaard, 1961); Rediker, *Between the Devil and the Deep Blue Sea*, 186–89; David Cordingly, *Women Sailors and Sailors' Women: An Untold Maritime History* (New York: Random House, 2001), 156, 158–59; Pablo E. Pérez-Mallaína, *Spain's Men of the Sea: Daily Life on the Indies Fleets in the Sixteenth Century*, trans. Carla Rahn Phillips (Baltimore: Johns Hopkins University Press, 1998), 129-38, 237-38; Greg Dening, *Mr. Bligh's Bad Language: Passion, Power, and Theatre on the Bounty* (Cambridge: Cambridge University Press, 1992), 19–20, 71, 73, 76–83.

[21] Bermuda Naval Office Shipping List, 1716, PRO CO 41/6–7; Horace Beck, *Folklore and the Sea* (Middletown, Conn.: Wesleyan University Press, 1973), 5–6, 12–29; Cordingly, *Women Sailors and Sailors' Women*, 156–63.

[22] Cary Carson et al., "Impermanent Architecture in the Southern American Colonies," *Winterthur Portfolio* 16 (1981): 135–96; Richard Bushman, *The Refinement of America: Persons, Houses, Cities* (New York: Knopf, 1992); Kevin Sweeney, "High-Style Vernacular: Lifestyles of the Colonial Elite," in Cary Carson, Ronald Hoffman, and Peter Albert, eds., *Of Consuming Interest: The Style of Life in the Eighteenth Century* (Charlottesville: University Press of Virginia, 1994), 11–40; James Deetz, *In Small Things Forgotten: An Archaeology of Early American Life* (New York: Anchor Books/Doubleday, 1996), 52–67, 125–64; Carole Shammas, *A History of Household Government in America* (Charlottesville: University Press of Virginia, 2002), esp. chs. 1-2.

# IV

# JOHN BLATCHFORD'S NEW AMERICA

Sailors, Print Culture, and Post-Colonial American Identity

## SARAH J. PURCELL

An analysis of the *Narrative of the Life and Captivity of John Blatchford* reveals how a very humble American sailor could help to define American national identity in the post-Revolutionary period by participating in the burgeoning culture of print. John Blatchford was a poor Massachusetts fisherman and merchant sailor in 1788 when he first published the story of his maritime service in the Revolutionary War, a sensational tale of repeated capture, imprisonment, and escape that reached across the globe. Paul Gilje has used Blatchford as a main example to prove his contention that Revolutionary sailors possessed an often divided form of American patriotism and that they gave first priority to their own personal sense of "liberty" as seamen.[1] It is true that Blatchford took part in the complex experience of transatlantic maritime culture and that he was willing to serve a variety of naval masters, as Gilje describes. But at the same time, Blatchford's narrative, published after the war was over, stressed overwhelmingly that his sailor's heart always belonged to the United States.[2] The narrative ultimately affirmed American national identity, albeit a complex and personal vision of that identity. At the same time that Blatchford offered a complicated picture of the life and politics of a Revolutionary sailor, he also contributed a unique voice to the print culture of the early republic that helped to create an "imagined community" in the early United States.

The Revolutionary War brought home to many Americans their previous status as colonial subordinates in the transatlantic world, even as they were seeking to become independent of British rule. Scholars have shown over the past thirty years how Americans' expectations that they were true possessors of "British liberty" were dashed by the colonial crackdown during the Imperial crisis and the beginning of the Revolutionary War.[3] The status of "American" was unloosed from its colonial moorings and in need of a new definition.

[73]

So, just as Americans won the Revolutionary War, declared political independence, and went about trying to create a new kind of political and social order, they also had to find new ways of thinking about themselves as Americans. Many Americans saw themselves only as liberated Englishmen and women, but the idea of America as a special place separate from England also had existed since at least the seventeenth century and John Winthrop's city on a hill. Not yet taken with exceptionalism and manifest destiny, but no longer defined by mercantilism, deference, or political subordination, Americans had to seek a new post-colonial identity that could define their special nature in new terms. If the American Revolution created the United States of America, it remained to be seen how the feeling of being American might be established.

Although not everyone approached American national identity in the same way, the Revolutionary War itself offered many ways for American identity to begin to take shape. The real violence of war provided a bloody break with the old order for many in America, but even those who experienced no actual violence used the war as a way to understand their separation from Great Britain. In sermons, Fourth of July celebrations, and in the burgeoning print culture of newspapers, pamphlets, and books, Americans in the Revolutionary and Post-Revolutionary period could be heard to ask themselves "What does it mean to be American?" and "What is our new place in the world?"[4]

One unlikely individual who offered answers to these questions during the early republic was John Blatchford. Blatchford made a contribution to his country by serving in the Revolutionary War, and his narrative elevated that service to a wider importance. Blatchford had enlisted in 1777 at the age of fifteen aboard the continental ship *Hancock* and had spent most of the Revolutionary War far from home. He was captured just one month after his enlistment when the *Hancock* was taken by the British ship *Rainbow*. John Blatchford endured several prison terms, trials, beatings, narrow escapes, and other adventures over the next six years as he was transported all over the world as a British prisoner of war and pressed into service on board several British ships and in the British army. Blatchford returned home to Cape Ann, Massachusetts, in 1782. He then married and settled down in Essex County to earn a humble living as a fisherman and merchant seaman. He died in 1794 while serving on a merchant vessel in Haiti.[5]

But Blatchford, along with a growing number of average veterans of the Revolutionary War, did not live a life of completely quiet obscurity. In 1788 he published the memoir of his wartime experiences, the *Narrative of Remarkable*

*Occurrences, in the Life of John Blatchford,* making him one of the first Revolutionary War veterans to publish the story of his service to his country. Blatchford's *Narrative,* a remarkably straightforward book, which in all probability he dictated to publisher Timothy Green, told the exciting tale of his captivity and transportation around the world as a British prisoner in unsentimental terms. Blatchford no doubt agreed to print his story in part hoping to make money to augment his seafaring income.

John Blatchford put the story of his life and Revolutionary service into print at an extremely important moment in the United States and at a time when not very many men like him made such a contribution to public culture. Stories about wartime heroism formed an important part of the print culture that helped to define the United States during the Constitutional period in the late 1780s and beyond. But most of the firsthand accounts of Revolutionary War service before 1800 were authored by officers, and very few addressed life in the navy, let alone from the perspective of a lowly enlisted sailor.[6] The early prisoner-of-war narrative most like Blatchford's was Ethan Allen's *A Narrative of Col. Ethan Allen's Captivity,* but Allen was a high-ranking officer from a politically powerful Vermont family who wrote in more refined terms.[7] Sailors and captives who wrote in later decades, most famously Israel Potter, employed a far greater degree of sentimentality than Blatchford and relied more openly on literary flourish.[8] Blatchford offered a very unusual perspective—that of the poor, ordinary sailor, who had traveled widely but who spoke in plain prose—and it was a perspective readers would gain for many subsequent decades.

Blatchford's narrative attracted readers because it was a cracking good story, but it also served a higher purpose. Blatchford's narrative went beyond just a straightforward record of his wartime actions or a way for him to make money; it also defined in subtle ways a vision of America that helped its readers to imagine their place in the world. Even if Blatchford, the sailor, worked for the British at several points in order to get through the war, which might be read as evidence of conflicted patriotism, his published story did the cultural work of American nationalism nonetheless. Blatchford's narrative, as it fit into the tradition of prisoner-of-war writings and captivity narratives, helped to affirm the power of the American nation, even though at times he flirted with his captors as a means of survival in the transatlantic maritime world.[9]

John Blatchford's narrative helped to define a new post-colonial role for America in the transatlantic world and beyond. Blatchford's narrative, like several other memoirs of naval prisoners of war in the surrounding decades, used conventions of the traditional captivity narrative, popular in America since the seventeenth century. But instead of a strong reliance on religion or faith to bring the captive home, Blatchford usually substituted a mild and straightforward American patriotism as his saving grace. Blatchford described for his American audience the exotic locations in which he found himself in a manner calculated to define, by contrast, a uniquely "American" experience. As Blatchford met a number of trials that seemed powerful enough to break his spirit as a Revolutionary sailor, he clung to his American identity as a badge of honor, almost as a protection in the harsh world outside his part of North America. Blatchford defined America in contrast to other parts of the Atlantic world as he helped his readers imagine a new "American" place in the post-Revolutionary Atlantic world.

While it is not possible to discern everything that American nationality meant to John Blatchford himself, or to his readers, it is possible to see how the text provided some opportunities for readers to ponder the nature and capacity of their nation. Blatchford's vision of America was tied to his vision of "home," what Alon Confino has called a sense of local nationalism.[10] Although the home which Blatchford sought was very specifically a site in Cape Ann, Massachusetts, his far-flung tale invited readers to contrast that home to points across the globe and in the process to think about their entire nation. As a captured sailor, Blatchford created himself as a character who was a national actor in a very personal tale.

The *Narrative of Remarkable Occurrences, in the Life of John Blatchford*, while not extensively studied by scholars, has found many readers for over two hundred years. After the original 1788 pamphlet sold out, several more editions appeared. In 1797, Philip Freneau published long sections of the narrative in his New York newspaper the *Time Piece*. Blatchford's tale found new readers in the mid-nineteenth century when it was published twice in the Cape Ann, Massachusetts, *Gazette* in 1860 and when the antiquarian Charles I. Bushnell published an annotated version of the text in 1865. Bushnell's edition was itself reprinted by the New York Times and the Arno Press in 1971. Many libraries around the United States own copies of the eighteenth- and nineteenth-century editions of Blatchford's story, and the British Library also holds several editions of the narrative. Although he was probably illiterate, the sailor John Blatchford made a long-lasting contribution to American print culture.

The popularity of Blatchford's narrative over the years is not surprising, given the exciting story it relates. Although Blatchford used plain language, he related the kind of adventures that readers hungered for in the late eighteenth and early nineteenth centuries.[11] Blatchford's tale recorded very little about his actual service aboard the *Hancock*, which was captured by the British on the very first page of the narrative. Instead, Blatchford transported readers along with him to Nova Scotia, the West Indies, Great Britain, France, and the East Indies as he bounced from ship to prison to ship, all the while pining to return to his home in Massachusetts. Along the way Blatchford escaped from British jails, killed a man, was acquitted of murder, was stabbed, received 800 lashes, escaped a firing squad, labored on an East Indian pepper plantation, wandered through the jungle in Sumatra, was rescued by a half-naked "Female Indian," and served on board half a dozen ships as he struggled to make his way back to Massachusetts. All of this action took place in under fifty pages of easy-to-read text, which wasted little space on details but still managed to present a palpable sense of excitement. Blatchford's story fit well into the tradition of eighteenth-century captivity narratives and gestured at the tradition of sensationalist literature, especially as it emphasized both his suffering and the fantastic (possibly even exaggerated) details of his voyages.[12]

The structure and drama of Blatchford's story bear some similarities to Indian captivity narratives, such as the tale by Mary Rowlandson that remained very popular at the turn of the nineteenth century, but Blatchford resisted casting even the primitive East Indians whom he met as wanton savages, and he relied little on religious solace. Blatchford's impressment and his forced labor on a pepper plantation in Sumatra prefigure themes that would become very popular in American Barbary captivity narratives during the late 1790s and 1810s.[13]

Blatchford was one of the earliest and poorest Revolutionary War veterans to publish a memoir or personal narrative, and he managed effectively to combine high adventure and plain-spoken common sense. Blatchford mixed the trope of the plain-spoken American into his prisoner of war tale. While other Revolutionary prisoners, most notably Ethan Allen, had published narratives or newspaper accounts of their captivity (and many more would do so in the decades following the 1780s), Blatchford's narrative was unique in its global scale. Blatchford provided the means for Americans to imagine themselves transported around the world, and he provided points of comparison between American society and what he found abroad. Blatchford's tale shared with other captivity narratives—both Indian captivity narratives and tales written by prisoners of war—an attempt to define the identity of the narrator and a series of

American "types" against examples of the foreign "other." As June Namias put it in her comprehensive study of Indian captivity: "The experience of living with members of other societies heightened awareness and functioned as a foil for one's behavior, testing which values could endure."[14] While Blatchford did use mild patriotic rhetoric and included a few sentimental flourishes, by and large his narrative speaks in a plain and humble voice that matches his vision of America.

As the self-conscious product of a poor, white man who was decidedly shaped by his identity as a sailor, Blatchford's captivity narrative stands out among a whole host of other publications of its kind to provide an interesting perspective on how one version American national identity was constructed. The narrative, more than what happened to Blatchford, challenged the American imagination to help create that identity. Perhaps because they sensed that more was at stake even than a humble man's personal reputation, Blatchford and his publisher took pains to assure their readers of the authenticity of his story. While Blatchford's narrative might be taken as a blueprint for American survival even if it were exaggerated or fictionalized, readers put a premium on truth, and captivity narratives almost always assured their readers of their veracity (even if they were manufactured).[15] The publisher of Blatchford's pamphlet included the following statement at the end of the text:

> Those who are acquainted with the narrator will not scruple to give full credit to the foregoing account—and others may satisfy themselves by conversing with him. The scars which he carries are proof of a part of his narrative—and a gentleman belonging to New-London, who was several months with him, was acquainted with part of his sufferings, tho' it was out of his power to relieve him.—He is a poor man, with a wife and two children—His employment fishing and coasting.[16]

The emphasis on Blatchford's humble social and economic status is particularly interesting, as is the assurance that "a gentleman" of New London could vouch for him. Blatchford's humble station made him suspect, a fact faced by other sailors who published memoirs in the years following Blatchford. Joshua Davis, a sailor who published his own Revolutionary War captivity tale in 1811, wrote that readers of his similarly fanciful tale might "wonder how I could keep so correct an account of dates and transactions while on board of so many ships," but that they should be assured because he kept a journal hidden in his stockings and because he had sworn his statements before the copyright clerk.[17] Blatchford offered no evidence that he kept notes during his captivity, but he asked the reader to believe him, and, much as the slaves and former slaves who were just beginning their own tradition of publishing personal narratives, he had a rich, white witness vouch for him. The patriotic function and the flat-out thrill of reading Blatchford's naval memoirs worked to overcome the suspicion of a poor and humble man telling fantastic tales.[18]

Although Blatchford kept political commentary in his narrative to a minimum, he set a patriotic tone from the outset, which makes it clear how Americans might have used his tale to imagine their role in the world. Blatchford's narrative is not the single most important source for understanding burgeoning American national identity in the late eighteenth and early nineteenth century, but the text does help us to reconstruct the raw materials from which Americans had to choose when creating what Linda Colley has called the "mental furniture" necessary for a diverse group of people to form themselves into a social and political unit.[19] As Benedict Anderson and the host of other scholars influenced by him have shown, the work of early Americans was to imagine their nation into existence, and John Blatchford's narrative provided a particular aid to the process.[20]

Taken as a whole, Blatchford's narrative encouraged readers to imagine several different aspects of their own American nature. He created himself as a humble, yet virtuous example of the average American, committed to home and willing to persevere in order to return to his beloved country. Blatchford was resolutely a sailor steeped in maritime culture and practices, but he also became an "everyman" who asked the landlocked reader to imagine him or herself in sympathy with his own (white) American struggle. Blatchford was, like other sailors, willing "to jump into the fray in the name of liberty or for the pure joy of it."[21] Blatchford contrasted an image of himself and other examples of virtuous American behavior to evil, traitorous, and foreign characters, and thus encouraged his readers to ponder the nature of true patriotism. Where religious captivity narratives usually stressed the "morally instructive nature of the experience," Blatchford offered himself as a more subtle example of patriotic behavior.[22] The narrative especially offered Americans a chance to compare themselves to the British and urged them not only to find some fundamental differences, but also to face the fact that the British did not respect them. The worldwide sweep of the narrative also allowed Blatchford to contrast North America with more exotic locales and peoples.

Blatchford first used his narrative to contrast American and un-American "types" by comparing his own virtuous and patriotic behavior to that of the evil character of Knowles, a fellow American sailor who betrayed Blatchford's plan to escape from his first imprisonment in a sugarhouse in Halifax, Nova Scotia. In what was surely a swipe at disloyal Americans, Blatchford wondered "what could have induced him to commit so vile an action cannot be conceived, as no advantage could accrue to him from our detection and by his treachery lost his country the lives of more than a hundred valuable citizens— fathers and husbands—whose return would have rejoiced the hearts of now weeping fatherless children, and called forth tears of joy from wives, now helpless and disconsolate widows." This passage contains the most sentimental language in the entire text and established at the outset that Blatchford would hold no truck with such betrayal. Knowles tormented Blatchford, causing Blatchford to wish "for nothing more than for an opportunity to convince him that I did not love him." Blatchford got his chance one day in the prison yard: "I suddenly drew one hand out of my irons, flew at him and struck him in the face, knocked out two or three of his teeth, and bruised his mouth very much."[23] Blatchford taught both Knowles and the reader a violent lesson about proper American behavior and loyalty. By punching the traitorous Knowles, Blatchford upheld his sailor's honor, and in the way he presented the incident he showed his readers an extreme example of how "valuable citizens" must stand up for themselves.

Blatchford pursued the theme of violent resistance. Following the incident with Knowles, Blatchford related that he was bound out to the frigate *Greyhound*, which cruised between Halifax and the West Indies. Though the crew watched him carefully, Blatchford took his first opportunity to escape and tried to slip away into the southern part of Halifax, known as "Irishtown." When an official tried to detain him, Blatchford at first lied, but then admitted he "was an American and making my escape."[24] The man refused to let Blatchford pass and then wounded him with a bayonet. Blatchford responded by knocking him down with a stone, a blow he later learned to have been fatal. Blatchford was arrested, and his captors threatened to bring him before the Canadian governor, but he demanded to be tried in England. So he was shipped to Portsmouth to appear at a court-martial (after trying unsuccessfully to escape again when his ship was detained for a time in Ireland).

The section of Blatchford's story that related his transportation for trial set up the perfect opportunity for him to contrast Americans and the English. Up until he reached England, Blatchford's narrative, in a departure from the captivity narrative trope, said very little about his British captors. But once he arrived in Portsmouth, Blatchford found himself to be the exotic object, and his narrative drew clear lines of conduct between the English and himself, as the narrator with whom the reader sympathizes.

Blatchford presented the English as overly effete and ignorant, even as he accepted help from some of the same Englishmen he mocked. An English "gentleman" named Mr. Thomas helped Blatchford gain acquittal on his murder charges, and before being consigned to his next ship he was allowed to explore the town with his new protector. Mr. Thomas took Blatchford in as a guest in his home, where Blatchford noted a marked contrast between himself and the gentleman's family. Blatchford did not speculate about the identity or the motives of this gentleman who provided help and comfort, but he returned a service by becoming an object of fascination in Mr. Thomas's household. Blatchford related the following story:

> In the evening Mr. Thomas came into the kitchin [sic] and asked me to walk into the parlour, to satisfy the curiosity of some ladies, who had never seen a Yankee, as they called me: I went in, and they seemed greatly surprized to see me look like an Englishman; they said they were sure I was no Yankee, but like themselves. The idea they formed of the Americans was nearly the same as we have of the natives of this country. When the ladies had satisfied their curiosity, Mr. Thomas put a guinea in to his hat, and carrying it round asked the ladies to contribute for the poor Yankee.[25]

Blatchford was able to repay the kindness of Mr. Thomas by putting himself on display to the curious Englishwomen, and the story serves a greater function of allowing Blatchford's readers to compare themselves to the English as well.

By allowing himself to be put on display, both to Mr. Thomas's household and in the narrative itself, Blatchford played himself off of the expectations of his audiences. His description of the incident stressed how *similar* Americans and the English were, but also exposed and mocked the complete ignorance of the English about America. In this humorous anecdote, English refinement in Mr. Thomas's parlor comes off as artifice and ignorance instead of something to be admired. Though some Americans may have confirmed their own class identities at the end of the eighteenth century by admiring English taste and refinement, Blatchford shows himself, as the humble American sailor, to be superior in his own way.[26] By carefully relating the anecdote in his memoirs, Blatchford changed himself from an object of curiosity into the subject of superiority—from colonial object to national subject.

This contrast to the English formed an important part of a set of military memoirs that would shape public memory of the Revolution over the first decades of the nineteenth century. Other soldiers' and sailors' captivity narratives echoed the way Blatchford lampooned upper-crust English ignorance while maintaining his pride as an American and showing himself off as an American specimen. Ethan Allen's narrative, which was first published in the 1770s and which remained in print during the period when Blatchford's narrative was popular, struck a similar note. Allen wrote that he would often entertain onlookers who gathered outside his English prison cell by speaking on American courage and freedom. He got his chance to declare his true national allegiance on one such occasion when a belligerent onlooker challenged American military competence and said that surely Allen "was an Irishman; but I assured him I was a *full blooded Yankee*."[27] Allen commented that the English seemed particularly surprised by his level of civility, because "to see a gentleman in England, regularly dressed and well behaved, would be no sight at all; but such a rebel, as they were pleased to call me, it is probable was never before seen in England."[28] Allen and Blatchford both set themselves apart by sneering at the assumptions of English upper-class gentility, although Blatchford was surely from humbler and poorer American stock than Allen, and Blatchford certainly never would have been mistaken for a "gentleman."[29]

Equally suspicious of arrogant English gentility and of the English lower-sort, American prisoners' narratives created a fantasy of the middling American, comfortably settled outside the English context and somewhere in between the extremes of its class system. Sailors' and soldiers' memoirs imagined Americans as a middling sort. The memoirist Israel Potter, who claimed to have lived clandestinely among the English for twenty-four years after escaping from a prison, rejoiced that he was "born among a moral and humane people" instead of the "rogues, thieves, pimps and vagabonds" of the English working class.[30] Blatchford's narrative created the sense that a sailor, not usually the most respectable of characters, could nonetheless stand for lower-middle-class respectability.

The eighteenth-century sailor's reputation for rough and plain speech, in this case, helped to convince the reader in the context of Blatchford's narrative how he survived his ordeal with American principles firmly intact.[31] After his acquittal in England, Blatchford was pressed into service aboard an Indiaman, the *Princess-Royal*, where he tried to adapt to life aboard an English trading ship. Following in the tradition of the captivity narrative, Blatchford told his readers that he now decided to try and accept his lot:

> Our captain told me, if I behaved well and did my duty, I should receive as good usage as any man on board:—this gave me great encouragement. I now found my destiny was fixed—that whatever I could do, would not in the least alter my situation, and therefore was determined to do the best I could, and make myself as contented as my unfortunate situation would admit.[32]

In this passage, as in the rest of the narrative, Blatchford related little about his treatment aboard ship. In contrast to other naval narratives, perhaps most notably sailor Joshua Davis' memoir that intended to whip up righteous indignation about impressment on the eve of the War of 1812, Blatchford made it clear that naval life in and of itself was not what he found oppressive. The only privations Blatchford ever described arose as a result of trying to assert his independence to escape, for he seemed perfectly accommodated to a seafaring life.

Blatchford himself was a man of the sea, but his narrative elevated his character to an even larger stage. In the pages of his life story, Blatchford became not only an archetypal sailor, but also a good American, even as he tried to accept his lot in the British navy. Blatchford's penchant for escape seemed to be an outgrowth of his Americanness, but even when he decided to give in to his "destiny" he stood out from the other eighty-six Americans pressed into service on board the *Princess-Royal* in his willingness to fight back. Upon arriving in Bengkulu, the British province on the otherwise Dutch-controlled Island of Sumatra, all of the American captives were put off the ship and forced into service as soldiers. Blatchford much preferred the naval life, and he wrote: "I offered to bind myself to the captain for five years, or any longer term, if I might serve on board this ship:—he told me it was impossible for me to be released from acting as a soldier, unless I could pay fifty pounds sterling. As I was unable to do this, I was obliged to go through the manual exercise with the other prisoners."[33] Blatchford stressed in print that being a naval captive did not strike him as a form of slavery, as did the captivity experienced by many sailors during the Barbary Wars or the impressment faced by others during the years leading up to the War of 1812, but he clearly found being a British soldier degrading.

Sumatra provided the setting for Blatchford's most dramatic experience and the most dramatic stories in his book. The section of the narrative set in Sumatra allowed Blatchford's readers to imagine a geographic and racial contrast between Blatchford, as American, and a very exotic set of "others." Blatchford despised being a soldier. He was beaten daily by a harsh drill sergeant, put to work harvesting pepper on a plantation for the East India Company, and fried by "the amazing heat of the sun," which was "too much for an American constitution, unused to a hot climate" and which killed several of his fellow Americans. The story of Blatchford's misery provided the classic turning point of the captivity narrative, when he threw off his resigned acceptance of fate and once again decided to escape. He believed that things could not get worse, but assured his readers that "Providence still preserved us for greater hardships."[34]

The narrative then turned to even higher adventure. Blatchford and two of his compatriots ran away from camp, but were apprehended by seapoys, some of whom they killed in a fight. Blatchford was court-martialed, but spared the firing squad at the last minute on account of his youth, a pardon which was normal, but one which he attributed to "Divine Providence." The leader of Blatchford's band of escapees, Josiah Folgier, was not so lucky, and, by contrast to the duplicitous American Knowles earlier in the book, Blatchford sets Folgier up as a true American patriot willing nobly to sacrifice himself to save the others. On the night before he was to die, Blatchford related, Folgier "who hated the name and sight of an Englishman" rejected the ministrations of a British clergyman, "for, said he, the sight of Englishmen, from whom we have received [poor] treatment, is more disagreeable than the evil spirits of whom you have spoken."[35] Blatchford told his readers that he was so full of emotion and admiration that when he was allowed to speak with Folgier just before he faced the firing squad, "my feelings were such at the time that I had not power to utter a single word to my departing friend, who seemed as undaunted and seemingly as willing to die as I was willing to be released—and told me not to forget the promises we had formerly made each other, which was, to embrace the first opportunity to escape."[36]

These men clearly evinced the sailors' love of personal liberty, but Blatchford also identified himself and his compatriots as Americans, and a greater sense of liberty seemed to be at stake. As Blatchford continued, he presented his quest to live up to his promise of solidarity with Folgier. After receiving 800 lashes as punishment for his escape and spending three weeks in a hospital, Blatchford found that his will to run away and his "hopes of regaining my liberty" were almost exhausted. But Blatchford's last remaining American friend, William Randall, convinced him to try another escape. Blatchford described how the two men gathered rudimentary supplies and slipped away from their hospital before the guards suspected that they were well enough to travel. Even though they were certainly not in top physical condition, the two set out on foot for the Dutch settlement of Croy.[37]

Thus began the most exotic portion of the narrative, which provided both the extremely fanciful adventure that could delight his readers and insure his narrative's popularity and also symbolically provide what was perhaps the truest test of Blatchford's American strength. Blatchford used the tale of his next series of adventures to invite the readers to compare themselves to people very unlike themselves. Blatchford and Randall wandered in the jungle for thirty days, "living on fruit, turtle-eggs, and some turtle." Randall poisoned himself on jackfruit and died, leaving Blatchford to carry on by himself. Wandering alone, Blatchford entered a kind of dream state, the narrative of which allowed him to muse on the blessings of home:

> The weather being at this time extreme hot and rainy.—I frequently lay down and would wish that I might never rise again;—despair had almost wholly possessed me; and sometimes in a kind of delirium would fancy I heard my mother's voice, and my friends calling me, and I would answer them:—at other times my wild imagination would paint to my view scenes which I was well acquainted with, then supposing myself near home I would run as fast as my feeble legs could carry me:—frequently I fancied that I heard dogs bark, men cutting wood, and every noise which I have heard in my native country.[38]

The imaginative contrast here was remarkably striking as Blatchford juxtaposed the mundane sights and sounds of his delirium to his sensationalist surroundings. In the midst of a foreign jungle, where he was pursued by lions, tigers, and monkeys, Blatchford told his readers that he fastened on the sounds of home and his mother's voice. Although he avoided any heavy-handed instruction to his reader, the message was clear that Americans should appreciate their everyday experiences. Even the sounds of dogs barking and men cutting wood could stand as a kind of American lifeline. Blatchford invited his readers to consider their "native country" and its atmosphere as comfortable and normal by contrast to the Sumatran jungle.

Blatchford's narrative pushed the contrast between "home" and the jungle even further. Just when Blatchford was about to be overcome by his exotic surroundings, he was saved by natives of Sumatra, who allowed him to ponder the nature of race along with nationality and placed this portion of his book firmly in the colonial captivity narrative genre. Blatchford, now reckoning that he had been wandering for fifteen weeks, was about to collapse from thirst. He discovered a brook and looked up to see a "Female Indian" fishing at the brook, but was taken aback that "she had no other dress on than that which mother nature affords impartially to all her children, except a small cloth which she wore round her waist."[39] Although neither spoke the other's native language, the pair managed to communicate in Malay, and the woman took pity on Blatchford when he told her, "that I was making my escape from the English, by whom I had been taken in war.—She told me that she had been taken by the Malays some years before—for that the two nations were always at war; and that she had been kept as a slave among them three years, and was then retaken by her countrymen."[40]

The narrative measured Blatchford as an American "type" against an exotic (yet attractive) "other." As he did when putting himself on display in Mr. Thomas's English parlor, Blatchford established sympathy between himself and the "other"—this time the much more exotic "Female Indian." By revealing her similar history of captivity and their ability to communicate in a common language, Blatchford invited his readers to see her sympathetically.[41] Blatchford showed his readers that both he and the "Female Indian" were escaped war captives, who were able to establish a connection in the jungle when Blatchford needed it the most.

Yet the narrative still made it manifestly clear that the woman and her society were exotic and out of the ordinary. Blatchford accepted her help, but he resisted the urge to "go native" as many other eighteenth-century captives had done.[42] Beginning with the description of her nudity, which marked the sexual exoticism of this former female captive, Blatchford clued the reader in that the Indian population would be notably different than "civilized" Americans and Europeans. The woman took him to her village, where he found her people suspicious but hospitable. After some food and a night of sleep, Blatchford attempted to explain his origins to the natives: "Early in the morning numbers came round the hut, and the female who was my guide, asked me where my country was? I could not make her understand, only that it was at a great distance. She then asked me if my countrymen eat men. I told her no—and seeing some goats, pointed at them and told her we eat such as them."[43]

Although Blatchford presented the village as somewhat savage, he was very clear that "nature" had not made it so, but rather stressed the curiosity of the villagers and the fact that lack of education and information about the outside world was all that prevented them from understanding his origins. Perhaps because of his open-mindedness and worldliness as a sailor, in his narrative Blatchford was willing to contrast his homeland and the native society along a cultural continuum, not as absolute opposites.

In case the reader established too much sympathy or missed the fundamental difference between Blatchford and the islanders, the narrative then continued to draw a starker comparison along explicitly racial lines. Blatchford's conversation with his female host continued:

> She then asked me what made me white, and if it was not the white rain [snow] that come upon us when we were small? And as I wished to please and satisfy them, I told them that I supposed it was—for it was only in certain seasons of the year that it fell, and in hot weather when it did not fall the people grew darker till it returned and then the people all grew white again—this seemed to please them very much.

This remarkable exchange suggests that Blatchford considered some of the difference between cultures to be based on race, but also that he hesitated to assume that his hosts were naturally childlike and unable to understand him. He supposed to his reader that the islanders had only mistakenly been informed that snow made people white because "while she was over with the Malays she had heard something of snow from them, as they carry on some trade with the English."[44] Blatchford accepts an environmental explanation for skin color, but he does so in a way that nonetheless recognizes white superiority.

While Blatchford explicitly used race to separate himself from the islanders of Sumatra, he did not paint them in derogatory terms, and in fact they appeared far more helpful and good-hearted than the British in his narrative. Blatchford referred to the woman as "his protectress," and he conveyed to his readers that he was genuinely grateful for her help. She sent her brother (who seemed more simple-minded and afraid of Blatchford) to help him find the Dutch port, and with their guidance he recounts that he was able to enlist on a Dutch trading ship bound for China and Batavia, on which he continued his quest to return to America.[45]

In Blatchford's retelling of his encounter with the natives of Sumatra he revealed himself to be something of a cultural relativist, ready to accept help from other races and to respect their cultural differences. At the same time, he invited his readers to compare their homes favorably to the wilds of the jungle far beyond the reaches of civilization. In contrast to Indian captivity narratives of the period, Blatchford neither embraced the islanders nor rejected them as a savage threat.[46] They provided just one more adventure along his journey home, and they seemed far less hostile to him than the British. The plain-spoken American sailor survived the most extreme test of his manhood. Blatchford was able to construct a vision of the jungle that emphasized the cultural superiority and normative whiteness of the United States by contrast without necessarily completely devaluing the "exotic" natives he relied upon for help. In this way, Blatchford's narrative hints at an American national identity that is strikingly similar to that created by British captivity narratives, which often simultaneously embraced exotic cultures while seeking to dominate them in a colonial relationship.[47]

The Sumatran jungle was only one of many difficult obstacles on Blatchford's quest to return home. After the natives helped Blatchford, he related in rapid succession his remaining voyage back to Massachusetts on board various Dutch, Spanish, Portuguese, English, and French ships. The simple conclusion of the narrative stressed that Blatchford was less concerned with the many masters he served at sea than with his return to Massachusetts. The clear goal of the whole narrative is Blatchford's American home. In May 1783, Blatchford at last arrived in Beverly, Massachusetts, "only 15 miles from home.—I immediately set for Cape-Ann, went to my father's house, and had an agreeable meeting with my friends, after an absence of almost six years."[48]

In the final analysis, the story of his very roundabout trip home allowed Blatchford to help imagine one form of national identity for his new nation. Aside from his personal uncertainty, Blatchford's narrative created his American "home" as a goal and as an international point of reference. Blatchford drew a series of comparisons between himself as a humble sailor and those who were unwilling to sacrifice for the quest for liberty, between virtuous Americans and brutish traitors and Brits, and between the United States and other exotic locations around the globe. Blatchford used elements of the traditional captivity narrative to elicit sympathy from the reader, but he primarily attributed his survival to American strength and common sense rather than to "Providence."

Blatchford's narrative was very much a sailor's story, and he managed simultaneously to present himself as part of the pragmatic transatlantic maritime culture and also as the quintessential American. Blatchford willingly allowed that he signed on to serve several foreign masters during his ordeal, but he clearly did so in an effort to regain a solid footing at home as an American. Blatchford communicated how he, as an American and a poor, but respectable, white man, was superior to those he encountered in Europe and Sumatra. In the process, it becomes clear how John Blatchford, as a humble sailor, set himself up as a model of perseverance and why so many people might have subsequently been drawn to his story. Blatchford did not assign one, specific meaning to American national identity, but he did create a mental space for readers to imagine their own versions. Readers could travel on the high seas with the humble sailor and imagine just exactly how they weren't English or Sumatran or even Loyalists. John Blatchford committed his life to the page, provided his own take on the captivity narrative, and left the American public to imagine for themselves what they might become in the future.

**NOTES**

1 Paul A. Gilje, *Liberty on the Waterfront: American Maritime Culture in the Age of Revolution* (Philadelphia: University of Pennsylvania Press, 2004), 97-99, 119, 127.

2 John Blatchford, *The Narrative of John Blatchford* (New York: Arno Press, 1971); all page numbers in this paper come from this edition; see also John Blatchford, *Narrative of the Life and Captivity of John Blatchford. . .a Prisoner of War in the Late American Revolution* (New London: T. Green, 1788).

3 For a good summary of this scholarship, see T. H. Breen, "Ideology and Nationalism on the Eve of the American Revolution: Revisions Once More In Need of Revising," *Journal of American History* 84 (1997): 13-39; see also David Waldstreicher, *In the Midst of Perpetual Fetes: The Making of American Nationalism, 1776-1820* (Chapel Hill: University of North Carolina Press, 1997).

4 Sarah J. Purcell, *Sealed with Blood: War, Sacrifice, and Memory in Revolutionary America* (Philadelphia: University of Pennsylvania Press, 2002); Len Travers, *Celebrating the Fourth: Independence Day and the Rites of Nationalism in the Early Republic* (Amherst: University of Massachusetts Press, 1997); Charles Royster, *A Revolutionary People at War: The Continental Army and American Character, 1775-1783* (Chapel Hill: University of North Carolina Press, 1979).

5 Charles Bushnell provides genealogical and biographical information in the notes to his version of Blatchford's text, Narrative, 111-12; Blatchford appears in a well-organized genealogy, *The Wainwright Family of Essex County Massachusetts, John Blatchford of Gloucester, Essex County Massachusetts and Some of His Descendants, http://www.wainwrightfamily.org/blatchfordfhr.htm* (accessed May 30, 2005).

6 Purcell, *Sealed with Blood*, 73, 114-16, 140-43.

7 Ethan Allen, *A Narrative of Col. Ethan Allen's Captivity. . .* (Philadelphia: Bell, 1779).

8 Israel Potter, *Life and Remarkable Adventures of Israel R. Potter, a Native of Cranston, Rhode Island* (Providence: Henry Trumbull, 1824); Potter's memoir inspired Herman Melville's later novel about the exiled Revolutionary captive.

9 Linda Colley, "Perceiving Low Literature: The Captivity Narrative," *Essays in Criticism* 53 (2003): 215.

10 Alon Confino, *The Nation as a Local Metaphor* (Chapel Hill: University of North Carolina Press, 1997).

11 On the popularity of captivity narratives see Christopher Castiglia, *Bound and Determined: Captivity, Culture-Crossing, and White Womanhood from Mary Rowlandson to Patty Hearst* (Chicago: University of Chicago Press, 1996), 2-5.

12 Michael Sturma, "Aliens and Indians: A Comparison of Abduction and Captivity Narratives," *Journal of Popular Culture* 36 (2002): 319.

13 Robert John Denn, "Prison Narratives of the American Revolution" (PhD Diss., Michigan State University, 1980); Paul Baepler, "Introduction," in *White Slaves, African Masters* (Chicago: University of Chicago Press, 1999), 1-10.

14 June Namias, *White Captives: Gender and Ethnicity on the American Frontier* (Chapel Hill: University of North Carolina Press, 1993), 11.

15 Kathryn Zabelle Derounian-Stodola and James Arthur Levernier, *The Indian Captivity Narrative, 1550-1900* (New York: Twayne Publishers, 1993), 10-14.

16 Blatchford, *Narrative*, 46.

17 Joshua Davis, *A Narrative of Joshua Davis, an American Citizen, Who Was Pressed and Served on Board Six Ships of the British Navy* (Baltimore: B. Edes, 1811), 3.

18 Ann Fabian, *The Unvarnished Truth: Personal Narratives in Nineteenth-Century America* (Berkeley: University of California Press, 2000); Thomas Couser, *Altered Egos: Authority in American Autobiography* (New York: Oxford University Press, 1989); on claims of authenticity in slave narratives see John Sekora, "Black Message/White Envelope: Genre, Authenticity, and Authority in the Antebellum Slave Narrative," *Callaloo* 10 (1987): 482-525; Jean Fagin Yellin, "Introduction," *Incidents in the Life of a Slave Girl* (Cambridge, Mass.: Harvard University Press, 1987), xiii-xxxiv.

19 Linda Colley, *Britons: Forging the Nation, 1707-1837* (New Haven: Yale University Press, 1992), 7; Colley has also extensively investigated how captivity narratives and the experience of captivity helped to reinforce the British Empire and its imaginative structure of power in *Captives* (New York: Pantheon Books, 2002).

20 Benedict Anderson, *Imagined Communities: Reflections on the Origins and Spread of Nationalism*, rev. ed. (New York: Verso, 1993).

21 Gilje, *Liberty on the Waterfront*, 105.

22 Richard VanDerBeets, "Introduction," in *Held Captive by Indians: Selected Narratives, 1642-1836*, rev. ed. (Knoxville: University of Tennessee Press, 1994), xxiii.

23 Blatchford, *Narrative*, 12, 13.

24 Ibid., 16.

25 Ibid., 21, 22.

26 See Colley, *Captives*, 214-15; Sheldon S. Cohen, *Yankee Sailors in British Gaols: Prisoners of War at Forton and Mill, 1777-1783* (Newark: University of Delaware Press, 1995).

27 Allen, *Narrative*, 16; Larry G. Bowman, *Captive Americans: Prisoners During the American Revolution* (Athens: Ohio University Press, 1976); Francis D. Cogliano, *American Maritime Prisoners in the Revolutionary War: The Captivity of William Russell* (Annapolis: Naval Institute Press, 2001).

28 Allen, *Narrative*, 38.

29 Richard Bushman, *Refinement of America: Persons, Houses and Cities* (New York: Knopf, 1992); note the contrast to the transatlantic notion of refinement in David S. Shields, *Civil Tongues and Polite Letters in British America* (Chapel Hill: University of North Carolina Press, 1997).

30 Potter, *Life*, 61; on class and sailors see Simon Newman, *Embodied History: The Lives of the Poor in Early Philadelphia* (Philadelphia: University of Pennsylvania Press, 2003), 104-24.

31 See Marcus Rediker, "Chapter 4: The Seaman as Plain Dealer, Language and Culture at Sea," in *Between the Devil and the Deep Blue Sea* (Cambridge: Cambridge University Press, 1987), 153-204.

32 Blatchford, *Narrative*, 24.

33 Ibid., 25.

34 Ibid., 26.

35 Ibid., 28, 29.

36 Ibid., 30.

37 Ibid., 31.

38 Ibid., 33-34.

[39] Ibid., 35.

[40] Ibid., 36-37.

[41] Colley, "Perceiving Low Literature," 205.

[42] Linda Colley, "Going Native, Telling Tales: Captivity, Collaborations and Empire," *Past and Present* 168 (2000): 170-93; I. C. Campbell, *"Gone Native" in Polynesia: Captivity Narratives and Experiences from the South Pacific* (Westport, Conn.: Greenwood Press, 1998).

[43] Blatchford, *Narrative*, 38.

[44] Ibid., 39.

[45] Ibid., 39-40.

[46] Namias, *White Captives*, 11; for a more hierarchical version of race and captivity see Jeremy D. Popkin, "Facing Racial Revolution: Captivity Narratives and Identity in the Saint-Domingue Insurrection," *Eighteenth Century Studies* 36 (2003): 511-33.

[47] Colley, "Going Native"; Colley, *Captives*.

[48] Blatchford, *Narrative*, 45.

# V

## "RELICS OF THE PAST GENERATION"
### Maritime Prisoners of War
### and the Memory of the American Revolution

### FRANCIS D. COGLIANO

His scars proved his only medals. He dictated a little book, the record of
his fortunes. But long ago it faded out of print—himself out of being—
his name out of memory.

—Herman Melville, *Israel Potter*, ch. 26.

During the War of Independence approximately twenty thousand Americans
were imprisoned for prolonged periods by the British. The overwhelming
majority of these were mariners, privateersmen as well seamen from the
Continental and state navies. Although prisoners were held in such disparate
locations as Halifax, Nova Scotia, Kingston, Jamaica, and Edinburgh, Scotland,
most were incarcerated on prison hulks in New York Harbor or in naval prisons near Plymouth and Portsmouth, England. The majority of prisoners ended
up on the prison hulks in New York where crowding, poor hygiene, inadequate
food and water, neglect, and cruelty led to horrific conditions. More than eight
thousand men perished on the New York prison ships.[1]

During the early nineteenth century several former prisoners published
memoirs and diaries which brought their wartime experiences to the attention
of the public. In 1818 and 1832 the United States government offered pensions
to men who had fought in the War of Independence (as well as their widows).
This legislation compelled tens of thousands of veterans, many of whom were
illiterate, to appear before local courts and testify to their wartime experiences.
Taken together the wartime memoirs and pension applications provide invalu-
able sources as to the complex way that revolutionary prisoners expressed and
used memories of their captivity. This essay contrasts the pension applications
with the memoirs. It demonstrates that although former prisoners were reluctant to testify about their captivity when making pension applications, they were
more forthcoming about their internment in their memoirs. It concludes by

considering how the public responded to the former prisoners by considering the efforts to commemorate their suffering during the early nineteenth century. It argues that former prisoners, while proud of their activities as seamen during the War of Independence, were ambivalent about where their captivity fit into a national narrative of heroic service.

The first decades of the nineteenth century were characterized by an increasingly robust nationalism and a surge in interest in the American Revolution. These years marked both the fiftieth anniversary of the Declaration of Independence and the deaths of John Adams and Thomas Jefferson on July 4, 1826, that seemed to signal, in a dramatic fashion, the passing of the revolutionary generation. It was during this period when nostalgia for the Revolution was at its height. As a women's magazine declared in 1846, "A Fourth of July celebration ungraced by a revolutionary warrior ... is like—like something flat."[2] It was during the 1820s and 1830s that interest in memories and reminiscences of former prisoners was greatest.[3] During this period most former prisoners also made their pension applications and the majority of prison memoirs were published. Taken together, the pension applications and the memoirs are quite revealing with respect to how revolutionary prisoners expressed memories of their captivity.

While the burst of nationalism which characterized the 1820s is crucial to reading the pension applications and memoirs, it is also important to note their regional aspect. A sample of more than 1,100 privateersmen imprisoned in Britain during the war reveals that more than two-thirds of the captives came from New England—with nearly 60 percent from Massachusetts. The smaller cohort of pension applicants and memoirists reflects this New England predominance (although some of the pension applicants made their application from the Old Northwest where they had migrated after the Revolution). Although the prisoner memoirs were published (and republished) throughout the country, the New England-centeredness of the applicants and writers *may* in part account for the relative lack of national support for the former prisoners discussed below.[4]

For pension applicants and memoirists credibility was essential. The pension applicants sought to convince the government of the legitimacy of their claims. The memoir-writers were eager to win the approbation of the public and posterity. Both relied on their memories of their wartime experiences. Their different objectives led them to use those memories in very different ways. A comparison of the two types of documents reveals that pension applicants tended to downplay or skip over their imprisonment whereas memoir writers placed prison experiences—usually stressing their ill treatment—at the heart of their narratives.

In 1818 Congress enacted a pension plan for officers and enlisted men who could demonstrate that they had served in the Continental Army or Navy. In 1832 Congress adopted a more comprehensive program that offered pensions to anyone who had served in the War of Independence. Under this legislation former militiamen and privateersmen were also eligible for pensions. Because many, if not a majority of, veterans could not produce discharge certificates or other proof of their service, they relied on oral testimony to prove their service (with corroborating testimony from neighbors, friends, relatives, and fellow veterans.) The veterans normally swore depositions before local courts. Given the public interest in the veterans, the depositions were often witnessed by curious members of the public. As *Niles' Weekly Register* reported in October 1832, "The assemblage of revolutionary soldiers yet remaining . . . constituted an interesting occasion to them and those who could look upon them as relics of the past generation."[5] The depositions of pension applicants were public expressions of memory by revolutionary veterans.[6]

Because they sought to prove that they were entitled to a pension, and they frequently lacked documentation to support their claims, the applicants often provided detailed accounts of their wartime service. They recounted the units and vessels in which they served as well as the names of their officers and friends. Despite their detailed recollections, the veterans provided relatively little information about their imprisonment. The testimony of William Evans is a case in point. In 1832, aged seventy-six, Evans, a native of Limerick, Ireland, testified about his wartime service before the Schenectady County Court in New York. Evans, who was a resident of Warren, Rhode Island, when the war broke out, joined the crew of the galley *Spitfire* which was charged with guarding the coast of Rhode Island. After thirteen months of service Evans and several of his crewmates were captured by the British. Evans recalled, "[we] were taken to Rhode Island and put on board a Prison ship and after remaining there 8 or 10 days placed on board of a prison ship in New York harbor." Evans spent more than five months on board the prison ships, yet his initial public account of the experience was confined to one sentence.[7]

Evans's account was not unusual. William Chadwell, aged eighty-two, told the Cumberland County Court in Portland, Maine, on January 1, 1840, that after extensive land service in the Massachusetts militia, he joined the crews of several privateers out of Boston and Salem including "the Ship *Oliver Cromwell*, Capt. Thomas Simmons, out of said Salem; that he was taken in a Prize of this latter ship carried to New York & Put on board the *Invincible* Seventy-four, thence transported to Mill Prison in England, & kept a Prisoner until the Peace." Mill Prison records reveal that Chadwell was held at the facility for nearly three years, from July 1779 until June 1782, yet he, like William Evans, had little to say about the experience when he made his pension application.[8]

The depositions of Chadwell and Evans are quite typical in their treatment of imprisonment. In the main, most former prisoners were reluctant to provide detailed public statements concerning their incarceration. Their reluctance did not arise because they had forgotten their experiences. Indeed more than four years after his original deposition Evans, who was approaching his eighty-first birthday, provided the following testimony:

> He was . . . imprisoned on board the British Vessel called the *Ardent*, which lay during said five months in the port of New York, which was then in the possession of the British. The prisoners on board the *Ardent* were very much stritened [sic] for provisions which was given them by the British being hardly sufficient to sustain life. General Washington became acquainted with their situation and sent them two pounds of bread and two pounds of beef or pork per week. . . . The number of prisoners in all was about three hundred of whom about one half were Frenchmen.[9]

Evans had testified a second time because his original application had been rejected. It seems that he was reluctant to provide details about his imprisonment until he was compelled to do so out of desperation to obtain a pension. Former prisoners may have been reluctant to testify to their experiences because they felt that such details might jeopardize their chances for a successful application.

Despite their reluctance to testify to their experiences in open court, former prisoners were much more willing to discuss their captivity in detail under other circumstances. Some pension applications provide tantalizing hints to a thriving oral culture among former prisoners. Sixty-nine-year-old Elisha Sherman of Waldo County, Maine, testified in 1847 in support of the application of the children of a former prisoner Prince Hatch, "I have frequently heard the said Prince Hatch tell of his sufferings during the time he was engaged in said war, particularly while he was in Prison."[10] Similarly Mary Lambert of Martha's Vineyard testified in 1845 to the experiences of her late husband, former prisoner Samuel Lambert, which "I have always understood from his own words... during his lifetime and from the uniform testimony of his shipmates, many of whom were Inhabitants of the Vineyard, but are all now dead." With respect to Samuel Lambert's wartime adventures and captivity his widow claimed "that he frequently conversed with his neighbours after his return home on the subject." Among those neighbors was Anthony Luce, the son of one of Lambert's shipmates who was blind from birth. In 1845 Luce, then aged fifty-one, testified:

> During a long succession of years I have attentively listened to the frequent conversations between my late Father & said Samuel Lambert respecting their services together in the Revolutionary Navy and all the Incidents connected therewith, the truth of which was never called into question by any person to my knowledge, and from hearing the circumstances often repeated for a long succession of years, they became imprinted in my memory.[11]

One can easily imagine the old sailors regaling the young blind boy with tales of the war during long winter nights on Martha's Vineyard. Since Samuel Lambert spent twenty-six months in Mill Prison it is highly unlikely that he did not share the details of his experiences with his friends and neighbors. It is probable that thousands of other former prisoners likewise shared their memories of incarceration with friends, neighbors, and relatives via oral tradition. Unfortunately this oral tradition, in the main, was not preserved in the pension applications made by prisoners and their widows. It did find expression in some of the prison memoirs.

Soon after the war the first of fourteen memoirs published by prisoners appeared in print. All told, four narratives appeared between 1788 and 1811 and five between 1847 and 1865. Five memoirs appeared in the relatively brief period from 1824 to 1833. These memoirs proved to be very popular. Eight of the fourteen memoirs were printed in second editions prior to 1865. Some went through three editions. John Blatchford's *Narrative of the Life and Captivity of John Blatchford*, for example, was published in New London, Connecticut, in 1788 and 1794 and reprinted in New York in 1865. Similarly, Nathaniel Fanning's *Memoirs* was published in New York in 1806, Boston in 1810, and Lexington,

Kentucky, in 1826. The table below shows the pattern of publication of the prison memoirs. It demonstrates that more first and second editions were published during the relatively brief period from 1824 to 1833 than at any other time. This period largely falls between the pension acts of 1818 and 1832 suggesting that the pension acts may have prompted some former prisoners to take up their pens and write their memoirs.

Table: Prison Memoirs
Timing of Publication

| Time Period | First editions Published | All editions Published |
|---|---|---|
| 1788-1811 | 4 | 7 |
| 1812-1823 | 0 | 0 |
| 1824-1833 | 5 | 8 |
| 1834-1846 | 0 | 0 |
| 1847-1854 | 2 | 4 |
| 1855-1865 | 3 | 4 |

When pension applicants made their depositions they did so under oath before judges or other court officials. Frequently they were accompanied by neighbors and family members who attested to the truth of the deponent's testimony. The authors and editors of prison narratives had to establish their credibility in other ways. Some, such as Nathaniel Fanning, a former naval officer, relied on simple and direct declarations. "He pledges himself," wrote Fanning, "that he has in the compilation of, kept truth on his side." Others had to rely on more elaborate forms of proof. For example when former *Jersey* prisoner Thomas Dring died in 1824 he had previously completed a draft manuscript of a memoir describing his wartime experiences. When Albert Greene of Providence undertook to edit and publish Dring's manuscript he went to pains to assert, "Although it was finished but a few months previous to his decease, his faculties were then perfect and unimpaired, and his memory remained clear and unclouded even in regard to the most minute facts." To substantiate this assertion Greene noted, "The manuscript has been sought for and eagerly perused by several gentlemen of high respectability, who were either prisoners on board the *Jersey*, or placed in situations where they had ample opportunity of being acquainted with the facts. They have uniformly borne testimony to the

[100]

correctness of its details." Fanning's declaration was akin to an oath in court and Greene and the "respectable gentlemen" whom he consulted very much assumed the role of the neighbors and acquaintances who corroborated the testimony of prisoners.[12]

By contrast with the pension applications, the published memoirs are much more varied documents. They were written and published for a variety of reasons. Joshua Barney's *Biographical Memoir* was the result of oral tradition as it was compiled by Barney's daughter after his death. Thomas Andros, who became an evangelical Baptist minister as a result of his wartime internment, wrote his narrative "to give glory to that kind and merciful Providence, which alone could rescue me in the midst of so many deaths."[13] Nathaniel Fanning prepared his 1806 narrative at the height of British-American diplomatic tension in order to oppose "the zeal of with which certain characters in this country have strove lately to debase the American name, by branding it with the epithet of coward."[14] Ebenezer Fox and Christopher Hawkins prepared their narratives late in life for the benefit of their descendants who subsequently published them.[15] Mary Herbert, the widow of a Mill Prisoner, and an unsuccessful pension applicant, published her husband's prison diary in the hope that "liberal sales will enable the publisher to render to the widow of Herbert a liberal donation."[16]

Despite their varied purposes the revolutionary prison memoirs fit into a broader literary genre—the captivity/prison narrative. From the earliest accounts of colonists abducted by Native Americans during the seventeenth century to those of service men and women captured during the 1991 Gulf War, American captivity accounts follow a similar pattern. They share the same features including descriptions of the captive's service before capture; the moment of capture and removal to prison; the physical confines of prison and treatment by captors; the captive's adjustment and/or resistance to life in confinement; the captive's release through escape, parole, cartel etc.; and a reflection on the meaning of the captivity experience. The revolutionary prison memoirs closely follow this narrative arc.[17]

Unlike the pension applications, which tended to ignore the details of the applicants' imprisonment, the prison memoirs place captivity and suffering at the center of their narratives. This was particularly true among those who had the misfortune to be incarcerated on the New York prison ships. In a typical passage, Thomas Dring described the smell which emanated from the *Jersey* as "far more foul and loathsome than any thing which I had ever met with . . . and produced a sensation of nausea far beyond my powers of description." In a typical passage another *Jersey* prisoner, Christopher Hawkins recalled:

> ev'ry prisoner was infested with vermin on his body and wearing apparel. I one day observed a prisoner on the fore-castle of the ship, with his shirt in his hands having stripped it from his body and deliberately picking the vermin from the plaits of said shirt, and putting them in his mouth . . . He had been so sparingly fed that he was nearly a skeleton, and in all but a state of nudity.

Prisoners held in Halifax, Kinsale, and in the English prisons provided equally detailed memoirs. Undoubtedly such tales were a staple of the oral tradition among former prisoners as they told their children and neighbors about their wartime experiences in the years after their release.[18]

The level of detail in the prison memoirs suggests that former captives remembered far more about their captivity than they revealed in their pension applications. This can be dismissed as the result of faulty memory and a tendency to exaggerate among writers who had an eye on the marketplace and thus an interest in providing entertaining, graphic, and shocking accounts that would attract a wide readership. Indeed, scholars and apologists for the British treatment of American prisoners have criticized the memoirs on just these grounds.[19] Such an interpretation, while plausible, fails to take account of the similarity between accounts, some of which were published simultaneously as well as the corroborating details to be found in unpublished sources (mainly diaries kept by prisoners) which substantiate the published accounts. The difference between the way pension applicants and memoirists presented their memories of captivity stems from the form and purpose those memories took. This is perhaps best exemplified by considering one man, Andrew Sherburne, who was a pension applicant as well as the author of a memoir.

Andrew Sherburne was a thirteen year-old boy from Kittery, Maine, when he joined the crew of the USS *Ranger* in April 1779. He was captured with the crew of the *Ranger* in May 1780 when Charleston fell to the British. After being detained briefly Sherburne was released. He subsequently served on board several rebel privateers. He had the misfortune to suffer capture twice more and was imprisoned both in Mill Prison and then on board of the *Jersey*. After the war Sherburne, who endured ill-health for the remainder of his life as a result of his captivity, struggled for a poor living as a small farmer and part-time teacher in Maine and Ohio.

In 1818 and 1820 Sherburne, then in his early fifties, made depositions in support of a successful pension application. He provided a detailed account of his service aboard the *Ranger* and at the siege of Charleston. In his 1820 deposition Sherburne referred only indirectly to the nearly two years he spent as a prisoner: "The imprisonment and sickness alluded to in my previous declaration, together with two subsequent imprisonments in each of which I endured a long and distressing fit of sickness—one in Mill Prison in great Briton, and the other on board the *Old Jersey Prison Ship* in New York harbour."[20] However, in 1828 Sherburne published a narrative of his experiences, *Memoirs of Andrew Sherburne: A Pensioner of the Navy of the Revolution*, in which he provided a wealth of detail on his captivity.

Andrew Sherburne's *Memoirs* closely follow the narrative arc characteristic of captivity narratives, describing his capture, imprisonment, and release. He recalled an argument he had with his father over joining the crew of a privateer and described his service in the Continental Navy and at the siege of Charleston as well as aboard several privateers before recounting his capture. At this point Sherburne's *Memoirs* provide a much fuller description of his captivity than in his pension depositions. Indeed, Sherburne the author devoted twenty-one pages to his experiences in Mill Prison and a further eleven to his recollections of life aboard the *Jersey*, events to which Sherburne the pension applicant devoted only a sentence.

In his *Memoirs*, Andrew Sherburne provided a detailed picture of life inside Mill Prison. His account of the serving out of prisoners' rations is typical. As at sea the men were divided into messes.

> At eleven o'clock, we drew a three pound loaf to each mess. [T]he bread was very dark colored and was supposed to have been composed of rye, oats, barley, and peas; the members of each mess would generally convene when the bread was served out. One person would divide the loaf into quarters, as exactly as he could; and then one of the mess would turn his back, and another, in the presence of the rest would touch a piece of bread, saying to him who had turned his back, "who shall have that?" "John," "Who shall have that?" "myself," and "who shall have that?" "you shall have it"; of course the fourth quarter must fall on the one not named.

Sherburne described a similar routine that was employed by all the messes when dividing up their meat and broth.[21]

Sherburne further related that when he was in Mill Prison, his townsmen from Kittery banded together to insure that the teenager received tutoring within the jail. The prisoners had organized schools within the prison so that ships' boys like Sherburne could master rudimentary skills such as record-keeping and basic mathematics so that they could acquire the skills to learn navigation. Sherburne claimed that when he started under the tutelage of a Mr. Tibbits, "I could not write my name. I do not know that I had ever written a line in my life, nor could I enumerate three figures." He claimed that his schooling was a success and that by the spring of 1782 he had advanced to the point where he could start learning navigation, but that an outbreak of illness in the prison prevented him from continuing his studies.[22]

As Sherburne's accounts of the dividing of bread and of prison education suggest, the Mill prisoners enjoyed a degree of autonomy in organizing their affairs. They went so far as to draw up a list of rules to govern their behavior that included prohibitions on swearing, stealing, gambling, and blackguarding. On one level the prisoners simply adapted the articles of war that governed their behavior at sea to life within the prison. Sherburne claimed that there was a political aspect to the adoption of the rules. He wrote that "the prisoners, notwithstanding they were located within the absolute dominions of his Britannic Majesty, adventured to form themselves into a republic, framed a constitution and enacted wholesome laws with suitable penalties."[23] Almost five decades after his imprisonment, Sherburne made a direct connection between his captivity and the republican cause for which he had been imprisoned. He claimed that he and his fellow captives had a clear understanding of the principles of the Revolution and were, by implication, held because of their loyalty to them.

What becomes apparent when Andrew Sherburne's pension application is set against his memoir is not that he failed to remember his prison experiences when he made his pension deposition but that he chose not to include those experiences. The issue is not whether Sherburne remembered but which memories he chose to share. The 1818 pension act limited pensions to those who had served in the Continental Army or Navy. Since Sherburne was imprisoned after capture while a member of the crew of privateering vessels it is likely that he did not provide detail about his experiences in "private" service because it was not directly relevant to the success or failure of his application. His memoir, however, makes a clear connection in his mind between his capture and imprisonment and the revolutionary cause. The 1832 pension act broadened pension eligibility to all those who had served in the war. This act was primarily aimed at rewarding those who had served in the state militias and navies. Privateersmen still found themselves in an ambiguous position. They had been captured while fighting for independence, yet they had been in private service at the time. Under such circumstances, applicants may have been wary about placing undue emphasis on their experiences as privateersmen, including their captivity.

While the anomalous legal position of privateersmen may have played some part in the reluctance of prisoners to testify to their experiences, it is also possible that they were unsure about how to interpret their imprisonment. One of the requirements of the pension application process was for applicants to testify to how long they served. Time and again, applicants noted their time in captivity but did not add it to their time of service. Thomas Rose of Dighton, Massachusetts, was typical. Rose, aged seventy-four, told the Bristol County Court on August 16, 1832, that he had "served all fifteen months; unless he allowed for the time as a prisoner . . . in which case he would be entitled for a much longer service."[24] Rose's comment reveals an ambivalence toward their time as captives. In a culture that lauded the exploits and venerated the memories of wartime heroes, prisoners may have felt that they failed as warriors and were reluctant to go on public record about their failure.

If former prisoners were reluctant or even ashamed to testify in court about their captivity, why then did so many memoirs appear that provided so much graphic detail about the prison experience? Many were not published until after the deaths of their authors (Dring, Barney, Hawkins, Bickford). Others placed the author's imprisonment in the context of other wartime exploits and adventures, which offset any stigma that may have been attached to capture (Blatchford, Fanning, Barney, Fox). Others were written with a specific purpose, such as Mary Herbert's attempt to win a pension after failed applications, or Thomas Andros's efforts to turn his captivity into an evangelical vehicle.

What then of Andrew Sherburne, who produced a pension application that epitomizes the stigma of capture, barely acknowledging his imprisonment, yet also was the author of a detailed account of his captivity? Although his pension application was successful, Andrew Sherburne was a poor man. In 1819 he had moved his family, which included two young children, from Maine to Ohio in an effort to make a new start. Ill health, contracted while in captivity, prevented him from prospering during the early republic. Sherburne and his family barely eked out a living. It is possible that Sherburne, who had grown increasingly embittered in the years between his pension application and the appearance of his memoir sought to tell the world how he had suffered during the war and that his sacrifices were ongoing. The words Melville wrote of Israel Potter, another memoirist who struggled after the Revolution, apply to Andrew Sherburne: "His scars proved his only medals. He dictated a little book, the record of his fortunes." Sherburne's failures and struggles in Jacksonian America were a direct result of his contributions to the cause of American independence two generations before. Most likely other revolutionary prisoners, those who described their experiences to their closest friends and relatives before the fire on winter evenings but glossed over them in court, shared Sherburne's ambivalence. If imprisonment lacked the heroism of shipboard or battlefield exploits, prisoners, though "failed" warriors, had played their part and paid the price for American independence and wanted someone to know it and remember it.

The contrast between the ways pensioners and memoirists remembered their captivity stemmed from the profound ambivalence prisoners had about their experiences. This ambivalence was shared by their countrymen, who largely excluded the prisoners from the public memory of the Revolution. The first decades of the nineteenth century witnessed the emergence of a popular festive culture that commemorated the American Revolution. In the main this culture neglected prisoners of war. This is perhaps best illustrated by the one celebration that did focus on prisoners.

On May 26, 1808, a remarkable funeral procession took place on the streets of New York to honor those who had died in British custody on board prison ships in the city's harbor during the War of Independence. The parade was led by a trumpeter on a black horse, dressed in black trimmed with red, who wore a helmet with black and red feathers. From his trumpet hung a black silk flag, edged with black and red crepe, which bore a motto in gold letters:

Mortals Avaunt!
11,500
Spirits of the Martyred Brave
Approach the tomb of Honor, of Glory, of
Virtuous Patriotism

The trumpeter was followed by a herald on a white horse who bore a staff and cap of liberty. Two former prisoners came next, followed by a procession of cavalry, artillery, infantry, and members of the Society of Cincinnati, members of the clergy, various trade associations, and the membership of the Tammany Society, which had organized the event. The mourners were followed by thirteen coffins, which contained the remains of the prison-ship dead. More than one hundred revolutionary veterans acted as pallbearers. The coffins were followed by groups of sailors, local and national politicians, foreign diplomats, and Masons. The mourners were followed by the central feature of the parade a "grand national pedestal"—an oblong stage on a large draped carriage—which bore the inscription:

Americans! Remember the British
Youth of my Country! Martyrdom prefer to Slavery.
Sires of Columbia! Transmit to posterity the cruelties
Practiced on board the British prison ships.
Tyrants! dread the gathering storm,
While Freemen, freemen's obsequies perform.

From a staff on the pedestal flew a blue silk flag with the arms of the USA. A figure representing the "Genius of America" garbed in a blue silk underdress, a white robe, a crimson scarf, a black cape, sandals, and a cap of large feathers "in the Mexican" style stood on the pedestal. The figure was surrounded by nine young men representing Patriotism, Honor, Virtue, Patience, Fortitude, Merit, Courage, Perseverance, and Science—who were styled in the attributes of the "Genius of America" and wore feathered plumes in their hats and crescent-shaped scarlet badges.

The procession made its way through the streets of New York and crossed the East River in boats to Brooklyn, where the march continued. Many Brooklynites, including twenty women dressed in white with black crepe veils, joined the mourners. When the procession reached a tomb overlooking Wallabout Bay, the Reverend Ralph Willotson offered a prayer and then Dr. Benjamin De Witt delivered the funeral oration. At the close of the ceremony the thirteen coffins were placed in the tomb and the procession returned to New York City. According to a local newspaper "The Concourse of spectators in the streets, the houses, and upon the housetops was immense. It seemed as if every man, woman, and child in the city, was anxious to view this scene of national piety. The wharves and places of embarkation were so thronged as seemingly to menace personal safety, and yet in the passage to and from Brooklyn of many thousand persons, no accident happened—so admirably were the arrangements made and executed."[25]

The ceremonies took place at a time when the reputation of sailors was improving. Although Jack Tar had played a crucial role in the protests over British policy prior to the Revolution, most of the eighteenth-century seafarers were viewed by the public as rootless, dangerous, and irresponsible men who lived dangerous lives at sea and irresponsible lives ashore. At the turn of the nineteenth century, as American prosperity came, increasingly, to depend on overseas trade, seafarers came to be seen in a more sympathetic light as promoters and protectors of American wealth and independence. There was particular public sympathy for captured sailors. In the twenty years prior to the procession honoring the prison ship dead, thousands of American sailors had been imprisoned and held for ransom by North African potentates and impressed into the Royal Navy by the British. These captives elicited stronger public sympathy than had their predecessors during the War of Independence. They were seen as symbols of American nationhood as the fledgling republic sought to defend its interests in a dangerous world. In the context of these events the support for 1808 funeral procession—the only public ritual during the period that was dedicated to honoring the memory of revolutionary prisoners of war—suggests that the public at last recognized and appreciated that suffering and sacrifices of the revolutionary prisoners.[26]

The apparent public enthusiasm for the procession and what it represented, however, was deceptive. David Waldstreicher has demonstrated that the unity and consensus that apparently characterized many public celebrations during the early republic often masked profound political and social divisions. Americans fostered a culture of commemorative national displays in order to discredit and exclude their political rivals. Robert E. Cray has persuasively argued that this is precisely what occurred during the 1808 ceremonies for the prisonship dead. Under such circumstances, the apparent unity displayed in ceremonies such as those held in May 1808 to honor the revolutionary prisoners was an act of political partisanship by its sponsors. The ceremonies occurred at a time when Jefferson's embargo policy threatened the livelihoods of those who worked at sea and on the waterfront. The Republican-oriented Tammany Society may have sought to appropriate the seemingly apolitical public memory of the revolutionary prisoners in order to demonstrate Republican sympathy for seafarers and to assert seafarers' support for Republican policies—especially the embargo. Indeed, the *New York Evening Post* was critical of the partisan nature of the rites and condemned the procession for exploiting the memory of the Revolution for partisan advantage. Subsequent events demonstrated that the crowd may have been attracted more by the spectacle than a desire to commemorate the prison ship dead.[27]

Despite the large crowds that turned out for the funeral procession, the public was not especially eager to commemorate those prisoners who had made the ultimate sacrifice on behalf of American independence. The May procession was part of an unsuccessful campaign to erect a permanent memorial to the seamen who died in British custody. In April 1808 members of the Tammany Society had laid a cornerstone for a monument and vault in Brooklyn where the remains of the prisoners could be interred. The ceremony in May was intended to mark the official internment of the remains with a suitable monument to be erected, paid for with funds raised from among the public at a later date. Due to a lack of public support, the funds for the monument were not raised and the memorial was not erected. Neither did the Tammany Society provide the money, suggesting that its interest in the prisoners may have been primarily political. Once its members realized that the public had little interest in the project, and after the Embargo was repealed in 1809, it was allowed to die quietly. The failure of the project to build a monument in honor of the prison ship dead speaks volumes about public indifference and discomfort with remembering the more unpleasant aspects of their revolutionary heritage.[28]

The first decades of the nineteenth century were a period of intense interest in the American Revolution, as evidenced by the appearance of many published memoirs of revolutionary veterans as well as public enthusiasm for, and interest in, the dwindling number of revolutionary soldiers and sailors. Among these veterans, former prisoners found themselves in an anomalous position. They were lauded for their contributions during the war, yet they were reluctant to speak publicly about their experiences in captivity. While they might share their experiences with relatives, neighbors, and close friends, they were, in the main, reluctant to testify to them in court or publish their accounts during their lifetimes. The failure of the public to raise the funds necessary to erect a memorial to the prison ship dead in Brooklyn indicates that the reluctance of the former prisoners was well-founded. In the robust nationalism that characterized the early republic and the Jacksonian era there was little room for failure. The silence among former prisoners and the public suggests that the former revolutionary prisoners had about them the whiff of failure. The public and the veterans themselves therefore chose to forget those whose experiences did not easily conform with an heroic narrative of national independence.

## Acknowledgments

Early versions of this essay were delivered as papers at the 1999 meeting of the Society for Military History and the 2004 meeting of the Society for Historians of the Early American Republic.

# NOTES

[1] For the revolutionary prisons see Francis D. Cogliano, *American Maritime Prisoners in the Revolutionary War: The Captivity of William Russell* (Annapolis: Naval Institute Press, 2001), and Sheldon S. Cohen, *Yankee Sailors in British Gaols: Prisoners of War at Forton and Mill, 1777-1783* (Newark: University of Delaware Press, 1995). The *Connecticut Gazette*, April 25, 1783, published the claim that 11,644 prisoners died on the prison-ships. This unsubstantiated claim was repeated by the *Pennsylvania Packet*, April 29, 1783, and the *New York Packet* on May 8, 1783. This figure was widely accepted during the nineteenth century. See, for example, Henry Stiles, *Account of the Internment of the Remains of the American Patriots* (New York: Priv. reprint, 1865), 5. Alice Morse Earle claims that this figure is accurate because it was in circulation immediately after the Revolution when those who were responsible for the ships could have disputed it, Earle, *Martyrs of the Prison ships* (Philadelphia: Historical Register Publishing Co., 1895), 7. The most recent and scholarly estimate of the prisonship deaths is that of Howard Peckham, who estimates that approximately 8,500 out of 18,152 prisoners (46.8 percent) died in captivity, see Howard Peckham, ed., *The Toll of Independence* (Chicago: University of Chicago Press, 1974), 132.

[2] *Godey's Lady's Book and Magazine* 33 (1846): 147, as quoted in Edward Tang, "Writing the American Revolution: War Veterans in the Nineteenth-Century Cultural Memory," *Journal of American Studies* 32 (1998): 63-80, 68.

[3] The most complete study of the memoirs is Robert John Denn, "Prison Narratives of the Revolution" (PhD diss., Michigan State University, 1980). The narratives consulted for this study are (in the order in which they were first published): John Blatchford, *Narrative of the Life and Captivity of John Blatchford* (New London: T. Green, 1788); *Historical Sketch to the End of the Revolutionary War, of the Life of Silas Talbot, Esp. of the State of Rhode Island, lately the Commander of the United States Frigate, the Constitution, and of an American Squadron in the West Indies* (New York: G. and R. Waite, 1803); Nathaniel Fanning, *Fanning's Narrative, Being the Memoirs of Nathaniel Fanning An Officer of the Revolutionary Navy* (1826; New York: DeVinne Press, 1912); Joshua Davis, *A Narrative of Joshua Davis an American Citizen, who was Pressed and Served on Board Six Ships of the British Navy* (Boston: B. Edes, 1811); *The Life and Remarkable Adventures of Israel R. Potter* (1824 New York: J. Howard, 1962); Thomas Dring, *Recollections of the Jersey Prison-Ship from the Manuscript of Captain Thomas Dring*, ed. Albert Greene (Providence: H. H. Brown, 1829); Andrew Sherburne, *Memoirs of Andrew Sherburne: A Pensioner of the Navy of the Revolution*, 2nd ed. (Providence: H. H. Brown, 1831); Joshua Barney, *A Biographical Memoir of the Late Commodore Joshua Barney*, ed. Mary Barney (Boston: Gray and Bowen, 1832); Thomas Andros, *The Old Jersey Captive: or a Narrative of the Captivity of Thomas Andros (now Pastor of the Church*

*in Berkley) on board the old Jersey Prison Ship at New York, 1781* (Boston: W. Pierce, 1833); Ebenezer Fox, *The Adventures of Ebenezer Fox in the Revolutionary War* (Boston: C. Fox, 1847); Charles Herbert, *A Relic of the Revolution* (Boston: C. H. Peirce, 1847); Christopher Hawkins, *The Adventures of Christopher Hawkins*, ed. Charles I. Bushnell (1864; New York: Arno Books, 1968); Eli Bickford, *A Memoir of Eli Bickford, A Patriot of the Revolution*, ed. Charles I. Bushnell (New York: n. p., 1865); Alexander Coffin, *The Destructive Operation of Foul Air, Tainted Provisions, Bad Water, and Personal Filthiness upon Human Constitutions, exemplified in the Unparalleled Cruelty of the British to the American Captives at New York, ... in a Communication to Dr. Mitchell dated September 4, 1807* (New York: n. p., 1865). Occasionally memoirs were reprinted with variant titles.

[4] Cogliano, *American Maritime Prisoners*, 1.

[5] *Niles' Weekly Register*, October 6, 1832, 89.

[6] Thus far I have located forty-two pension applications by imprisoned seamen. These are:

| | | | |
|---|---|---|---|
| Adams, Isaac | S17811 | Ingersoll, John | R4425 |
| Bacon, Jacob | S15306 | Jillson, Oliver | W26670 |
| Bagwell, Isaiah | S6550 | Johns, Jacob | W1192 |
| Balch, Thomas | S44338 | Knowles, James | W14036 |
| Barber, Daniel | S6573 | Lambert, Samuel | W20418 |
| Barber, George | S8050 | Luce, Thomas | S33018 |
| Brown, Thomas | S19569 | Maddocks, Caleb | R6824 |
| Bunker, Benjamin | S19575 | Marshall, Joseph | R69 |
| Campbell, John | S12425 | Parker, Joseph | W21944 |
| Casey, John | S40811 | Peabody, Andrew | S22438 |
| Chadwell, William | S19242 | Perkins, Joseph | W21944 |
| Collins, Isaac | S12527 | Potter, Israel | S8369 |
| Curtis, Samuel | S4276 | Rose, Thomas | S30069 |
| Curtis, Samuel | W3956 | Sherburne, Andrew | S42275 |
| Daniels, John | R2651 | Tarr, John | W19429 |
| Edgar, Thomas | S37905 | Trask, Israel | S30171 |
| Evans, William | R3398 | Warner, Nathaniel | S30191 |
| Harris, John | W19679 | Webb, Samuel | R11246 |
| Hatch, Prince | S17994 | Wilson, Ephraim | S29554 |
| Herbert, Charles | W15175 | Wilson, William | S32606 |
| Hunt, Abijah | S23271 | Woodworth, Abel | S23496 |

The original pension applications are in the National Archives in Washington. I consulted the applications on microfilm in the David Library of the American Revolution,

Washington Crossing, Penn. Also see John P. Resch, "Politics and Public Culture: The Revolutionary War Pensions Act of 1818," *Journal of the Early Republic* 8 (1988): 139-58.

[7] William Evans, deposition October 12, 1832, pension file R3398.

[8] William Chadwell, deposition, January 1, 1840, pension application S19242. Also see List of American Prisoners who have been committed to the Mill Prison, April 15, 1782, HO 28/1/139-52, Public Record Office, London, which records that Chadwell was committed to Mill on July 28, 1779.

[9] William Evans, deposition April 25, 1837, pension file R3398.

[10] Elisha Sherman deposition, April 17, 1847, pension file S17994 (Prince Hatch).

[11] Depositions of Mary Lambert and Anthony Luce, March 18, 1845, pension file W20428 BLW34844-16055 (Samuel Lambert).

[12] Fanning, *Narrative*, 1; Greene, *Recollections of the Jersey Prison Ship*, iv, v.

[13] Andros, *Old Jersey Captive*, 5.

[14] Fanning, *Narrative*, 1.

[15] Fox, Adventures of Ebenezer Fox, iv; Hawkins, *Adventures of Christopher Hawkins*, x.

[16] Herbert, Relic of the Revolution, 16. For Mary Herbert's unsuccessful application see Pension file W15175.

[17] Diaries and unpublished accounts—excluding pension applications—follow a similar arc. See Cogliano, *American Maritime Prisoners*. For a discussion of prisoner-of-war narratives as a genre see Robert C. Doyle, *Voices from Captivity: Interpreting the American POW Narrative* (Lawrence: University Press of Kansas, 1994), especially chapters 1 and 4. For a more general discussion of captivity narratives in the context of British imperialism see Linda Colley, *Captives* (New York: Pantheon Books, 2002).

[18] Greene, *Recollections of the Jersey Prison Ship*, 12; Hawkins, *Adventures of Christopher Hawkins*, 71.

[19] Denn, "Prison Narratives of the Revolution," ii. Also see pages 4-5 and chapter 3.

[20] Deposition of Andrew Sherburne, August 4, 1820, pension file S42275.

[21] Sherburne, *Memoirs*, 85-86, 87.

[22] Sherburne, *Memoirs*, 83-84, 91. For the prison schools, see Cogliano, *American Maritime Prisoners*, 71-73.

[23] Sherburne, *Memoirs*, 83.

[24] Deposition of Thomas Rose, August 16, 1832, pension file S30069.

[25] Alice Morse Earle, *Martyrs of the Prison-Ships of the Revolution* (Philadelphia: Historical Register Publishing Co., 1895), 9-11; *The American Citizen* (New York) May 28, 1808.

[26] For the place of mariners in American culture during the period see Paul A. Gilje, *Liberty on the Waterfront: American Maritime Culture in the Age of Revolution* (Philadelphia: University of Pennsylvania Press, 2004).

[27] Robert E. Cray, Jr., "Commemorating the Prison Ship Dead: Revolutionary Memory and the Politics of Sepulture in the Early Republic," *William and Mary Quarterly* 3rd ser., 56 (1999): 565-90. This is the best analysis of the 1808 internment ritual. For public rituals during the early republic see David Waldstreicher, *In the Midst of Perpetual Fetes: The Making of American Nationalism, 1776-1820* (Chapel Hill: University of North Carolina Press, 1997), especially chapters 3-4; Simon P. Newman, *Parades and the Politics of the Street: Festive Culture in the Early American Republic* (Philadelphia: University of Pennsylvania Press, 1997); Len Travers, *Celebrating the Fourth: Independence Day and the Rites of Nationalism in the Early Republic* (Amherst: University of Massachusetts Press, 1997). *New York Evening Post*, May 27, 1808. For the Embargo and its impact see Gilje, *Liberty on the Waterfront*, chapter 5.

[28] The subsequent story of the proposed monument and the remains of the prisoners is an interesting one. Eventually the vault was covered and its remains sold for taxes. A former New York prisoner and Tammany member, Benjamin Romance, took possession of the remains of his fellow prisoners, which were kept in his basement until his death in 1844. In 1855 a Martyr's Monument Association was established to revive the project. It too failed to raise the necessary funds to build a monument to the prisoners. On June 17, 1873, in a small ceremony the association interred the remains on a hill at Fort Greene overlooking Wallabout Bay. In 1888 the Society of Old Brooklynites tried to raise $100,000 for a monument from Congress without effect. In 1895 the Long Island Society of the Daughters of the American Revolution tried to raise money for a monument. They too were unsuccessful. Eventually the Prison Ship Martyrs' Monument was completed in the early twentieth century and it can be found in Fort Greene Park, Brooklyn. See Earle, *Martyrs of the Prison-Ships*, 8-14 and Barnet Schecter, *The Battle For New York: The City at the Heart of the American Revolution* (New York: Walker & Co., 2002), 387.

# VI

## BEFORE AND AFTER THE MAST

James Fenimore Cooper and *Ned Myers*

HESTER BLUM

A profligate, alcoholic, half-crippled lifetime seaman, Ned Myers was among a class of laborers who registered in the annals of nineteenth-century American literary history either as objects of charitable sympathy, or as harlequins or otherwise comic figures. The aging sailor, unlike the robust Jack Tar of familiar fiction, hardly animated the popular imagination. Like many sailors of his generation who had come of age during the War of 1812, and who continued in the merchant service throughout the subsequent boom decades of the American maritime economy, Myers found himself in retirement without pension or prospects. He had spent his life in and out of the naval and merchant services, and in and out of trouble with the law. Myers deserted ships he did not fancy, earned and then imbibed fortunes, and established few human connections, despite attempts at moral reform. In many ways his career exemplified the vicissitudes of early-nineteenth-century maritime life.

Some sailors in these straits tried to support themselves by writing and circulating narratives of their youthful maritime adventures. This practice was enabled in the first half of the nineteenth century by growing charitable interest in seamen, and particularly by an increasingly democratic literary marketplace. In America in the 1830s, innovations in print technology helped fuel an explosion of magazines and cheap editions of books. By making bookmaking less expensive and faster, these technological advancements allowed non-elites to enter the world of literary production.[1] Myers himself could read more successfully than he could write. His maritime career, however, included one passage with future literary greatness: as a boy, in 1806-07, Myers had shared a transatlantic voyage with seventeen-year-old James Fenimore Cooper. Nearly four decades after their voyage the debilitated sailor contacted the now-famous writer; Cooper subsequently offered himself as amanuensis for a reform narrative of Myers's adventures with war, impressment, tyranny, and riotous port life.

The resulting work, *Ned Myers; or, A Life Before the Mast* (1843), is known to literary history as the product of Cooper's authorship, not Myers's. Even so, *Ned Myers* earns scarce mention in the genealogy of Cooper's own literary output. Part of this oversight, notable even within the context of the relatively limited attention paid to Cooper's sea novels as opposed to his frontier tales, may have to do with the hybrid form of *Ned Myers*. The narrative is described as the "biography" of a common sailor, yet it is told in the first person singular, and "edited" by Cooper.

This essay explores how Ned Myers's unusual form helps to illustrate both the status of sailors in the antebellum literary marketplace, and the pressures upon Cooper's later career as a writer of maritime fiction. Neither strictly first-person account nor biography, neither wholly Cooper's own imaginative work nor his editorial production, *Ned Myers* is peculiar within both the body of first-person narratives written by working seamen, and the measure of Cooper's novels. Cooper's sea novels, which were esteemed by contemporary readers and reviewers, mocked by many nineteenth-century sailors, and little noticed by present-day critics, initiated the genre of sea fiction in America.[2] When he began publishing nautical historical romances in the 1820s, Cooper represented the solitary voice of the American mariner; when his last sea tales appeared in the late 1840s, they jostled for shelf space with the explosive number of seafaring narratives and novels that had been produced in the previous decade, usually by seamen-authors themselves.[3] Cooper's later maritime fictions are thought to respond to the marked generic shift in the demands and interests of sea writing in antebellum America, when the romanticism of the early nautical reminisces of the 1820s gave way to increasingly realistic portrayals of nautical experience in the 1840s. Most critics have followed Thomas Philbrick in concluding that Cooper answered to market demands and a climate of reform in refashioning the focus of his novels, often unsuccessfully, both critically and commercially.[4]

As an unsentimental portrayal of the trials endemic to a life at sea, *Ned Myers* would seem to embrace the 1840s model of the sea narrative genre. Yet its recognizable subject matter is at odds with the anomalous form of the narrative itself. It was highly unusual for a sailor's narrative to appear under the imprint of another's authorship, for one. American sea writing set its own value in terms of the authentic portrayal of maritime life offered by its authors, however rudely delivered. Of the scores of antebellum sea narratives in American maritime archives, for instance, I have found only two others besides *Ned Myers* that required an amanuensis. One such narrative was dictated by a blind sailor; the other is that of a former Barbary captive, a mulatto sailor whose narrative bears the editorial apparatus of slave narratives. Neither of these, it should be noted, cite their amanuenses on their title pages, but instead credit the sailors themselves.[5] Yet the title pages of the 1843 first American edition of *Ned Myers* by Lea and Blanchard (as well as the 1844 first British edition by Richard Bentley) credit Cooper as the editor of the volume, but do not list an author; Myers's own name appears only in the title. If, as contemporary and present-day critics maintain, *Ned Myers* represents Cooper's most "authentic" portrayal of maritime life, then the narrative's form and production call into question the terms of authenticity stipulated by the broader genre of sea writing.

The voice of Myers, in the narrative's conclusion, stresses that "this is literally my own story, logged by my old shipmate."[6] The use of a nautical metaphor in summoning the figure of the logbook is provocative: for many of his reviewers, Cooper's sense of maritime "reality" was widely seen as the best recommendation of his work. Stressing the admirable prosaic (i.e., not poetic) quality of Cooper's writing, one contemporary reviewer remarked of his portrayal of the sea: "[h]e is not her poet, but her secretary and copyist."[7] It is this sense of Cooper as "secretary" to, or "copyist" for, maritime experience that is of interest to this essay. Whereas in the 1820s Cooper felt compelled to ally his sea writing with the cultural value of historical romance, by the 1840s he tried to refashion his writerly genesis in the technical nautical terms authorized by scribbling sailors and an appreciative public.

There is a deep inconsistency, though, between Cooper's proficient use of realistic techniques in *Ned Myers*'s nautical scenes, and his misapprehension—and therefore misuse—of a tacit but fundamental aspect of the sea narrative genre. By this I refer to the sailor's own belief in the value of his story, however humble, which customarily lends a sense of confidence and authenticity to even the most injured sailor's history. Cooper errs in misplacing his narrative's authority, yoking it to his own editorial pen rather than to the voice of his subject. Ned Myers the sailor proves to be a subaltern in his own narrative.

*Ned Myers* attempts to claim a freshness or immediacy of narrative tone, as the narrative is presented in the first person; yet Cooper's editorial voice intrudes awkwardly at points. For one, the narrative distinguishes between the "old shipmate" that Cooper had been, and the "gentleman" he had become. By associating himself in print with the semiliterate Myers, his "old shipmate," Cooper attempted to reenlist in nautical life and labor. Yet Cooper's absorption of Ned Myers's "own story" betrays his misreading of the formal elements of the sea narrative genre and its definition of authenticity. At the same time, it suggests Cooper's broader devotion to social and economic hierarchies, which are further enforced within *Ned Myers* itself.

## Cooper's Realities

*Ned Myers* has been described as anomalous within Cooper's body of work because of its clarity, directness, and unsentimental voice—what one contemporary review called Cooper's "unusual perspicuity."[8] Yet this very quality marks the narrative as prosaic within the broader body of sea narrative writing, such as Richard Henry Dana's super seller *Two Years Before the Mast*, as well as the host of imitators that had emerged in the years following its 1840 publication. The subtitle to Myers's narrative—*A Life Before the Mast*—appropriates Dana's language, just as many narratives did in stressing that their subjects sailed "before the mast" as common sailors, rather than as officers. Just a few examples of this one-upsmanship include Nicholas Isaacs's *Twenty Years Before the Mast* (1845), Samuel Leech's *Thirty Years from Home, or A Voice from the Main Deck* (1843), and William Nevens's *Forty Years at Sea* (1845). The geometric growth of the number of years spent before the mast is not simply due to competitive increases, it must be noted. Dana's relatively scant "two years" expose him as a temporary sailor (despite his lowly shipboard status) rather than a lifetime tar. Therefore, sailors by trade could invoke their longevity at sea as a sign of their narratives' greater authenticity. The apotheosis of the genre in the nineteenth century, Dana's narrative explicitly invoked the founding influence of Cooper's novels in its preface, noting that "[s]ince Mr. Cooper's Pilot and Red Rover, there have been many stories of sea-life written."[9]

Cooper's correspondence in the 1840s makes clear his desire to remain relevant to the burgeoning sea narrative genre. In several letters to Richard Henry Dana Sr., famous literary father of the author of *Two Years Before the Mast*, Cooper is eager to report the times young Dana's authorship is called into question. After first reading *Two Years*, Cooper writes to the senior Dana, "I do not know whether your son will be inclined to take it as a compliment or not, it was first introduced to me by a question from Jos. R. Ingersoll, who wished to know whether Dana were not a nom de guerre I had taken to write a sea narrative. He did not suppose the book fiction, but *truth* barbacued a little" [sic].[10] Several years later, when young Dana had not published anything new other than the nautical manual *The Seaman's Friend*, Cooper takes up the theme anew with the father: "What has become of your chap? [...] I do not know whether the compliment is to me, or to himself, but many persons asked me if I had not written his book, when it first appeared."[11] Cooper is at pains to clarify that the misrecognition of authorship does not invalidate the stamp of truth assigned to Dana's nonfictional narrative. He does this not so much to praise Dana, however, as to esteem his own "fiction" for having the taste of *"truth* barbacued a little." More palatable, presumably, to a reader, Cooper's *"truth"* is the product of a literary transformation. The larger degree of transformation registers in two ways: first in Cooper's own late-career espousal of the intellectual utility of maritime truths; and second in the larger literary historical interest in the materiality of literary texts. Still, if Cooper thought that *Ned Myers* would capitalize on the popularity of Dana's narrative, he was mistaken, as the book failed to meet his expectations. Although a commercial disappointment, *Ned Myers* offers an illuminating glimpse not only of life before the mast, but of the professionalization of authorship in America.

The standard of literary value set by *Two Years Before the Mast*—that is, the degree to which a sea narrative could represent the experience of maritime "work"—was in part a logical response to an increasingly urbanized population that appreciated increasingly realistic literature. In fact, Dana's narrative explicitly invokes the mechanized and repetitive nature of sea labor in disavowing any romantic notions of maritime life, pointing out, "The romantic interest which many take in the sea, and in those who live upon it, may be of use in exciting their attention to this subject, though [...] the sailor has no romance in his everyday life to sustain him, but that it is very much the same plain, matter-of-fact drudgery and hardship, which would be experienced on shore."[12] Whereas the publication and popularity of James Fenimore Cooper's sea novels in the 1820s had signaled the moment when the instruments of sea navigation and labor became expressive media in sea novels and narratives, it was not until Dana's narrative that such tools could be employed on behalf of imaginative work. In other words, even though sea narratives and their sober accounts of shipboard life might be thought to cause it to be "all over with dreaming now" for "those who know nothing of the sea, and those who know everything," the reality, according to the *North American Review*, is that "it would be juster to say, that we have surrendered our false fancies, and with full compensation, so much more animating and productive is the truth, as here [in *Two Years Before the Mast*] set forth, than our former guesses."[13]

The economic and technological conditions that engendered America's nautical successes, Cooper understood, also included what he called "the restlessness of moral excitement." This inducement to a life at sea was propagated in part by a literary culture of adventurous enterprise. "This cause is more active in America," Cooper argued, "where the laboring classes read more, and hear more of adventure than any where else."[14] Laboring men—who "read more" adventure literature in America—were inspired by their reading in turn to help swell the ranks of working seamen and to continue America's maritime prosperity. Yet in the case of *Ned Myers*, Cooper, decades removed from the authenticating experience of actual nautical labor, felt the need to generate the writing subject of the narrative from a fusion of the seemingly at-odds figures of the "gentleman" author, and the "old shipmate" Cooper had himself once been. The lack of harmony between these roles, as will be seen, was detrimental to the successful publication and marketing of *Ned Myers*.

When, in fact, Cooper revisited his early sea novels such as *The Pilot* in the late 1840s, writing new prefaces for editions published by George Palmer Putnam, he likewise cited the value of representing the "truth" of maritime life versus the "false fancies" readers might have entertained. And since Dana's narrative had been saluted as much for its antiflogging reform tendencies as for its portrait of maritime reality, Cooper was eager to reestablish himself within the genealogy of popular sea writing. In the wake of the reform movements of the 1820s-1840s, Cooper is therefore able to reevaluate one key function of the success of *The Pilot*. "Sea-tales came into vogue"—among landsmen—as a result of its healthy sales, Cooper notes in his new preface to his first sea novel, "and as every practical part of knowledge has its uses, something has been gained by letting the landsman into the secrets of the seaman's manner of life. Perhaps, in some small degree, an interest has been awakened in behalf of a very numerous, and what has hitherto been a sort of proscribed class of men, that may directly tend to a melioration of their condition."[15]

The kind of "interest" described by Cooper here refers to the rash of "Peace Societies, Temperance and Moral Reform societies" that included sailors as objects of their charitable attentions. Aiming to modify the laborers' avowed habits of swearing, godlessness, and Bible illiteracy, charitable societies for seamen had private and public sponsorship. Other, more secular movements, especially those that concentrated on the working conditions of wage laborers, included sailors in their efforts. Unlike the great majority of seaman authors who invoked reform, though, Cooper was not himself uniformly against the practice of flogging, an issue of terrific concern for sailors; many men, he opined, "would be greatly benefited by a little judicious flogging."[16]

While it is nevertheless fair for Cooper to credit *The Pilot* for the "awakened" interest in seamen, it is also fair to point out that Cooper did not express particular concern for the conditions of seamen in his early sea fiction. The officers of *The Pilot* are able to move successfully from ship to shore, from the longboat to the parlor, yet the one common sailor characterized in the novel, the towering Long Tom Coffin, cannot exist independently of his ship, and goes down with her. Out of touch, perhaps, with the concerns of the common seaman (an accusation made by Dana and others), Cooper's call for landsmen to become involved in sailors' lives was the kind of impulse that other mariners, such as Nathaniel Ames, rejected: reformers, wrote Ames in his popular memoir *Mariner's Sketches*, "have volunteered a feeble crusade against the vices and sins of seamen and have accordingly stuffed ships full of tracts which have entirely defeated their own object."[17] What Cooper calls the "secrets of the seaman's manner of life" could almost constitute the rhetorical equivalent of the city mysteries genre, which had similarly flourished in the 1840s (and had similarly drawn both excited readership, and the attentions of reformers). Cooper's newly expressed interest in the "melioration of [sailors'] condition" speaks powerfully to the social changes that had both inspired and responded to the generic changes in literary production, and helps underscore *Ned Myers*'s own attention to reform.

### Falling Astern

Cooper's editorial preface to *Ned Myers*, tellingly, advertises the narrative primarily as a reform manual that possesses "interest and instruction for the general reader." This reader presumably would learn frugality and sobriety from Ned's own mistakes on this score. Even for those readers who might find "amusement" in Myers's "perils and voyages," Cooper hopes that "the experience and moral change of Myers may have a salutary influence."[18] Ned Myers struck Cooper as an exemplary figure for charitable interest. Indeed, he helped to procure employment for Ned and for his family members (including a step-daughter who served as the Coopers' maid). Furthermore, Cooper personally agitated on behalf of Myers for a naval pension for injuries sustained in the War of 1812, describing Ned to then-Secretary of the Navy George Bancroft as "a man who is deserving of some rewards for his sufferings and conduct in the last war."[19]

Yet within the narrative itself, Myers expresses a fatalism about his economic and societal position. Even while acknowledging that he has wasted his wages and the good will of charity-minded friends, Myers doesn't sustain any interest in advancement, whether spiritual, social, or economic. He knows his place—his role as a common sailor—and rarely seems to chafe at the restrictions of maritime hierarchy. In fact, Ned seeks clearly defined class systems, disdaining one group of relatively poor ship owners because "they were too near my own level to create respect."[20] He prefers the naval to the merchant service, because in the former a sailor is "pretty certain of having gentlemen over him, and that is a great deal."[21] Further, Myers is all too willing to take demotions—he repeatedly sails before the mast even after earning a mate's berths—and never negotiates for more favorable conditions. Desertion, usually, is Ned's mode of protest. Any chance for advancement, or "preferment," to use Ned's term, is suspect: early in his sailing career, Ned is offered a promotion to a master's mate's berth, but reports "I felt too much afraid of myself to accept it. I entered the navy, then, for the first time as a common Jack."[22] The reasons for his fear here are mysterious, as this moment predates his long struggles with drunkenness. This unexplained sense of fear prevents Myers from ever taking comfort in his one living family member, a sister, whose efforts to meet Ned are brusquely rebuffed—he "was afraid to venture on that," Ned says.[23]

As he reaches the sailor's middle age of thirty, Ned's unspecified fear turns to apathy—"I had felt a singular indifference whether I went to sea as an officer, or as a foremast Jack," he explains.[24] Part of this indifference can be attributed to Ned's inability to master mathematical navigation and "the lunars." He turns down an offer to work towards a captaincy because "I was honestly diffident about my knowledge of navigation. I never had a clear understanding of the lunars, though I worked hard to master them."[25] Yet, despite Ned's tough luck with math, he takes pleasure in reading the Bible's narratives: "The history of Jonah and the whale, I read at least twenty times. I cannot remember that the morality, or thought, or devotion of a single passage struck me on these occasions. In word, I read this sacred book for amusement, and not for light."[26] Easily influenced, when Ned reads Tom Paine he finds "practical evidence of the bad effects of his miserable system. I soon got stern-way on me in morals[...]. I began to think that the things of this world were to be enjoyed."[27] Even though the end of his narrative finds Ned embracing sobriety and Christianity—influenced by a Bible he is given with "prayers for seamen bound up with it"[28]—he died of alcoholism several years after his narrative was published. "I am sorry to say our friend Ned Myers has fallen astern," wrote Cooper during Ned's final debauch, and Myers passed without preferment.[29]

Myers's embrace of Cooper as the public face of his life story therefore registers as wholly consistent with Ned's longstanding comfort with clear, established hierarchies, and with his own relatively modest place within them. Myers is very happy to have Cooper serve as the "gentleman" who authorizes his narrative. Yet for Cooper, the value of *Ned Myers* lies not in his hierarchical remove from Ned, but rather in his presumed shared experience with his "old ship-mate." This is a paradox that the narrative itself struggles mightily to reconcile, especially because Cooper himself profited from his own lofty position within established hierarchies. How can Cooper stand both as an authentic former sailor before the mast, and a gentleman-editor enjoying literary status? If the narrative is designed, in part, to serve the interests of reform, then Myers's habitual self-deprecation would be inconsistent with the production of the narrative. That is, if Myers considered himself too unworthy even to meet with his only sister, or to accept a promotion, it seems unlikely that he would offer up his own life as a model for charitable attention to seamen's issues. Within this context, Cooper's role as Myers's "superior" is telling. Ned rekindles their acquaintance after a space of nearly thirty-five years, writing Cooper a letter in which he asks if the famous author is the young man whom he knew in 1809 ("I had taken it into my head this was the very person who had been with us in the *Sterling*," Ned reports.)[30] Myers addresses this letter to "Mr. Fenimore Cooper," and sends it to the town that bears the writer's widely known family name. Known to all as "the author of many naval tales, and of the Naval History," Cooper nevertheless replies familiarly: "I am your old ship-mate, Ned."[31]

This sense of intimacy doesn't penetrate the narrative to a great extent, however. In his career as a sailor, Ned had been indifferent to any personal claims for agency or self-definition, and the production of his narrative is no exception. Unlike slave narratives, many of which also feature amanuenses, *Ned Myers* lacks the full editorial apparatus testifying to the narrative's authenticity and truth-value: no one vouches for his story other than his editor. That is, Cooper's voice is presumed to have its own authority, both within the field of sea writing and in the broader literary marketplace, in endorsing Ned's story. And Cooper's authority is, ultimately, the point. The Preface to *Ned Myers* displays a provocatively elastic use of the terms "editor," "writer," and "author." This elasticity is precisely the interests of this essay: in which role is Cooper best cast in Ned Myers's narrative? If Cooper's fittest role, according to his critics, is to serve as "copyist" for maritime experience, then Cooper's position as amanuensis for Ned Myers's account of his life at sea should be transparent. Such, however, is not the case.[32] Cooper's eagerness to associate his own writing—as well as his own position as sailor-author—with that of Richard Henry Dana, for example, makes for some confusion in analyzing Cooper's influence over Myers's own *Life Before the Mast*. This difficulty occurs in part because literary historians have often overlooked *Ned Myers* in discussions of Cooper's body of work; some reprints of Cooper's complete works have even omitted it completely. Thomas Philbrick's landmark *James Fenimore Cooper and the Development of American Sea Fiction*, the only critical work devoted to thorough analysis of Cooper's maritime writing, devotes only two or three pages to *Ned Myers*, and does so mostly to praise the freshness and authenticity of its narrative voice when compared with what Philbrick finds to be the "hackwork" of other seamen authors. Finding the style of the narrative to be a "minor triumph," and exceptional within Cooper's body of work, Philbrick argues that Cooper preserves "the idioms and intonation of the seaman and imposing, at the same time, the order and control which are so conspicuously lacking in the narratives of other literary tars."[33] The authenticity that Philbrick values, in this case, is dependent more on Cooper's editorial skill than on Myers's unadulterated voice.

Cooper himself contributed in some fashion to the narrative's subsequent critical neglect and bibliographic confusion, however inadvertently. In a letter to Richard Bentley, his usual London publisher, Cooper explains that his newest book will be "*a real biography*, intended to represent the experience, wrecks, battles, escapes, and career of a seaman who has been in all sorts of vessels, from a man of war to a smuggler of opium in China" (emphasis Cooper's). Ned himself has been visiting him, he continues, and "I have been at work on him with great zeal."[34] Here, Cooper conflates the physical Ned with the text his narrative will produce. His preposition is telling: he has been working on Myers, not with him, and this suggests that Cooper views the old salt as a work-in-progress ready-made, a text for the taking. But the printed work is not, strictly speaking, a biography, as it is told in the first person. In claiming the category of "biography," rather than that of "narrative," Cooper may be attempting to elevate the status of both Myers's life and his life story. As Ann Fabian has persuasively argued in *The Unvarnished Truth*, the personal narrative genre in the antebellum period was embraced by destitute and forgotten men on the margins of society. "Biographies," on the other hand, more typically served to place the life of an individual (usually an elite) within a specific (usually richly evoked) historical or cultural context, and this broader perspective tended to be beyond the interests of the narrative form.

The Preface to *Ned Myers*, however, does not feature the word "biography," despite Cooper's promises to Bentley. In it, Cooper initially refers to himself as "the editor," but he is an editor who is also a writer, as he explains: "the reader will feel a natural desire to understand how far the editor can vouch for the truth of that which he has here written."[35] From this point in the Preface onward, Cooper proceeds to call himself "the writer" of the narrative, who was "determined to produce the following work" upon hearing Ned's story.[36] This slippage between editor and writer—with Cooper inhabiting both roles—creates some confusion for the reader. This confusion was reflected in the few reviews of *Ned Myers* that appeared in periodicals. *Graham's*, for example, was initially skeptical of the claim that Cooper served only as "editor" to the volume; its review begins "The words '*edited* by J. Fenimore Cooper,' in the title-page of this volume, have, no doubt, a suspicious appearance." Given the examples of works such as *Robinson Crusoe* and *Arthur Gordon Pym*, the review continues, "the reader will naturally be induced to suspect Mr. Cooper, who professes to *edit* '*Ned Myers*,' of having, in fact, composed it himself."[37] While *Graham's* ultimately endorses the volume, not all were so forgiving; another review finds *Ned Myers* to be "scarcely worth the attention bestowed upon it by its distinguished *editor*" (reviewer's emphasis).[38]

Such perplexity only increases in the narrative's footnotes. In one instance, a note to a given regimental number reads that "the writer" had in fact left a blank for this regiment[39]; yet, the next footnote is credited to the "Editor."[40] The presumption that the former footnote refers to Ned ("the writer") and the latter to Cooper ("the Editor") turns out not to be true, as in the course of single paragraphs Cooper refers to himself variously as editor and writer. He only intrudes upon the text to point out Ned's errors—"The names of Ned are taken a good deal at random, and, doubtless, are often misspelled,"[41] reads one note—although many of these errors are of the sort that, presumably, some one in the position of editor would be able to correct. Cooper appears to want to call attention to such minor errata, rather than silently correcting them, as a perverse way to authenticate this narrative of a common sailor.

Strange, though, are the terms under which Cooper does choose to correct Ned's own account. The value of Myers's narrative lies in part in Ned's extensive travels throughout the broader world, from Canton to Quebec; yet Cooper, referring to himself here in the third person, reveals that "In a few instances he has interposed his own greater knowledge of the world, between Ned's more limited experience and the narrative; but this has been done cautiously, and only in cases in which there can be little doubt that the narrator has been deceived by appearances, or misled by ignorance."[42] Cooper would have "greater knowledge of the world" than Myers in some senses, certainly, but not in the view of the world that matters here—the view offered by Ned's narrative of global voyaging. The "limited experience" Cooper here attributes to Myers likewise could not refer to any aspects of his life that would confer value on a travel or sea narrative; Ned's experiences are, in this regard, prodigious. Further, stamping Ned as an occasionally "deceived" or "misled" narrator of his own experience betrays many of the expectations of the narrative genre: that is, whereas readers or critics might disbelieve an account, the text itself should endorse its own veracity, from preface to endnote. Cooper's qualifications seriously undercut his observation that in Ned he finds "a man every way entitled to speak for himself; the want of the habit of communicating his thoughts to the public, alone excepted."[43] It is Cooper, after all, who suggests publishing the narrative, or as Ned puts it, Cooper is "disposed to put into proper form the facts which I can give him."[44] The result, Myers is made to proclaim, is "literally my own story, logged by my old shipmate."[45]

## Log-Book Truths

The figure of the log is telling. Shipboard experience is most commonly recorded in the form of the logbook, which in practice is the record of a nautical voyage, complete with distance, longitude and latitude readings, seamen's muster, and occasionally, events of note. Even though most actual logbooks contain almost no narrative detail, the logbook is often invoked figuratively in sea narratives as a stand-in for truth, or as an objective register of experience. In the mouths of Cooper's sailors, the logbook is primarily referred to as a standard of historical fact. In *The Pilot*, for example, Tom Coffin's boast of having killed over a hundred whales is met with skepticism, to which Tom rejoins, "It's no bragging, sir, to speak a log-book truth!"[46] Tom Coffin here alludes to the fact that a ship's official log is often replicated and amplified by a sailor's narrative or journal, as both record the circularity of a successful voyage. Indeed, logbooks are the narrative model for most sea writings, which adopt either the logbook's diary-entry form, or at least its insistence on a meticulous chronological progression. Logs likewise display the precision of navigational measurements and reflect the discipline of record-keeping practices aboard ship. They presume a linear narrative structure, and make date, time, and location a vital narrative preoccupation of sea fiction. The metaphor is elastic for Cooper; he makes the reach of the logbook far more expansive in his fiction than it would customarily be in practice. Ever alert to a useful nautical metaphor to describe mortality, Cooper observes in *The Pilot*, for example, that human intervention "can do but little to clear the log-account of a man whose watch is up for this world."[47] He recognizes the poetic value of the rigor of a log's documentation in the face of the inscrutability of a sea that permits no records.

More significantly, in his 1827 preface to the first edition of his second sea novel, *The Red Rover*, Cooper avows that "[t]he true Augustan age of literature can never exist until works shall be as accurate, in their typography, as a 'log-book,' and as sententious, in their matter, as a 'watch-bill.'"[48] In elevating the logbook and the watch bill (the schedule of sailors' labor) to serve as the standards of literary excellence, Cooper underscores several points. First, he stresses that technical accuracy and informational brevity will be goals of his literary efforts. This is a bold choice, given the skepticism magazines like the *North American Review* held in the early years of the nation's literary production for America's "matter-of-fact sort of people," presumably inadequate to literary attention.[49] Second, Cooper asserts the value of both the American mariner and his writings, since they will stand as a model for classic ("Augustan") literary achievement. But the final and most important point that Cooper makes in this passage from *Red Rover* concerns book-making. The "typography" of the logbook is what is most valued here, as well as the admirably pithy—or well-edited—watch bill. This sentence concludes a paragraph in the preface to *Red Rover* in which Cooper apologizes for inaccuracies any "keen-eyed critic of the ocean" might spot, such as "a rope rove through the wrong leading-block, or a term spelt in such a manner as to destroy its true sound."[50] And although he hopes critics will impute such errors simply to "ignorance on the part of a brother," Cooper's real target for blame is the book-maker. He continues, "It must be remembered that there is an undue proportion of landsmen employed in the mechanical as well as the more spiritual part of book-making, a fact which, in itself, accounts for the numberless imperfections that still embarrass the respective departments of the occupation."[51] The "landsmen" of the book trade bear responsibility for a sea novel's failures, which could be textual (in the form of inaccurate typography), or what Cooper calls "spiritual," which seems to indicate a failure of editorial or industrial support. Even as Cooper positions the publisher or printer as an antagonist to the seaman-author, he provides the possibility that the "undue proportion of landsmen" in the trade might someday be evened out. Sailors, he implies, should enter the trade in order to ensure the kind of literary accuracy that could have "mechanical" as well as "spiritual" dimensions.

For all Cooper's insistence on the logbook truth of his edition of *Ned Myers*, however, such truth-value proved of little interest to readers. In a letter Cooper wrote to his wife two months after the narrative's publication, he complained, "I am afraid 'Ned' has not done much after all. No one I meet, appears to know any thing of it, and, you know, these people wait to be told what to do, say, or think by the newspapers. The last have maintained a dead silence. Nothing but murders appear to move the public mind now, and even murders begin to be stale."[52] A public dining on critical opinion, and hungry for fresher and more startling tales of truth, chooses to pass on Cooper's latest fare. The truth-value of a narrative helps sell its story, in every sense. While his old friend, navy man William Bradford Shubrick, praises the volume as a "pleasant [...] compagnon de voyage," Shubrick does express concern that the narrative's value as a tale of truth might not be made evident in the literary marketplace: "it is to be regretted I think that the book is advertised in some of the papers as 'a novel.' There are many persons who would read it as a statement of facts who would not read it as a novel."[53] Cooper, in this case, cannot even enjoy the kind of readership that might prefer fiction, for as he frets to Shubrick,

> I am inclined to think you are mistaken as to the circulation of Ned Myers. It may have gone off pretty well at Baltimore, but I see no signs of any movement in New York, nor do I hear any thing from Philadelphia. Baltimore is only a secondary market for a book, the place yielding very little to authors I believe; less than any town of its size in America, I think I have been told. I can not even see an advertisement in a New York paper. In long lists of other works, Ned is not even named.[54]

The attention to the marketing and reception of the work that Cooper displays above is consistent with his method of promoting his works to publishers. A tireless agitator for American copyright law, Cooper tended to be very precise in his demands of publishers. Here, provocatively, *Ned Myers*'s progress as a text is discussed as a hopeful mimic of the real *Ned Myers*'s own maritime circulation.

[128]

*Ned Myers* was first published in November of 1843 in America by Lea and Blanchard of Philadelphia, and in Britain by Richard Bentley of London; both were Cooper's usual publishers. The quality of these simultaneous editions varied widely, however. The American edition was cheaply printed, in wrappers, and its front cover lists the price at 37 1/2 cents; it featured ads for volumes ranging from "The Complete Cook"—a domestic treatise, oddly, not the narratives of the famous explorer—to the novels of Smollett, Fielding, and Cooper himself. The quality of this edition was consistent with many of Lea and Blanchard's productions of the time. None of the advertised books cost more than 50 cents, with the exception of a handsome bound set of Cooper's *History of the Navy*.[55] The British edition, on the other hand, was bound in two volumes, the spine of which read "Edited by F. Cooper, Esq., Author of 'The Pilot,' 'The Spy,' etc."; it did not include advertisements, nor was the price listed. This discrepancy in the print quality of *Ned Myers*'s various editions reflects Cooper's own sense of the unusual status of this particular volume.

But the finer quality of the British edition was not, ultimately, predicative of the narrative's success. Cooper was anxious to see *Ned Myers* in a cheaper edition, as he wrote to Bentley: "I anticipate an extensive sale for this book, which has been read in sheets here, by two or three good judges, who think it must take.[...] I think you ought to get this book out in a popular form, though you know your own market."[56] When Bentley revealed that he intended a run of only 750 copies, Cooper became concerned by what seemed to him an "extraordinarily small edition," and pushed further for "a cheap edition to make returns of such a book," which Cooper told Bentley would become "a standard book of its class."[57] Cooper's distress increased when Bentley replied that the attention given to *Ned Myers* had been unfavorable, especially in comparison with Dana's *Two Years Before the Mast*; this, according to Bentley, obviated any advantage in issuing a cheap edition. Agitated, Cooper attempted one last sally, writing to Bentley nearly six months after the book was published, "Do you not mean to publish a cheap edition of Ned Myers? Or have you done it? That is the form in which to circulate such a work."[58] Bentley reported that since no copies of *Ned Myers* had been sold in the preceding three months; that he was "persuaded that a cheap edition would not succeed."[59]

Cooper's further justification to Bentley that the demands of veracity would not permit him to embroider Myers's narrative into a length of two volumes is arresting: "I was writing truth, and did not feel justified in spinning out the facts, and as to any comments of my own they would have

[129]

impaired the identity of the whole affair. I was forced to stop, when Ned had no more to say."[60] Caught between the literary market's interest in tales strictly of truth, and his own instinct for "spinning out the facts," Cooper finds that he must repress his drive to expand a narrative he hints is incomplete. To have intruded too much would have "impaired the identity" of the work, he writes. But what, finally, is the identity of *Ned Myers*? One that requires cheap publication, apparently, in order to meet an authenticating "standard" of its peculiar class. In writing to Bentley that he has "anticipated that [*Ned Myers*] will become a standard book of its class," Cooper reveals how strategic his embrace of the form of the first-person sea narrative has been. But this strategy did not earn Editor Cooper the esteem, or sales, of a narrative like Dana's. Myers's attitude is not typical of the genre of sea writing, in which sailors might acknowledge the comparatively debased status of seamen in the broader culture, but would almost never debase their own value. That is, Dana's reform-minded sea narrative had insisted upon the value of the individual laboring sailor, whereas Ned Myers could not bring himself to accept a promotion. *Ned Myers* registers both the changes and distortions of the genre of the maritime narrative between the 1820s and 1840s, and Cooper's own struggles in the face of these changes. His unease with the form is a reminder that the impetus to introduce Ned's narrative to a reading public did not, crucially, come from the laboring sailor himself. Sea narrative writing may not be of the highest class, but it has its standards.

# NOTES

[1] On the place of paupers' narratives in the literary marketplace, see Ann Fabian, *The Unvarnished Truth: Personal Narratives in Nineteenth-Century America* (Berkeley: University of California Press, 2000). For more on the explosion of print in the early nineteenth century, see Nina Baym, *Novels, Readers, and Reviewers: Responses to Fiction in Antebellum America* (Ithaca: Cornell University Press, 1984); William Charvat, *Literary Publishing in America, 1790-1850* (Amherst: University of Massachusetts Press, 1993); *The Profession of Authorship in America, 1800-1870: The Papers of William Charvat* (Columbus: Ohio State University Press, 1968); and Cathy N. Davidson, *Revolution and the Word: The Rise of the Novel in America* (New York: Oxford University Press, 1986).

[2] See, for example, the four brief papers on Cooper included in William S. Dudley and Michael Crawford, eds., *The Early Republic and the Sea: Essays on the Naval and Maritime History of the Early United States* (Washington, D.C.: Brassey's, 2001). Literary scholars, of which I am one, have largely ignored Cooper's sea writing. Two exceptions are Thomas Philbrick, *James Fenimore Cooper and the Development of American Sea Fiction* (Cambridge, Mass.: Harvard University Press, 1961), which provides an excellent overview of Cooper's nautical fiction, and Hugh Egan, "Cooper and His Contemporaries," in *America and the Sea: A Literary History*, ed. Haskell Springer (Athens: University of Georgia Press, 1995). While the existing scholarship on Cooper's writing is able, it is not diverse; the scholars mentioned above—Philbrick, Dudley, and Egan—have themselves provided the bulk of criticism on Cooper's sea fiction.

[3] Cooper's eleven sea novels are *The Pilot* (1824), *The Red Rover* (1827), *The Water-Witch* (1830), *Homeward Bound* (1838), *Mercedes of Castile* (1840), *The Two Admirals* (1842), *The Wing-and-Wing* (1842), *Afloat and Ashore* (1844), *The Crater* (1847), *Jack Tier* (1848), and *The Sea Lions* (1849). Cooper was also the author of naval histories including *The History of the Navy of the United States of America* (1839); *The Battle of Lake Erie* (1843); *Lives of Distinguished American Naval Officers* (1846); and a lengthy review included in the *Proceedings of the Naval Court Martial in the Case of Alexander Slidell Mackensie* (1844).

[4] See Philbrick, *James Fenimore Cooper*, and Egan, "Cooper and His Contemporaries," 64-82.

[5] See George Little, *Life on the Ocean; or, Twenty years at sea: being the personal adventures of the author. By George Little, for many years Captain in the Merchant Service out of the Port of Baltimore, but now entirely blind* (1843; Boston: Waite, Peirce and Company, 1845), and

Robert Adams, *The Narrative of Robert Adams, an American Sailor, who was wrecked on the Western coast of Africa, in the year 1810; was detained three years in slavery by the Arabs of the Great Desert, and resided several months in the city of Tombuctoo* (Boston: Wells and Lilly, 1817).

[6] James Fenimore Cooper, ed., *Ned Myers; or, A Life Before the Mast*, introduction and notes by William S. Dudley (1843 Annapolis, Md.: Naval Institute Press, 1989), 278.

[7] Quoted in George Dekker and John P. Williams, eds., *James Fenimore Cooper: The Critical Heritage* (London: Routledge, 1973), 121.

[8] Anon., Review of *Ned Myers; or, A Life Before the Mast, Graham's Lady's and Gentleman's Magazine* 25:1 (January 1844), 46.

[9] Richard Henry Dana Jr., *Two Years Before the Mast*, edited and with an introduction by Thomas Philbrick (1840; New York: Penguin Classics, 1986), 37. The full elaboration of Dana's motives in the preface stresses his experience as a common laboring seaman, as opposed to an officer, such as Cooper was.

[10] Cooper to Richard Henry Dana Sr., October 15, 1841, *The Letters and Journals of James Fenimore Cooper*, 6 vol., ed. James Franklin Beard (Cambridge, Mass.: Harvard University Press, 1960), 4:181.

[11] Cooper to Dana Sr., 30 Oct. 1845, *Letters*, 5:94.

[12] Review of *Two Years Before the Mast*, North American Review lii:110 (Jan. 1841), 60.

[13] Review of *Two Years Before the Mast*, 60.

[14] James Fenimore Cooper, *Notions of the Americans, Picked Up by a Travelling Bachelor*, 2 vols. (1828; New York: Frederick Ungar, 1963), 1:337 [Note B].

[15] James Fenimore Cooper, *The Pilot*, in *Sea Tales* (New York: Library of America, 1991), 7.

[16] Cooper, *The Pilot*, 8, 7.

[17] Nathaniel Ames, *A Mariner's Sketches* (Providence: Cory, Marshall and Hammond, 1830), 241.

[18] Cooper, *Ned Myers*, 1.

[19] Cooper to George Bancroft, June 5, 1845, *Letters*, 5:36.

20 Cooper, *Ned Myers*, 146.

21 Ibid., 212.

22 Ibid., 52.

23 Ibid., 108.

24 Ibid., 172.

25 Ibid., 203.

26 Ibid., 206.

27 Ibid., 241.

28 Ibid., 271.

29 Cooper to William Bradford Shubrick, October 6, 1849, *Letters*, 6:73-74.

30 Cooper, *Ned Myers*, 276.

31 Ibid., 277.

32 The few critics who have devoted attention to *Ned Myers* agree that little can be known about the specific form Cooper's and Myers's collaboration took in practice. It should be said that the structure of this collaboration is not a source of curiosity for such critics, generally speaking.

33 Philbrick, *James Fenimore Cooper*, 129.

34 Cooper to Richard Bentley, July 18, 1843, *Letters*, 4:391-92.

35 Cooper, *Ned Myers*, 1.

36 Ibid., 2.

37 Anon., *Review of Ned Myers; or a Life Before the Mast, Graham's Lady's and Gentleman's Magazine*, 46.

38 Anon., *Review of Ned Myers; or a Life Before the Mast, Editors' Table* (January 1844), 155.

39 Cooper, *Ned Myers*, 6, n. 1.

[40] Ibid., 8, n. 2.

[41] Ibid., 16, n. 3.

[42] Ibid., 2-3.

[43] Ibid., 3.

[44] Ibid., 5.

[45] Ibid., 278.

[46] Cooper, *The Pilot*, 202.

[47] Ibid., 249.

[48] James Fenimore Cooper, *The Red Rover*, in *Sea Tales*, 425.

[49] W. H. Gardiner, Review of *The Spy* [1821], *North American Review* 25 (July 1822), 250.

[50] Cooper, *The Red Rover*, 425.

[51] Ibid., 425.

[52] Cooper to Susan Augusta Cooper, January 14, 1844, *Letters*, 4:332.

[53] William Bradford Shubrick to Cooper, November 23, 1843, quoted in *Letters*, 4:431.

[54] Cooper to William Bradford Shubrick, December 9, 1843, *Letters*, 4:428-29.

[55] A testimonial from the *American Traveller* regarding this edition, quoted in the advertisement, praises Cooper's ability to give the subject "all the richness of romance, with the method and accuracy of strict history," advertisement in *Ned Myers, or a Life Before the Mast* (Philadelphia: Lea and Blanchard, 1843).

[56] Cooper to Richard Bentley, September 25, 1843, *Letters*, 4:415.

[57] Cooper to Richard Bentley, January 9, 1844, *Letters*, 4:440-41.

[58] Cooper to Richard Bentley, April 16, 1844, *Letters*, 4:456.

[59] Richard Bentley to Cooper, May 21, 1844, quoted in *Letters*, 4:456.

[60] Cooper to Richard Bentley, January 9, 1844, *Letters*, 4:440-1.

# VII

## BROADSIDES ON LAND AND SEA
### A Cultural Reading of the Naval Engagements
### in the War of 1812

### DAN HICKS

The War of 1812 on land began disastrously for the United States with the surrender of William Hull's forces on August 16, 1812, less than two months after war was declared. Although the military situation improved over the course of the war, American land forces scored few signal victories before Andrew Jackson's trouncing of British invaders at the Battle of New Orleans. The main goal of the U.S. Army, moreover, the conquest of Canada, ensured that a large body of Americans would withhold their applause for soldiers on the scattered occasions of success—particularly Federalists and "Old Republicans," conservatives like John Randolph who had broken with the administration. Americans did, however, have one nearly unanimous source of martial pride during the conflict: single ship actions that seemingly demonstrated American maritime superiority over the British. These sea battles may not have had a huge impact on the outcome of the war, but they did help to boost American morale, a role they acquired early in the war, when news of the destruction of HMS *Guerrière* by the USS *Constitution* on August 19, 1812, partially offset the disgrace of American arms in Canada. These battles also helped to fuel an American naval mythology that has continued to the present. Looking beyond this naval heritage, we need to understand these ship-to-ship contests within their historical context. There are several ways of "reading" these sea battles as cultural artifacts. First, they represented affairs of honor peculiar to the era of the early republic. Second, ship-to-ship engagements helped to define a nascent American nationalism. Third, celebrations of victories were used to push partisan agendas. And finally, the feting of the common seamen after the battles accentuated class divisions and highlighted the problematic role of sailors in the new American nation.

Honor was integral to early American politics, and was of central concern to leading political figures. The War of 1812 had to be fought, many Americans

[135]

believed, to uphold the nation's honor.[1] Once the fighting began, codes of honor maintained through violence guided the conduct of many American combatants, especially the men who held commissions in the army or navy. Indeed, American officers serving on the Lakes sometimes seemed more intent on thinning their own ranks through internal duels than they did in confronting the nearby British foe.[2]

Honor also came into play in encounters with the British, as naval engagements were particularly well suited to exhibit. Single-ship engagements especially were imagined as duels: two combatants met as equals, sometimes after one of the sides issued a written challenge to the other, and they fought according to accepted rules of equal combat. In theory, the combatant who possessed superior qualities would claim the laurels. Success was believed to depend more on intangible factors than on the strength of the ship or the number of its guns (though these factors assumed considerable importance in explaining defeats).

"Equal combat" and "fair play" were crucial terms in narratives of naval battles.[3] During the war, both British and American commanders challenged their opponents to ship-to-ship duels to "try the fortune of our respective flags."[4] In the interest of fair play, they promised that their escorts would stand off and not interfere. Naval officers gained glory only through victories over near-equals or superiors. A commander added no luster to his name by defeating a weaker opponent. Commodore John Rodgers, commander of the USS *President* during its controversial engagement with the smaller HMS *Little Belt* in 1811, confessed that the affair "has given me much pain, as well on account of the injury she sustained; as that I should have been compelled to the measure that produced it, by a vessel of her inferiour force."[5] Similarly, Captain David Porter of the USS *Essex*, after capturing the smaller HMS *Alert*, which was pursuing the more equally matched USS *Hornet*, wrote the secretary of navy that "it is a source of regret to me that she did not fall in with that vessel instead of the *Essex*, as the forces would then have been more equal."[6] An officer who eschewed equal combat for the safety of more favorable odds opened himself to the bitter recrimination of his peers. Captain David Porter of the USS *Essex* denounced Captain James Hillyar of HMS *Phoebe* for this reason. "For six weeks I daily offered him fair and honorable combat on terms greatly to his advantage," Porter growled. Yet Hillyar had refused his offer, postponing his attack until joined by his consort, HMS *Cherub*. What made Hillyar's character worse, in Porter's assessment, was that he attacked the USS *Essex* as it lay within Chile's neutral waters. The crippled *Essex* mounted a valiant defense, but ultimately surrendered, with scores of its men dead or wounded. Because of Hillyar's dishonorable conduct, Porter concluded, "the blood of the slain must be on his head, and he has yet to reconcile his conduct to heaven, his conscience and to the world."[7]

In some degree, Porter had himself to blame for losing his ship. From a strategic standpoint, Porter accomplished more than any other American commander during the War of 1812. His foray into the heart of Britain's Pacific whaling territory devastated the industry. It also cost the American people little, as Porter and his growing force "lived off the land," as it were, provisioning themselves with supplies pillaged from their prizes. Unfortunately, after having "done all the injury that could be done to the British commerce in the Pacific," Porter "still hoped to signalize my cruise by something more splendid before leaving that sea."[8] He therefore cruised in search of a fight, finding one in his ill fated encounter with the *Phoebe* and the *Cherub*.

Porter's desire "to signalize" his cruise was a common one. Secretary of the Navy William Jones had repeatedly to order his commanders from "giving or receiving a Challenge, to, or from an Enemy's Vessel." The navy's strategy was to attack Britain's shipping, Jones admonished, "for there he is indeed vulnerable." Jones reminded his officers that, "it is not even good policy to meet an equal, unless, under special circumstances, where a great object is to be gained, without a great sacrifice." As for the glory to be won by single-ship victories, Secretary Jones insisted that, "The Character of the American Navy does not require those feats of Chivalry."[9] Even victorious engagements might subvert strategic goals, forcing a triumphant vessel to abandon its mission and return to port for repairs. By the spring of 1813, American ships that docked at home ports rarely faced long odds at evading the Royal Navy's blockade and returning to sea.[10] Excepting the Battles of Lake Erie and Plattsburg, which respectively helped to restore American control of the Northwest and halted a British invasion into New York, the most widely celebrated naval victories—*Constitution* vs. *Guerrière, United States* vs. *Macedonian, Constitution* vs. *Java,* &c.—had little impact on the course or outcome of the war. Single-ship engagements, in short, were not strategically beneficial; they risked more than they could return; they undermined the navy's designs; and they brought the country no closer to an end to the war. Yet Americans celebrated them enthusiastically.

Although the strategic significance of many naval battles was negligible, the symbolic significance could be of great importance, and that is what Americans cheered. The symbolic importance of naval battles can be gauged well by

Americans' reactions to their worst maritime loss: the USS *Chesapeake* vs. HMS *Shannon*. An unmitigated defeat for the American navy in terms of strategy (not only did the *Chesapeake* fail to complete its mission, it was also captured by the enemy), Americans nonetheless succeeded in transforming it into proof of American superiority. Tellingly, they did so not only through their own commemorations of the battle but also through references to British ones.

The battle took place on June 1, 1813, off the shore of Massachusetts. The *Chesapeake* had been bottled within the port of Boston by a British frigate, HMS *Shannon*. The *Shannon* stood off the port, either to accept a challenge from the *Chesapeake* or to force it into a fight if it attempted to slip past. The recently transferred commander of the *Chesapeake*, James Lawrence, gambled that he could lead the ship to victory despite his unfamiliar and somewhat disgruntled crew. The *Chesapeake* sailed out to meet the *Shannon*, which was manned by a well-seasoned crew under Captain Philip Broke. The *Chesapeake* suffered a series of accidents early in the encounter, not least of which was the fatal wounding of Captain Lawrence. Fifteen minutes after the battle began, boarders from the *Shannon* took control of the American ship and sailed it to Canada alongside the victor.[11]

The defeat was a spectacular one—quite literally, as the battle occurred near enough to the shore that the residents of several Massachusetts towns were able to witness it from rooftops and hillsides.[12] Americans were shocked by the loss. They cast about for explanations. Lawrence's leadership was not open to question. The young captain had already become a hero to the American people before his death, thanks to the earlier destruction of HMS *Peacock* by the USS *Hornet* under Lawrence's command. The loss of the *Chesapeake* only enhanced his reputation, making a martyr out of him. An alternative explanation was needed. Some commentators blamed a treacherous Portuguese boatswain in the *Chesapeake*'s crew who helped the English boarders take the ship; some blamed a black bugler who hid in a boat when the battle began rather than call the men to action with his horn. In the courts-martial that followed the loss, the bugler, George Brown, suffered the worst punishment of all personnel tried: 300 lashes and the mulcting of his future wages. In effect, the bugler's service ended as slavery. Another popular theory was that someone on the *Shannon* had cheated. Witnesses swore they saw an explosion on the *Chesapeake* early in the encounter, which they attributed to a grenade, or "stink pot," tossed by someone on the *Shannon* in violation of the codes of honorable conduct: "Though a frigate we've lost, it was not by fair play, / And in spite of their '*Stink Pots*' we'll lather away," as one song avowed.[13]

Whatever the particular explanation, Americans insisted that the character of their nation had not been compromised by the defeat. After learning the particulars of the loss, an American prisoner of war in Ashburton, England, grinned and declared, "I knew the Chesapeake must have been taken by surprize, not by a fair fight, yard arm and yard arm, broadside and broadside. We have lost no honour."[14] An Independence Day oration of 1813 asserted that the Americans on the *Chesapeake* "were overpowered, but not subdued, accident baffled our skill, and slaughtered our officers, and at the moment when victory was almost within our grasp, an act of foul play by a desperate foe, aided by an extraordinary complement of men, overpowered the brave remnant of our countrymen."[15] Americans could not transform the battle into a victory, but they could, and did, interpret it in a light favorable to their national character. They did so partly by claiming that the battle somehow had not been fair and that naval battles were only valid insofar as they were fair (as opposed to strategically efficacious).

Americans found their greatest solace in England's jubilant reaction to *Chesapeake* vs. *Shannon*. An American who was in England when news of the *Shannon*'s victory arrived in the country recalled that, "the loyal inhabitants of Plymouth, had just illuminated with much splendour, for the joint victories of Vittoria and the Chesapeake, and the names of Wellington and Brock [that is, Broke, commander of the *Shannon*] were entwined together in one wreath." To the American spectator's mind, this dual commemoration "bestow[ed] upon us the highest honour they possibly could bestow, by comparing the accidental capture of one American frigate, to a splendid victory, which in effect, drove the French from the peninsula, and paved the way for those extraordinary events which have since occurred in Europe [that is, the initial abdication of Napoleon]." Other Americans, reading similar accounts in newspapers, noted proudly that England, a nation that hardly blinked at the receipt of news of the capture of a French fleet, had erupted into paroxysms of joy for the capture of a single American frigate.[16]

American newspapers echoed these sentiments. One widely reprinted editorial judged that, "the great exultation of the British, both in and out of parliament, upon receiving the news of the capture of the Chesapeake, may be considered the greatest compliment that has yet been paid to our gallant navy."[17] Newspapers throughout the nation agreed that British celebrations were inadvertent admissions of American superiority: "what an encomium did those guns pay to our tars! what a peal of joy did the bells ring in the ears of

Americans! Yes, the bravery of our tars is such, that we have compelled the enemy to proclaim it themselves: so difficult was it to gain a single victory or a single ship from us, that when gained, as much was done to celebrate it, as used to be done after a battle in which twenty ships of the line were taken."[18] Several newspapers carried a comical dialogue between Brother Jonathan and John Bull in which the latter hailed the victory of the *Shannon* as "certainly the greatest achievement which the world ever saw." In reply, Jonathan asked, "Are you proud of conquering a man whom you despise? No, it is because you were afraid of us, & envy our superiority, that you croak so much at this victory." Then Jonathan reached the crux of the matter: "In the very excesses which you are indulging, you bow to our ascendancy."[19] Clearly, the ways in which battles were remembered could matter as much as their tangible effects.

The close attention that contemporaries paid to interpretations of naval victories is illustrated by the satirical American piece, *British Glory*. This extended poem parodied the exculpatory accounts of British defeats that appeared in British commanders' official letters, parliamentary proceedings, and newspapers. At one point in the poem, Admiral Herbert Sawyer of the Royal Navy sadly informed the Admiralty Board of Captain James R. Dacres's defeat in the battle of the USS *Constitution* vs. HMS *Guerrière*. "He's drubb'd sir, to his heart's content," wrote the poem's caricature of Sawyer; "Nor can he yet a lie invent / By which to prop his sinking fame, / And save the glory of our name." Sawyer held out hope that he and Dacres could still "Raise some good story of the fight, / Disgrace from him and us to drag off"—in other words, that Dacres might weave a tale to transform the defeat into a victory, the same way Americans would later do when they lost the *Chesapeake*. The narrator of the poem, in the guise of a Briton, provided a string of flimsy excuses to explain the *Guerrière*'s defeat—rotten hulls, a green crew, and so forth. He began to despond, however, as American forces accumulated more and more successes. The narrator's ultimate solution, since the British could not defeat the American Navy at sea, was to fight "against them in the papers."[20]

Naval victories gave Americans an opportunity to celebrate their national character. They provided the opportunities to reaffirm sentimental union which other national festivals failed to do during the war. As Admiral E. M. Eller wrote of naval celebrations, "Here lies the real importance of the unexpected naval victories against the mighty ruler of the sea. The nation that had expected little of its infant navy against the overwhelming power of the British fleets now joined in widespread exultation over the victories. The diverse states were suddenly wielded with a unifying national interest."[21] Praise for the navy was indeed one of the few sentiments upon which Americans across party lines could agree. John Adams, a stalwart supporter of the navy, contended that the victories would "ferment in the Minds of this People till they generate a national Self respect, a Spirit of Independence and a national Pride which has never before been felt in America."[22] The navy had become, one army officer growled, "the Idol that all sects & parties in this country, have agreed to worship."[23] As another contemporary observed, "The deeds of our naval heroes have ... created one universal feeling of admiration and delight, from Maine to Georgia."[24] The fervor with which so many Americans throughout the country feted naval heroes and cherished their achievements would seem to prove that celebrations of naval victories were instruments of unification and nationalization.

The superficial unanimity with which Americans celebrated naval victories during the War of 1812, however, obscures the important truth that those celebrations were often vehicles of partisan dispute and other forms of disagreement. Naval commemorations were complicated phenomena. They contained a multiplicity of meanings. To say that Republicans and Federalists celebrated the victories of the U.S. Navy together is true, but to suggest that they were united by those victories is not. The different meanings that different Americans derived from the same event emerge clearly, if inadvertently, at the dinners hosted throughout the war in honor of victorious naval officers and crewmen.

These dinners were sentimental affairs. They were intended, "to reward, by every possible demonstration of respect and gratitude, those gallant men who had so nobly supported their country's honor," and to evince "the grateful feeling of our citizens to our gallant countrymen."[25] The dinners would prove that a republic could properly honor its heroes. The dinners put sentiments on display. They allowed Americans, within the dining halls and without, to show their appreciation of sailors' achievements. They offered Federalists and Republicans opportunities to meet in a single space for a common purpose, proving that national sentiments remained paramount. They also provided elites with the means to test the sentimental fitness of the "lower sorts." Common sailors were sometimes invited to and honored at these dinners. These sailors needed to show simultaneously that they felt the stirrings of patriotism, but that they would not lose control of their passions. In a word, they tested whether or not the masses had the sentimental capacities to preserve the republic.

The organizers of celebratory naval dinners favored lavish spectacle over republican simplicity. Perhaps thousands of persons participated in the larger dinners, from the onlookers, "thick as a hive of bees before swarming," who crowded the streets to cheer the officers and their men as they processed from their docked ship to the dinner hall, to the three to four hundreds of gentlemen seated there.[26] The dining halls were elaborately decorated. Paintings of naval officers and battles, hundreds of feet wide, festooned the walls, alongside banners that read, "Don't Give up the Ship" and "We Have Met the Enemy, and He Is Ours." Centerpieces in the shape of frigates adorned each table. The celebrants feasted on "every dainty the season affords," accompanied by "the best of liquors and the choicest wines."[27] A miniature frigate, an exact replica of the *Constitution* or the *Essex*, floated over an artificial lake twenty feet wide at the front of the room (sometimes filled with grog instead of water). Model frigates dangled from the ceiling. An eagle with its wings outspread hovered behind the guests of honor, painted on a backdrop set to furl during the ritual toasts to reveal behind it an illumination of the battle chiefly celebrated.[28]

These dinners ostensibly promoted an uncomplicated sense of patriotism and unity that transcended party divisions. The first major dinner, held in Boston early in September, 1812, and commemorating the battle *Constitution* vs. *Guerrière*, was hailed as the "Union Naval Dinner," because the participants eschewed partisan divisions.[29] Later dinners, too, were reportedly "attended by gentlemen of every denomination of party."[30] "Although persons of both parties" joined to celebrate their naval heroes, newspapers constantly remarked, "the greatest harmony and unanimity prevailed throughout."[31] Typical was the toast "*Party*—May our only contest be, who *most* shall *love* and *best* shall *serve* our country."[32] Another toast identified the role the dinners supposedly played as exemplars of unity for the American people to follow: "*Union of sentiment*—May it ever prevail as now, on the present occasion."[33] At such festivities, newspaper correspondents assured their readers, in an echo of Jefferson's first inaugural, "*All* were *republicans*; *all federalists* … an *American* sentiment was universal."[34] At one dinner, a Revolutionary War veteran turned to another guest, and said, "This looks like old times—The curse is removed from the town—May the country at large follow this good example: and God send us a happy and speedy deliverance from party spirit, the sorest of all evils that ever afflicted our country."[35]

Still, even seemingly innocuous toasts carried partisan undertones in those factious times. At a dinner in his honor in Boston, Oliver Hazard Perry toasted, "*The Town of Boston*—The birth-place of American Liberty; from whence, should she ever leave the country, she will take her departure."[36] A correspondent of Perry's, presumably a Republican, assailed him for this comment, which the correspondent seemed to believe reeked too much of Federalism.[37] Perry defended himself by stating that, while he could "see *some good* beyond the mists of party on both sides," his correspondent was "warped by party feelings," and hence had misconstrued the gracious sentiment behind Perry's toast.[38]

Perry's plight must have been a common one, as "warped party feelings" were hardly a rarity, and surely tinctured the way most persons who heard or read toasts understood them. Many toasts offered some room for interpretation. A toast to "the President of the United States" was substantially different from a toast to "James Madison," especially when the former ended without qualification, and the latter continued, "guiding the helm of our *National Ship* thro' a turbulent sea, he has evinced a skill, prudence and magnanimity, that has even called forth the admiration of his political opponents."[39] Indeed, an unqualified toast to the president became a mere matter of form when followed by, for instance, a toast to Federalist Governor Caleb Strong of Massachusetts, whose "*name* indicates his *character*-Strong in intellect-Strong in principles-and Strong in the *affections of the people*."[40] Similarly, a toast to "the United States" became a partisan statement with the simple addition of the line, "engaged in a just and necessary war."[41] The statement, "*the Union of the States*—May it never be endangered by foreign attachments, or by internal dissentions," was bipartisan insofar as stalwarts of either party could launch it against their rivals.[42] The same might be said of the toast, "Party Spirit—It can never be extinct in a free nation, may it in ours always be unmixt by foreign partiality."[43] The best proof that these dinners were often bipartisan affairs is that sometimes, at a single dinner, celebrants offered toasts seemingly oppositional in partisan spirit.

Many toasts were ambiguous or sly with regards to their political leanings. One naval dinner included the Federalist-toned warning, "French Alliance— Tenfold more dreadful than British war."[44] No one during the war would fail to see the Federalist apologia in another toast, "The founders of our Navy.— Honor to whom honor is due."[45] Similarly, it is hard to shake the suspicion that the toast, "The Constitution—When properly manned and managed, she did wonders," offered to William Bainbridge, formerly the commander of the USS *Constitution*, did not also voice a Federalist longing for the Washingtonian era, when the U.S. Constitution had been "properly manned and managed."[46] Sometimes celebrants expressed their partisan sentiments baldly. Republicans at Tammany Hall, for instance, toasted, "*Our Eastern Brethren*—Strayed Sheep from the American Flock—may they soon be sensible of their wandering, and return, with gladness, to the fold of their country."[47]

Accounts of naval dinners could be as ambiguous regarding partisan sentiments as the dinners themselves. Though often contending that the dinners were nonpartisan affairs, newspaper editors from different parties found ways to trumpet their party's cause. Toasts that might offend a particular journal's audience might disappear from an otherwise faithful account of the proceedings, or they might receive critical commentary. The Republican *Columbian*, for instance, footnoted an anti-Jeffersonian sentiment—"The Navy of the United States—Washington its founder; dry dock projects its destroyer"—with the not entirely relevant observation that *"the law for selling or* 'destroying' the navy, *was passed by a federal congress and signed by* John Adams."[48] (As one of his "midnight" measures, Adams had reduced the size of the navy in an attempt to forestall more drastic cuts by the incoming administration.) Sometimes editors impugned the motives behind their political opponents' participation in naval celebrations. The Federalist *Boston Daily Advertiser* compared a predominantly Republican celebratory naval feast to "the *Saturnalia* of the Romans, feasts, where all distinctions, civil and honorary were suspended, and every guest was at liberty to make himself as drunk and as ridiculous as he pleased."[49] Federalists also reported the rumor that, at one naval dinner, "Queen Dolly" Madison, when presented with the colors of HMS *Macedonian*, had trampled them under her feet.[50]

While Federalists accused Republicans of poor conduct, the latter retorted by charging the former with inconsistency. "Can it be possible that such men are the *real, cordial* friends of the *American Navy*, its officers and seamen?" demanded a Republican editor, after comparing the involvement of Federalists Harrison G. Otis and Christopher Strong at naval celebrations against their refusal to openly support the U.S. Navy in its conflicts with Great Britain.[51] Similarly, the Republican *Enquirer* imagined Federalist Oliver Wolcott Jr., a prominent guest at a dinner in honor of Hull, Decatur, and Jones, attempting to justify his opposition to the war to one of the officers, before finally admitting, "*entre nous*, I mean to cry down this war, to get my friends into power. Indeed, sir, I love the *Seamen* a great deal, but I love the *loaves and fishes* much better."[52] In a "humorous anecdote," one Republican newspaper warned Federalist merchants that they would find their accustomed protection from British seizure jeopardized by their party's celebration of American victories.[53]

Apostates from the Federalist party shared Republicans' suspicions regarding the sincerity of their former associates' enthusiasm. John Adams, a long-time advocate of a strong navy, believed that several unnamed Federalists lied about their admiration for the institution. He wrote privately that the "Hyper-" or "Ultrafederalists" secretly despised the navy, and that they wished that, "every one of our Frigates had been taken burnt or Sunk and every one of Our Naval Conquerors kill'd or carried Prisoners to British Dungeons. They are not only no Friends, but they are in their Hearts rancorous Enemies to an American Navy."[54] Although one must accept Adams's accusation with a grain of salt, he was not the only person to think such things. The same Oliver Wolcott Jr. whom Republican newspapers unfairly portrayed as an opportunistic opponent of the war (though, like Adams, he straddled Republicanism and Federalism and gave the war his support), received a letter from a Bostonian acquaintance who wrote, "on Tuesday we have a grand Festival in honour of the Navy; & the week following a Naval Ball, much to the secret dissatisfaction of some of our great folks."[55]

Appearance or absences from naval celebrations became issues of partisan speculation. On June 1, 1813, a collection of political notables gathered together in Washington, D.C., to celebrate recent naval victories. The guests included the vice president of the United States, the secretaries of state, war, and navy, and the speaker of the house, among other Republican personages. The list was impressive, but so were the no-shows. Under the headline, "Something Strange," a Federalist newspaper remarked that, "none of our Naval heroes, attended the grand naval dinner, given on Saturday last by the Democratic gentry of Washington and its vicinity."[57] The author of the notice left to readers to infer the lesson of the fact; not so the Federalist who recorded the presence of Monsieur Serrurier, the French diplomat, at the same dinner. Surely, this commentator suggested, the presence of the Frenchman and the absence of naval officers signified a tacit alliance between the United States and Napoleon. Serrurier had raised his glass to the rising glory of the United States, but, Federalists noted, "the only grandeur which can be ascribed to them [i.e., the United States] for some time past, has been reflected upon them as satellites, from the Grand Empereur, whose wars they are waging."[59] Republicans countered with references to a Federalist dinner commemorating the victory of Alexander I over Napoleon, held the same week and in the same city as the officer-free Republican naval dinner: "There were two public dinners lately given at Washington: one to celebrate the victories of our country over its enemy; the other to celebrate the victories of the ally of that enemy over a power with which we are at peace. This requires no comment."[60]

Republicans charged Federalists with hypocrisy for attending celebrations of victories won in a war that they opposed. The Republican *Providence Patriot & Columbian Phenix* generously applauded prodigal Boston Federalists' appearance at a dinner in honor of Perry: "and from whatever motive they joined the general sentiment, we are pleased at the result.—It shews that whatever their opinion of the justice of the war may be, they can no longer withstand the glorious effects of its operation."[61] After Stephen Decatur Jr. had proposed the toast "Free Trade and Sailors' Rights" at a dinner in his honor, a Republican newspaper wondered, "Why is not the sentiment of Decatur universal?—Ask the 'friends of Great Britain in Congress.'"[62] Josiah Quincy opened the Federalists to charges of hypocrisy and treachery when he shepherded through the Massachusetts Senate a resolution against participation in celebrations of naval victories gained in an unjust and immoral war.[63] In the autumn of 1813, Republican editors frequently referenced the resolution when describing naval dinners. The words of the resolution should be "echoed from one end of the continent to the other, as the leading sentiment, as the morality and religion of the leaders of a faction who would sell their country that they might enjoy the loaves and fishes of office," one Republican newspaper proclaimed.[64]

Although many Federalists continued to celebrate naval victories publicly, others took Quincy's resolution to heart: In early October 1813, Newburyport Federalists broke the windows of houses illuminated in celebration of the Battle of Lake Erie.[65] "A federalist was lately reprobating the Ball and Dinner," a Republican journal later reported on another event, "then preparing in honor of the Heroes of our gallant *Navy*, in the following manner—'How mortifying it is that we federalists (in order to prevent being run down as a party) should be obliged to celebrate victories we deprecate, and to do it in company with blackguard democrats.'"[66] More significant than the item's claim, the veracity of which cannot be confirmed, is the item's purpose—to deny that naval celebrations evoked a true spirit of unity. Patriotism, the Republican newspaper's editor contended, belonged solely to his party.

In truth, it is safe to say that celebrations of naval victories only superficially quieted partisan bickering. Federalists could embrace naval victories *because* they were strategically insignificant, and mattered only in terms of what they symbolized. The U.S. Navy could sting the British Navy, but it could not hope to cripple it. Federalists, therefore, could commemorate the victories with a clear conscience, and could attempt to foist their own interpretations of the victories' meanings on the American populace.

Federalists insisted that the victories the navy won proved the validity of Federalist principles. They claimed the navy as their "pet project," the last remnant of Washingtonian policy not dismantled by Republicans' visionary imbecility.[67] The navy's accomplishments, according to Federalist lights, redounded honor on the war's opponents, and enhanced the ignominy of its instigators, who had never supported the institution. "Thank Heaven!" exalted a speaker before the Pennsylvania chapter of the Federalist Washington Benevolent Society, with regard to the navy, "that source of joy, politically speaking, is peculiarly our own. To us and our associates, the disciples of Washington, does it exclusively belong."[68] Federalists seethed at Republicans who "arrogate to themselves all the honor, which the federal frigates have reflected on the country, and more impudent than the harlot before the tribunal of Solomon, claim for their own, that child they would have strangled in its cradle."[69] After all, a strong navy had long been snubbed by Jeffersonians "who were journeying to the moon, instead of traversing the ocean," and who preferred in its place "a *Lilliputian cordon* of *gun-boats* and torpedos."[70] "The Navy of the United States," according to a representative Federalist toast, offered on July 4, 1813, was "the first born of Federalism; but now claimed as the favorite of democracy; may its laurels survive the blighting fondness of its step mother."[71] Federalist Congressman Abijah Bigelow wrote to his wife about the celebrations in the capital in response to the taking of the *Macedonian* by the *United States*: "I kept, however, in my room minding my own business, and feeling a little satisfaction that even democracy is reluctantly compelled to do honor to federalism, for the Navy is not only of federal origin, but nearly all the officers are federal," Bigelow crowed, in a tone remarkably similar to that with which American newspapers described British celebrations of the *Chesapeake* vs. *Shannon*.[72]

Federalists believed that naval victories confirmed not only their political views, but their social ones as well. They saw naval society as rigidly and functionally hierarchical, with a spectrum of ranks capped by the divorcement of forecastle men from quarterdeck officers, and the ideally unquestioning obedience of the latter to the former. The navy's successes in the War of 1812, therefore, proved the correctness of Federalists' ideology. They verified a contention Federalists had put forth since falling from power—that only their return to power could preserve the nation in prosperity.

Republicans counterclaimed that these victories evidenced the justness of the war, and the correctness of Republican policies: Republicans had not misplaced their faith when they called for American men to defend their rights by an appeal to arms. They had not erred in their belief that, no matter how weak its military, America could nonetheless restore its honor in equal combat against a supposedly unconquerable opponent. Republicans facetiously granted Federalists "our undissembled approbation, for the employment of ingenious carpenters, and the use of most excellent timber" by which Federalists had created the navy; but they added, "To a republican administration, belongs the splendid honor of conducting her flag to immortality. She has become the proud avenger of our wrongs."[73]

Federalists and Republicans, in short, aggravated their differences through their naval commemorations, and only by glossing over these ceremonies and swallowing uncritically their participants' pretensions to harmony can they be painted retrospectively as unifying events. Through parades and speeches, ballads and poems, and various printed ephemera, partisans laid claim to partisan interpretations of naval victories. As the roar of broadsides subsided a new battle began, fought with a different type of broadside, over the battle's meaning.

Status arguably cleft the celebrations more distinctly than partisanship. Some dinners honored commissioned officers exclusively; others segregated the officers and the men into separate rooms, or held one dinner for officers and a later one for the men. Officers' dinners were both splendid and dignified affairs. As pageants, they explicitly endorsed the moral that republics were not stingy in honoring their heroes. Implicitly, they provided a miniature of the American political ideal. Each dinner was a gathering of men. The men, honorees and attendees alike, were of solid social standing. Local "gentlemen," sometimes numbering several hundred, attended dinners for naval officers (and were advised "not to bring their servants with them, as a sufficient number will be provided").[74] Although partisan slips and nods insinuated themselves into the proceedings, the celebrants maintained overall a veneer of unity. At officers' dinners, the participants consciously worked hard to embody the republican ideals of order and harmony.

Seamen's dinners were different affairs. At their dinners, crewmen typically dined with few men other than themselves and their hosts; even their officers appeared only briefly to drink a single toast and receive the men's applause. Accounts of crewmen's behavior at these dinners are worth investigation. They reveal an anxiety on the part of both organizers and correspondents that seamen might not play their roles in the celebration properly. Newspapers evidenced an implicit fear that sailors would run riot, their judgment clouded by alcohol, exaltations, or, perhaps, egalitarianism.

Describing the arrival of a body of sailors at a theatrical production in their honor following an elaborate dinner, one newspaper admitted that, "every body seemed desirous to see how such a body of sailors, coming directly from a jolly dinner would behave."[75] Correspondents remarked on sailors' orderly demeanor with an almost audible sigh. Referencing a dinner in honor of the crew of the USS *Hornet*, an observer noted that "though the bottle, the song and the toast passed in jocund glee, yet the most perfect order and decorum were observed."[76] An account of a different dinner noted that the sailors participated in the fete "without having been guilty of unseaman-like conduct or a single excess." One correspondent described the feted crewmen of the USS *Enterprize* as having a "healthy, hardy and cleanly appearance and correct deportment."[78] (The gentlemanly deportment of officers at similar occasions was taken for granted.) With sailors, there was always a potential for mischief, for rowdiness. At naval celebrations, Americans celebrated their ideal of their nation, and whether that ideal was Federalist or Republican, it was not purely egalitarian. Sailors should accept their place, the organizers of these fetes seemed to suggest, not blaze their own paths. One dinner featured a speaker who not only praised his audience, but also lectured them on the significance of their achievements, anxious that they drew the proper lessons from them.[79] Federalists might have expressed their preference for social hierarchies more blatantly than Republicans, but gentlemen of both parties feared sailors' alleged proclivity for disruptive behavior. Such a proclivity raised questions of the common people's capacity for self-government. Marks of deference from the crewmen, therefore, were especially applauded, and correspondents delighted in reporting the spontaneous cheers with which the "jolly tars" greeted the appearance of their commanders.

Sailors' sentimental excesses occasionally emerged to threaten the purpose of the festivities. The City Hotel in New York City hosted separate dinners for the officers and for the crewmen of the *United States*, each dinner being identical in its ornamentation (except that a twenty-foot-wide artificial lake at the front of the hall was filled with water for the officers' soiree and grog for the sailors').[80] Clearly, the two celebrations were intended to follow the same spirit. Yet despite superficial similarities, the dinners were not and could not be the same. The sailors did not comport themselves with the same refinement as their officers. The differences between the crewmen and the officers changed the meaning of the celebration. An otherwise flattering report recounted how sailors at their dinner "commenced their attack upon an excellent dinner, which was soon demolished"; officers' table manners were never described in such violent wording.[81] With regards to the men's behavior, the memories of one forecastle sailor differ from contemporary accounts of general good behavior. The sailor recalled that the dinner "was followed by rather more than a usual amount of drinking, laughing, and talking; for as liquor was furnished in great abundance, the men could not resist the temptation to get drunk." Furthermore, as the men left the hall "to go to the theatre, the poor plates on the sideboard proclaimed that 'Jack was full three sheets in the wind.' Almost every one, as he passed, gave them a crack, crying out as they fell, 'Save the pieces.'"[82]

Several dinners were followed by excursions to the theater, where the pit was laid aside for the honored crewmen. An unflattering description survives of one crew attending a play, to which "they paid little or rather no attention to it, for they could not understand it without a much greater exertion of the intellect than they were disposed to make." The sailors' attention did, however, peak when a fetching actress, Mrs. Daeley, appeared, and they voiced their appreciation for her beauty.[83] The "better sort" hoped for sentimental effusions from sailors that evidenced their patriotism in an orderly fashion; they expressed some discomfort when forced to admit that sailors might have other priorities besides republican unity. If sailors did not actively undermine the celebrations in their honor, their behavior did not, on such occasions meet the ideals of deference and subordination which newspaper commentators hoped to read back into the events.

Moreover, sailors' own statements and actions at naval dinners indicate that they did not regard the meaning of their victories in exactly the same way as their social superiors did. Sailors' toasts reveal that they formulated their own understandings of their victories and of the war as a whole. One commentator noted without elaboration that, "many an appropriate and many a hearty toast was given, and some of them in a language that could not be misunderstood by the dullest present."[84] Another commentator recorded several of the sailors' toasts; two of them mentioned money, a perennial concern for the common tar: "Officers and men, may each American hero receive his pay when he has earned it," and "Success to the frigate United States and plenty of prize money."[85] At a different dinner, sailors raised their glasses to themselves and their colleagues, wishing them to "have plenty of rhino [that is, cash] and hearts to spend it."[86] Clearly, sailors believed they had more due to them than an elaborate dinner; their countrymen would need to do more to express their appreciation.

Sailors voiced their disdain for the war's dissenters, offering nine cheers in favor of the toast, "Withered be the arm—palsied be the hand, that will not defend the rights of his country."[87] If dinner organizers believed that sailors needed instruction, sailors did not hesitate to instruct their compatriots in return: "*The Citizens of the United States*—May they never celebrate the downfall of our own government as they have that of Bonaparte; and may the downfall of Great Britain be like *Lucifer*, never to rise again."[88] Sometimes sailors' toasts aimed explicit threats at domestic enemies: "*Sailor's Rights and Free Trade*—The knot of *Jack Ketch* [that is, the hangman] and a *yard arm* [that is, the naval equivalent of a gibbet] to the lubber that would not support them."[89]

Indeed, sailors' toasts expressed animosity towards the British that transcended the contentions over abstractions that characterized the toasts of officer and gentlemen: "Free Trade and Sailors' Rights, / Shall ever be out boast— / When Johnny Bull those rights invade, / Then Johnny Bull we'll roast," as one rhyming toast avowed.[90] A dinner for the officers of the USS *Enterprize* gallantly toasted their defeated counterparts in the HMS *Boxer* as "Enemies by Law; but *in gallantry & worth* we pronounce them *Brothers.*" At a subsequent dinner on the same occasion, the less magnanimous tars of the *Enterprize* offered such toasts as "*Yankee Humanity*—Always ready to give the enemy a WARM *FIRE-SIDE.*" Such sentiments demonstrate that sailors freely interpreted battles according to their own concerns, and that those concerns did not necessarily square with the ones expressed by their officers and other members of the American elite. Contrasted to the disinterested rhetoric affected by officers and gentlemen, sailors personalized their confrontation with Great Britain. In the process, they confirmed their ties to the American nation: sailors' victories belonged to the nation, and the nation's victories belonged to sailors.

Evaluated by strategic criteria, few of the navy's accomplishments of the War of 1812 warranted the enthusiasm with which Americans greeted them, a fact that could not have been lost on the people of the time. Surely, no one believed that a handful of single-ship victories could force the thousand-ship British navy to its knees. Nonetheless, these victories did secure one war aim— they proved to the satisfaction of most Americans that under the right circumstances Americans could stand toe-to-toe with any competitor and best it in a fair fight. The achievements of the U.S. Navy showed that the American nation could play a part in the world, and that it could command respect even from the world's most powerful states—it could be, and act as, a truly independent nation. At the same time, naval victories showed that the American nation suffered from powerful divisions. Americans applauded the supposed nonpartisanship that prevailed at naval celebrations while they also claimed naval victories as victories for their own partisan ideologies. They praised the orderliness of their republic even as they fretted that raucous individuals were subverting that order. Ultimately, Americans hoped to emphasize the unity of their nation through naval commemorations, but divisions continually rose to the fore. Even as they united to celebrate their nation, they divided over what their nation was and should be.

# NOTES

1 For discussions of honor in the War of 1812, the early republic, and generally, see Norman Risjord, "1812: Conservatives, War Hawks and the Nation's Honor," *The William and Mary Quarterly*, 3rd Ser., 18, no. 2 (April 1961): 196-210; Bertram Wyatt-Brown, *Southern Honor: Ethics and Behavior in the Old South* (New York: Oxford University Press, 1982); Wyatt-Brown, "Andrew Jackson's Honor," *Journal of the Early Republic*, 17, no. 1 (Spring 1997): 1-36; Kenneth Greenberg, "The Nose, the Lie, and the Duel in the Antebellum South," *The American Historical Review* 95, no. 1 (February 1990): 57-74; Joanne Freeman, *Affairs of Honor: National Politics in the New Republic* (New Haven: Yale University Press, 2001).

2 For challenges and duels on the Lakes, see Usher Parsons, *Surgeon of the Lakes: The Diary of Usher Parsons 1812-1814*, ed. John C. Fredrikson (Erie, Penn: Erie County Historical Society, 2000), 20, 60, 85, 107.

3 For instances of uses of the phrases in naval correspondence, see William S. Dudley and Michael J. Crawford, eds., *The Naval War of 1812: A Documentary History*, 3 vols. (Washington, DC: Naval Historical Center, Department of the Navy, 1985), 1:49, 2:292 (hereafter Naval War).

4 The wording is from a challenge that Captain Philip Broke of the HMS *Shannon* sent to Captain James Lawrence of the USS *Chesapeake*. For Broke's challenge, see *Naval War*, 2:126.

5 Ibid, 1:44.

6 Ibid, 1:444.

7 Ibid, 3:737.

8 David Porter, *Journal of a Cruise Made to the Pacific Ocean, by Captain David Porter, in the United States Frigate Essex, in the Years 1812, 1813, and 1814*, 2 vols. (Philadelphia: Bradford and Inskeep, 1815), 2:150.

9 *Naval War*, 2:296. For similar advice from the Secretary, see *Naval War*, 3: 7, 29.

10 For an assessment of the navy's strategic failures, see Alfred Thayer Mahan, *Sea Power in Its Relations to the War of 1812*, 2 vols. (Boston: Little, Brown, and Company, 1919

[1903-1904]). See also Mark Russell Shulman, "The Influence of History upon Sea Power: The Navalist Reinterpretation of the War of 1812," *The Journal of Military History*, 56, no. 2 (April 1992): 183-206.

[11] For details of the battle, see Robert Gardiner, ed., *The Naval War of 1812* (Annapolis: Naval Institute Press, 1998), 57-61; Mahan, *Sea Power*, 2:132-147; Theodore Roosevelt, *The Naval War of 1812: Or, the History of the United States Navy During the Last War with Great Britain, to Which Is Appended an Account of the Battle of New Orleans* (New York: G. P. Putnam's Sons, 1902), 220-236.

[12] See Abigail Livermore Williams Diary 1809-1813, The Massachusetts Historical Society, Boston; William Bentley, *The Diary of William Bentley, D. D., Pastor of the East Church, Salem, Massachusetts*, vol. 6: January 1811-December 1819 (Gloucester, Mass.: Peter Smith, 1962), 172-73.

[13] *Offset of the Chesapeake* (Boston: Nathaniel Coverley, 1814); Bentley, Diary, 4:173.

[14] Mordecai Noah, *Travels in England, France, Spain, and the Barbary States, in the Years 1813-1814 and 15* (New York: Kirk and Mercein, 1819), 27.

[15] Louis M'Lane, *Oration Delivered before the Artillery Company of Wilmington, Commanded by Captain Rodney, on the 5th of July, A.D. 1813* (Wilmington, Del.: Porter, 1813), 22.

[16] Noah, *Travels*, 26

[17] *New York Columbian*, September 21, 1813.

[18] *Baltimore Patriot & Evening Advertiser*, September 9, 1813.

[19] *New-Hampshire Patriot*, October 12, 1813.

[20] See [An English Cossack], *British Glory, or Naval and Military Exploits from Original Documents* (Philadelphia, 1814), 6-7, 24.

[21] Admiral E. M. Eller, "Introduction" to A Wanderer [Noah Jones], *Journals of Two Cruises aboard the American Privateer Yankee* (New York: MacMillan Company, 1967), xiii-xiv.

[22] Adams to Waterhouse, Quincy, March 23, 1813, Adams-Waterhouse Letters, 1784-1837, typescripts, Massachusetts Historical Society, Boston.

[23] *Naval War*, 3:525. The author of the line was Major General Jacob Brown.

[24] David L. Parmelee, A*n Address, Delivered at Goshen, at the Anniversary Celebration of the 4th of July, 1814; at the Desire of the Young Men of the Town* (Hartford: Peter B. Gleason and Co., 1814), 7.

[25] *The Yankee* (Massachusetts), May 14, 1813.

[26] *New York Evening Post,* January 8, 1813.

[27] *Alexandria Daily Gazette Commercial & Political,* January 4, 1813.

[28] These details have been culled and compiled from a number of different dinners reported in various newspapers, memoirs, journals, and other sources. These sources include Amos Evans, *Journal Kept on Board the Frigate Constitution, 1812* (Lincoln, MA: Bankers Lithograph Co., 1967, Reprinted for William D. Sawtell from *The Pennsylvania Magazine of History and Biography*), 378-79; Samuel Leech, *Thirty Years from Home, or, A Voice from the Main Deck,* 15th ed. (Boston: Tappan, Whitemore & Mason, 1843), 160-61; Private Journal, 1814-1817, Papers of William T. Rodgers, Library of Congress, Manuscript Division, Washington, DC; *Free Trade and Sailors Rights: The Victories of Hull, Jones, Decatur, Bainbridge; as Detailed in Their Official Letters and the Letters of Other Officers. Together with a Collection of the Public Testimonials of Respect; and the Songs and Odes Written in Celebration of These Events* (Philadelphia: Dennis Heartt, 1813). Notices of the larger dinners appeared in newspapers throughout the country, not infrequently with detailed accounts of the proceedings. As was common practice at the time, newspapers cannibalized each other for these accounts. Major naval dinners (there were numerous smaller ones) included ones for Isaac Hull, Boston, September 5, 1812; Jacob Jones, Philadelphia, December 11, 1812; Stephen Decatur, Isaac Hull, and Jacob Jones (the latter in *absentia*), New York City, December 21, 1812; the crew of the USS *United States,* New York City, January 7, 1813; Stephen Decatur Jr., Philadelphia, February 4, 1813; William Bainbridge and the other officers of the USS *Constitution,* Boston, March 2, 1813; James Lawrence and the crew of the USS *Hornet,* New York City, May 4, 1813; miscellaneous naval victories, June 1, 1813 (this dinner included no naval guests of honor, but received wide coverage because of the high-ranking government officials in attendance); William Bainbridge, Portland, Massachusetts (Maine), August 30, 1813; the surviving officers of the USS *Enterprize,* Portland, Massachusetts (Maine), September 15, 1813; the crew of the USS *Enterprize,* Portland, Massachusetts (Maine), September 20; Oliver Hazard Perry, Albany, New York, November 8, 1813; Oliver Hazard Perry (and William Henry Harrison), Buffalo, New York, November 12, 1813; William Bainbridge, Georgetown, DC, November 23, 1813; William Bainbridge, Philadelphia, December 2, 1813; William Bainbridge, New York City, December 8, 1813; John Rodgers, New York City, March 7, 1814; Oliver Hazard Perry, Washington, DC, January 25, 1814, and Boston, May 10, 1814; Stewart and his officers, Salem, Massachusetts, March, 1814; Lewis Warrington and his officers, Savannah, Georgia, May, 1814; Thomas

Macdonough and the officers of his fleet, Burlington, Vermont, September 27, 1814; This list compiles the larger and more widely reported dinners. Small towns sometimes threw dinners for local heroes. Elkton, Maryland, for instance, feted naval surgeon Amos Evans, who served on board the Constitution, on June 15, 1813.

[29] *New-England Palladium*, September 8, 1812.

[30] *American Advocate* (Maine), January 29, 1814.

[31] *Northern Post* (New York), December 1, 1814.

[32] *New-York Commercial Advertiser*, February 5, 1814.

[33] *Columbian Centinel* (Massachusetts), September 4, 1813.

[34] *Baltimore Patriot & Evening Advertiser*, September 8, 1813.

[35] *Yankee* (Massachusetts), September 11, 1812.

[36] Ibid., May 13, 1814.

[37] I have not found the correspondent's initial letter, only Perry's response, from which the contents of that first letter are deduced.

[38] Oliver Hazard Perry to Samuel L. Anderson, Newport, June 22, 1814, War of 1812 Collection, box two, MS 1846, Maryland Historical Society, Baltimore.

[39] *Telegraph*, March 22, 1813.

[40] *Evening Post* (New York), March 6, 1813.

[41] *Telegraph* (New York), March 22, 1813.

[42] *Columbian* (New York), January 2, 1813.

[43] *New-York Commercial Advertiser*, February 5, 1814.

[44] *New Bedford Mercury*, March 12, 1813

[45] *Boston Gazette*, May 12, 1814.

[46] *The Columbian* (New York), December 10, 1813. The past tense gives the game away.

[47] *Baltimore Patriot*, March 12, 1814.

[48] *New York Columbian*, January 2, 1813.

[49] *Boston Daily Advertiser*, December 24, 1814.

[50] Samuel Taggart to John Taylor, Washington, D. C., December 21, 1812, Samuel Taggart Letterbook, 1803-1815, American Antiquarian Society, Worcester. Taggart admitted that he could not confirm the rumor because "I go to none of these entertainments."

[51] *Pittsfield Sun or Republican Monitor*, March 11, 1813.

[52] *Enquirer*, December 31, 1812. This attack was unfair. Wolcott distanced himself from mainstream Federalism by backing the War of 1812.

[53] *Native American*, April 21, 1813.

[54] Adams to Benjamin Waterhouse, Quincy, March 16, 1813, Adams-Waterhouse Letters, 1784-1837, typescripts, Massachusetts Historical Society, Boston.

[55] George Gibbs to Oliver Wolcott, Boston, February 28, 1813. Oliver Wolcott Papers, Microfilm (Mss. 19, 345). Library of Congress, Manuscript Division, Washington DC.

[56] Details of the dinner can be found in *New-York Commercial Advertiser*, June 4, 1813.

[57] *Alexandria Daily Gazette, Commercial & Political*, June 1, 1813.

[58] The Russian minister was also invited but, according to an article in the *New-York Gazette & General Advertiser*, June 6, 1813, declined on account of the amity his country felt towards both the United States and Great Britain.

[59] *Federal Republican* (Maryland), June 6, 1813.

[60] *New Jersey Journal*, June 29, 1813.

[61] *Providence Patriot & Columbia Phenix*, May 21, 1814.

[62] *Yankee* (Massachusetts), January 1, 1813.

[63] See Richard Buel Jr., *America on the Brink: How the Political Struggle over the War of 1812 Almost Destroyed the Young Republic* (USA: Palgrave Macmillan, 2005), 175-76.

[64] *New-Hampshire Patriot*, September 21, 1813.

[65] Bentley Diary 4:205; *Essex Register*, October 16, 1813.

[66] *Yankee* (Massachussets), March 5, 1813.

[67] For recent reevaluations of Jefferson's attitude toward the navy, see Gene A. Smith, *"For the Purposes of Defense": The Politics of the Jeffersonian Gunboat Program* (Newark: University of Delaware Press, 1995), and Craig Symonds, *Navalists and Antinavalists: The Naval Policy Debate in the United States, 1795-1827* (Newark: University of Delaware Press; London and Toronto: Associated University Press, 1980).

[68] Charles Caldwell, *An Oration, Commemorative of American Independence, Delivered before the Washington Benevolent Society of Pennsylvania* (Philadelphia: Office of the United States Gazette, 1814), 62

[69] William Ladd, *An Oration, Pronounced at Minot, Maine, on the Fourth Day of July, 1814* (Portland, ME: Arthur Shirley, 1814), 10-11.

[70] Francis Blake, *An Oration, Pronounced at Worcester, (Mass.) on the Thirty-Sixth Anniversary of American Independence, July 4, 1812* (Worcester: Isaac Sturtevant, 1812), 21.

[71] *Boston Gazette*, July 15, 1813.

[72] Abijah Bigelow to Hannah Bigelow, Letters of Abijah Bigelow Member of Congress to His Wife 1810-1815, American Antiquarian Society, Worcester.

[73] Rollin Carolus Mallary, *An Oration, Addressed to Republicans, Assembled at Poultney, Vermont, July 4, 1814* (Rutland: Fay & Davison, 1814), 18.

[74] *New York Columbian*, December 28, 1812.

[75] *New York Evening Post*, January 8, 1813.

[76] *Yankee*, May 14, 1813.

[77] *Salem Gazette*, January 12, 1813.

[78] *Eastern Argus*, September 23, 1813.

[79] The speaker was Mr. Alderman Vanderbilt. He addressed the crew of the USS *United States* in New York, January 7, 1813. See *New York Columbian*, January 8, 1813.

[80] *Commercial Advertiser*, January 8, 1813.

[81] *Salem Gazette*, January 12, 1813.

[82] Leech, *Thirty Years from Home*, 160-61.

[83] *New York Evening Post*, January 8, 1813.

[84] *The Evening Post*, January 8, 1813.

[85] *Salem Gazette*, January 12, 1813.

[86] *Eastern Argus*, September 23, 1813.

[87] *Baltimore Patriot*, January 11, 1813.

[88] *Yankee*, August 12, 1814.

[89] *Eastern Argus*, September 23, 1813.

[90] *Yankee*, August 12, 1814.

[91] *Essex Register*, September 22, 1813.

[92] *Eastern Argus*, September 23, 1813.

# VIII

## NEGOTIATING POWER
### Status and Authority in Anglo-American
### Shipwreck Narratives

### AMY MITCHELL-COOK

Shipwreck was a common occurrence in the early modern Atlantic world. An examination of insurance records suggested that 4 to 5 percent of all voyages ended in failure. As most ships went to sea again and again, chances were good that any given vessel would ultimately wreck, and it was possible that some survivors saw fit to record their experiences. These survivors wrote about shipwreck for a variety of reasons—to make money, to find a sense of closure, to demonstrate God's mercy, and to exonerate the living—to name but a few.

A study of shipwrecks *themselves* is useful because at this critical juncture, officers' control depended on their ability to assure crew members that officers could help them survive. Shipwreck *narratives*, however, in most cases demonstrated the officers' ability to maintain their authority in the face of adversity, and presented how a disobedient crew suffered for disregarding their superiors. The published narratives suggested that although the captain's supposed supremacy remained, only a veneer of unquestioned authority existed on ships and that the crew sometimes challenged and negotiated their power using a range of techniques from polite discussion and silent resistance to outright mutiny or desertion. Captain-authors often indicated that drunkenness or immorality were the usual reasons for insubordination, and the guilty paid for it, sometimes with their lives, before intelligent officers reasserted their authority and saved the vessel. Shipwreck narratives thus highlighted both the extent and the limit of shipboard authority in starker terms than accounts of maritime life under normal conditions.

Shipwreck narratives are short stories, typically less than twenty pages, which provide a precise account from the voyage's inception to the rescue of remaining survivors. This essay utilizes sixty British and American authors who survived and wrote narratives of their shipwreck experiences between the sixteenth and the early nineteenth centuries. Of the sixty, captains wrote twenty-two, officers six, and passengers fourteen. The identity of ten writers remains unknown: common sailors wrote only seven, and two narratives—Olaudah Equiano's and Briton Hammon's—by slaves exist.[1]

Authors printed these stories as cheap, or street, literature in the form of broadsides, chapbooks, or poems; however, many were collected and published together in larger volumes. Advances in printing technology and the increase of worldwide commerce expedited publishing in the nineteenth century, but later editions represented mere adaptations of earlier shipwreck accounts. Excluding minor editorial changes, narratives generally remained true to their original story and despite subsequent editions, related events as told in the first printing. The numerous reprints also demonstrated the continued popularity of the shipwreck genre and that the stories appealed to audiences over time.

Narratives in this study comprised those published both in America and in Britain. In early America, national identity often either linked to or defined itself in opposition to England. The new nation sought cultural independence, yet depended heavily on Britain for print culture and trade. Narratives and tales of wonder added to this connection as popular accounts in England often appeared in the colonies and vice versa.[2] For example, Jonathan Dickinson first published his narrative in Philadelphia in 1699. Within a year T. Swole printed a London edition.[3] In 1817, the first known accounts of the *Commerce* shipwreck became available in both New York and in London, and a year later both cities saw the earliest editions of the wreck of the *Oswego*.[4] Most early British narratives for this study were reprinted several times and eventually found their way to American printers. Usually the narratives crossed the Atlantic in the form of collections such as Archibald Duncan's six-volume London edition of *Mariner's Chronicle* (1804).[5] American printers reused the stories for single publications as well as in collected volumes. American editions incorporated older narratives with newer accounts to create their own anthologies. By the 1830s, Boston and New York, as well as Hartford, New Haven, and Salem, printed several American collections.[6]

Similar to other popular forms of literature such as captivity or travel narratives, accounts of shipwreck blended reality with fiction to produce a harrowing and affordable form of amusement.[7] These narratives furnished excitement and adventure as well as practical suggestions concerning proper survival behavior authors hoped might appeal to eager audiences. Shipwreck narratives also revealed what Anglo-Americans thought about society and of the importance of maintaining order. The published accounts provided an excellent medium to illustrate how mariners (as well as readers on land) understood status and place. Prescriptive by nature, published accounts taught audiences the correct forms of behavior. At the moment of crisis men revealed their true essence and either upheld or betrayed social hierarchy and the common good. The accounts validated a specific definition of conduct based on capability, leadership, and bravery. Disregarding the actual backgrounds of officers and captains (some from a social level barely above that of common sailors) the narratives promoted a definite class orientation. Audiences read the repeated lessons within these accounts that emphasized strength, moderation, and self-control; characteristics often associated with middle- and upper- class values.

Despite the narratives' potentially chaotic subject, the published accounts actually imparted a positive message that substantiated order and assured readers that social hierarchies remained intact.[8] According to the published accounts, sailors and officers chose to preserve social order and to maintain traditional hierarchies, even as the world they knew collapsed beneath them. This behavior was more surprising considering that once a ship went down, a crew could legally refuse to follow the captain. A careful reading of behavior in the accounts indicated sometimes the crew lost respect or confidence in the captain's authority. Mutinous behavior did happen, but the men who participated in these events frequently met with death and disaster. Such subversive behavior suggested the captain's authority was not absolute, and a wise leader balanced power with sympathy; he understood the crews' rights but never surrendered his command.

Despite the heroic vision of a captain going down with the ship, the high percentage of narratives written by captains and officers indicated otherwise. These individuals understood the necessity of justifying their actions to owners and insurance companies. Several authors even appended official protests or sworn testimonies to their stories to support their case. Their goal in publishing these accounts was to prove shipwreck as an "act of god" or a "peril of the sea." In doing so they exempted themselves from blame and from having to pay insurance or legal fees. Likewise, seamen's behavior during shipwreck affected whether an individual received wages or faced a breach of contract. The narratives inserted specific details concerning the crew's behavior to demonstrate their cooperation. Obviously, these factors affected the narratives' ultimate creation as each author tried to justify their actions, and the actions of others, in this terrifying moment.

The narratives also presented a public platform for personal glory that ignored rank and status. The accounts indicated that mariners, at all levels, contributed to the crew's survival, although they were often at odds with the captain and officers. These men did not represent a subversive threat, as depicted in other narratives, but instead worked as part of a team for everyone's survival. These sailor-authors promoted images of bravery and intelligence that all shared, regardless of rank, rather than one of mutiny and fear. Captains stressed teamwork and continued deference as honorable while sailors leveled hierarchies as a means for survival.

While the maritime world offered to release sailors from restrictions on land, it placed mariners in a well-defined chain of command. The ship's proper functioning necessitated a strict hierarchy, though as Daniel Vickers and Vince Walsh point out, there was no one type of class relationship at sea.[9] Status and power continued with masters or captains wielding supposed absolute authority. The means for doing so, however, differed from ship to ship and according to time and place. Kenneth Andrews studied seventeenth-century ships in which captains' personal backgrounds resembled their crews. Their status came from age, personality, and skill, with power derived from custom and necessity rather than deference to one's betters or economic status.[10] As the eighteenth century progressed, Andrews found that wealth consolidated in the hands of the few, and some captains, who became rich through the colonial trade, could assert a social superiority over their men.[11] In a 1789 parade honoring George Washington, for instance, sea captains held a prominent place, behind only merchants, professionals, and various government officials; sailors came second to last in the parade—ahead of common laborers.[12]

Theoretically, captains exercised supreme authority over everyone and everything in their vessel. Edward Ward, writing in the eighteenth century, provided a vivid, if somewhat sarcastic, view of captains. A sea captain is "a Leviathan, or rather a kind of Sea God, whom the poor Tars worship as the Indians do the Devil, more thro' fear, than affection; that he's more a Devil, then the Devil himself." He remains hidden "for such a Prostitution of presence, he thinks, weakens his authority, and makes his worship less reverenc'd by the Ship's Crew. It is impudence for any to approach him within the length of a Boat-hook."[13] Order required a degree of hierarchy and leadership for a successful voyage. The captain's primary directive was to "prosecute the voyage" and he devoted all his actions to this end. It was his responsibility to divide the men into watches, proportion food, take sightings, and determine courses; in essence to make sure everything ran accordingly.[14] To do so necessitated supposed control—

though not absolute. Alfred Conkling stated that by law the captain had the "right to compel prompt obedience to his orders" and "could subject the offender to corporeal punishment." But, the law also stated that this punishment be "moderate, just, and proportionate."[15] His authority was not "absolute," and although captains resorted to brutality, or the threat of it, to maintain order, the most successful captain exercised control judiciously knowing sailors refused to tolerate such extreme measures.[16]

One overarching theme in shipboard narratives was that the captain was a "father" and the crew his "children." This image fed into an emphasis on the family and the importance of showing deference to elders. In 1817, when Moses Adams was but fourteen, his father warned him to obey his master, saying "always remember that he knows best. He is a man, you are a child."[17] Sentimentalism added emotion to this bond that supposedly placed rank on ships within a nurturing familial setting.

Although captains technically maintained supreme authority and strict regulation, sailors asserted their power when necessary. The shipwreck narratives suggest the chain of command often incorporated a level of flexibility and individual agency. Even beyond shipwreck, common mechanisms included protests, walkouts, desertion, or mutiny.[18] At sea in the early eighteenth century John Cremer related that when unhappy or dissatisfied he often changed ships, quit a voyage, or at least made the motion to desert. The captain responded by either addressing his concerns or letting him leave.[19] Sailors had several options for creating a better situation. Word of mouth let mariners know of "good" captains and ships, and contracts provided legal assistance against owners who denied pay. Sailors could also act in a collective body to negotiate labor relations.[20] To gain better wages, to improve conditions, or to counter an overly brutal captain, sailors simply refused to sail. Such actions limited the captain's "absolute" authority and permitted sailors a modicum of power and agency in their daily lives.[21]

Some narratives authored by common sailors suggested hierarchy often failed in the face of disaster. A few sailors went further and directly blamed the captain for making a bad situation worse. Briton Hammon, a slave, declared the ship's captain failed to take proper action when the vessel ran aground off Florida in 1747 with a load of logwood. The crew and passengers begged the captain to throw over a part of the cargo to lighten the vessel and enable it to float free. According to Hammon, "which if he had done, might have sav'd his Vessel and cargo, and not only so, but his own life, as well as the lives of the Mate and Nine Hands." The captain's supposed superior character failed him, and his greed cost him his life. The ideal image of a sympathetic and understanding captain no longer held true, and Hammon, the sole survivor, persevered to tell his version. If the captain had listened to the crew's advice and allowed everyone to work as a team, he too might have lived to write his own tale.

Olaudah Equiano continued this theme when he was shipwrecked in 1767 on his way from St. Eustatius to Georgia. Several times he tried to alert the captain that the vessel was in dangerous waters but the captain disregarded these warnings. When the captain finally emerged from below decks it was too late; the vessel was upon the rocks. In the heat of the moment, and angry with the captain for attempting to nail down the hatches on the slaves below, Equiano yelled that the captain "deserved drowning for not knowing how to navigate the vessel." Equiano asserted that only with his ability, and the assistance of "three black men and a Dutch Creole sailor" did everyone make it to a nearby island.[22]

Additional narratives challenged the captain's hegemonic authority. In these accounts the captain begged the crew to follow his orders. Reversing roles, the captain of the *Mentor* (1832) wanted to abandon ship while his crew preferred to stay on the vessel. The captain, "with great earnestness entreated the men to assist him in lowering the boat." His requests were followed but, "as this was a time when but little attention could be paid to the distinctions usually kept up on board, I [Horace Holden] suggested that it might be well to cut away the masts." The crew followed Holden's advice, and they managed to lower a boat safely for the captain. In similar accounts the captain negotiated with the crew to maintain a level of hierarchy. Those written by sailors often pointed to a temporary flexibility during crisis. Authors minimized social distinctions and stressed the importance of continued teamwork. Rather than listening solely to the captain or officers, each man had the opportunity to impart his opinions and to participate in the crew's survival.

Narratives authored by captains told a slightly different story. These accounts highlighted the necessity of teamwork and related how the crew acted as a team, with each individual working within appropriate parameters. The captain's life as well as those of the seamen required each man to perform his specific duty: a captain who failed to command loyalty in a time of crisis risked his own safety as well as that of all onboard. When the *Boston* (1828) caught on fire only six days out of Charleston, the crew and passengers worked together to save the vessel. "The passengers had exerted themselves to the utmost to assist us," said Captain Mackay. "The officers had with unwearied exertion, coolness and persevering activity done all that men could do. The ship's crew worked like horses and behaved like men."[23] When Captain Riley's ship *Commerce* wrecked off the coast of West Africa (1818), the crew followed his every command, "Every man worked as if his life depended upon his present exertions; all were obedient to every order I gave, and seemed perfectly calm."[24] From a practical point of view, survival in the crisis situation necessitated such behavior from all men, regardless of rank or social standing. Captains and officers, however, inserted this information to demonstrate their continued status and to assure audiences of order in a chaotic event.

To guarantee a safe and prosperous voyage a competent captain had to remain calm and in control of himself and his crew. According to Barnabas Downs on the *General Arnold* (1778), Captain Magee provided an excellent example of leadership. "In the hour of difficulty and danger he was calm, hopeful, self-reliant. Without these qualities, the most experienced and energetic often fail . . . None would have survived if our master's spirit had not been there to cheer them by his works, and encourage them by his example."[25] In every instance, the captains who survived credited themselves with an innate character that allowed them to rise to the situation. In an effort to preserve future voyages, William Vaughn, the editor of Captain David Woodard's narrative, stated that in moments of danger "patience and perseverance are necessary." Though he admitted that no hard and fast rules maintained order, "a great deal may be done by management and good conduct, to alleviate the sufferings and distresses."[26] In these incidents, the authors presented captains as upper-class individuals who demonstrated self-control, strength, and civility.

Although in the best of all possible worlds everyone remained calm during shipwreck, this rarely occurred. Otherwise, the published narratives might lose much of their dramatic appeal. Mariners who read the narratives learned the necessity of following orders and to not flee the ship in a panic. William Vaughn included "Hints for a Society for Promoting the Means of Preserving Ships and Lives in Moments of Danger and Accidents," in his narrative of Captain David Woodward's voyage. He suggested that sailors should stay by the ship and remain calm, "that the buoyancy of a ship in itself, in all cases, will keep her afloat."[27] To minimize chaos and prevent undue injury or damage, someone—the captain, if possible—must organize and lead panicked crew and passengers. The narratives suggested that following traditional lines of authority prevented death.

In some accounts, sailors did not follow orders and put forth their own propositions for survival. In shipwreck, to ensure their survival, sailors spoke to captains in a manner not allowed under normal circumstances. In 1800, Captain Riley sought to convince his crew to stay aboard the *Oswego* rather than abandon her. Not satisfied, the crew came forward with a bargain: that if the captain allowed them to cut the masts "they would stay still till morning."[28] However, not everyone accepted this compromise. When Riley cut down the masts, the second mate, Judah Paddock, "raised himself up very deliberately and said, 'It is all d----d nonsense, we will go ashore.'" Realizing the tenuous situation, the captain wrote, "As grating as that expression was, prudence forbade me making a reply or noticing it."[29] Paddock forced the captain to acknowledge the crews' fears and in doing so Riley retained order on ship. In crisis, standard command fluctuated and ordinary seamen found openings to challenge traditional lines of power. Captains, however, emphasized that such opportunities were only temporary and that by the story's end, hierarchies once again firmly controlled the crew. Such behavior, rather than a form of teamwork, as represented by common sailors, became a threat to social order, and the narratives portrayed them negatively. Yet, while captains recovered their authority in print, no alternative accounts exist to question what really happened once a crew challenged a captain and survived on their rather than his terms.

In another case, in 1789 the *Tyrrel*, on a voyage from Sandy Hook to Antigua, began to leak. According to the chief mate, the "captain was now earnestly entreated to put for New York, or to steer for the capes of Virginia." The next day he agreed to sail for North Carolina.[30] Narratives authored by sailors indicated that good commanders understood their fragile position. Moderate behavior and a need to balance force with understanding made for a strong, not absolute leader. In contrast to their legal power, most successful captains maintained authority through consensus rather than coercion.

After abandoning ship, in 1756 the survivors of the *Betsy* found themselves in a small lifeboat with few provisions. On the fourth day they saw a sloop, but it failed to see them, and this threw two sailors into a deep depression. According to Captain Aubin: "In spite of all I could say, one of them would do nothing, not even bail out the water." He tried everything, even begging, but the man continued to refuse. Finally, with no other options the captain and his mate threatened, "to kill him instantly with the top-mast, which we used to steer by, and to kill ourselves afterwards, to put a period to our misery." These threats worked and the man began to bail water.[31] Far from absolute control, Aubin negotiated with the sailor and found that only with the threat of violence did he react. The rest of the survivors concurred: all had to pull their weight in this situation.

William Bligh, after the infamous *Bounty* mutiny, sailed with those who remained loyal to his command several thousand miles from Tofoa to Timor in a small open boat. While in the boat, Bligh managed to maintain authority, though at times it seemed a second mutiny might occur. He wrote that, "On this occasion, fatigue and weakness so far got the better of their sense of duty; one person in particular, went so far to tell me . . . that he was as good a man as myself . . . I determined to either preserve my command or die in the attempt; in seizing a cutlass, I ordered him to lay hold of another and defend himself; on which he called out that I was going to kill him, and immediately made concessions."[32] Desperate and far from land, sailors took survival into their own hands; however, once an authority figure appeared, old hierarchies fell into place. Chaos within the narratives, while a threat, rarely lasted. If men on the *Bounty*, *Betsy*, *Tyrrel*, *Oswego*, and many others vessels challenged authority, they never permanently inverted power.

And yet, in some narratives deference remained unquestioned. Sailors on the *Kent* (1827) found a box of oranges while waiting for rescue. Though exhausted, starving, and "beginning to experience the pain of intolerable thirst, [they] refused to partake of the grateful beverage, until they had afforded a share of it to their officers."[33] On the same ship one man went so far as to ask permission to use cordage from an officer's cot to tie a rope around his waist. He wished to "know whether there would be any harm in his appropriating it for his own use." In addition, the narratives suggested sailors allowed officers into life- or longboats or gave them special consideration with food and other necessities. On these vessels the chain of command remained intact. Perhaps sailors wanted to avoid retribution if rescued, or they realized that officers were often the only ones with navigational skills or who had knowledge of approaching coastlines. For some, as on the *Kent*, the authors stressed that deference persisted from a combination of "consideration, respect, and affection."[34] The narrative, written by a sympathetic passenger related a story of continued deference.

Even narratives not written by captains or officers suggested men of higher rank disproportionately survived. They often gained access to lifeboats, shelter, or food ahead of common seamen, and thus increased their chances for survival. On the rocks near Seacombe, the *Halsewell* (1785) struck ground with little hope of rescue. "It was agreed that the boats could not then be of any use, but it was proposed that the officers should be confidentially requested, in case an opportunity presented itself, of making it serviceable, to reserve the long boat for the ladies and themselves, and this precaution was accordingly taken."³⁵ There was no mention of the sailors or of the soldiers' wives, though elsewhere the narrative indicated their presence on board.

Published accounts repeatedly showed the advantages of status during ship-wreck. The crew of the *Margaret* (1810) faced the possibility of abandoning ship when they foundered on their way from Naples to Marblehead. When disaster struck, several individuals (including the captain) jumped into the longboat. These thirteen people remained close to the ship and promised not to leave those still stranded in the vessel. However, they kept at a distance to prevent additional crewmembers from swimming to the longboat and possibly capsiz-ing it. After several days the longboat separated from the ship and was eventu-ally rescued. The *Margaret* and those left on the wreck were never heard of again.³⁶ The captain lived to relate, and to justify, why he survived and how thir-ty-one individuals disappeared with the *Margaret*.

Not all captains abandoned their crews when they faced possible shipwreck. Many captains and officers worried about their reputations when, and if, they returned home. Lieutenant Archer of the *Phoenix* (1780) provided a heroic exam-ple of doing the right thing while facing difficult choices after the vessel wrecked. He initially offered to run a line to shore to enable the crew's escape when he real-ized: "This won't do for me, to be the first man out of the ship, and the first lieu-tenant; we may get to England again, and people may think I paid a great deal of attention to myself, and did not care for any body else. No, that won't do; instead of being the first, I'll see every man, sick and well, out of her before me."³⁷ Captain Cobb of the *Kent* (1827) also declared "his immovable resolution to be the last, if possible, to quit his ship."³⁸ Success in a commercial environment relied on a good reputation, and quitting the ship before others might demonstrate a lack of concern for the owners' cargo and vessel. Men needed to "preserve and earn the trust of other men" so they might one day sail another ship.³⁹ Despite such heroics captains and officers survived. Rarely did the accounts suggest a noble captain went down with the ship. Instead, authors justified their survival as a matter of necessity or as an accident.

While some captains remained in control of themselves and their crews, not all successfully commanded their vessels. In these situations sailors lost respect for their superiors' authority and no longer felt the need to obey. Marcus

Rediker and Paul Gilje found that sailors frequently resisted their superiors.[40] In shipwreck, crews often lost trust in their captain's abilities and instead looked to their own survival. For example, the captain of the *Oswego* ordered his crew to remain with the ship, but they insisted on leaving. The captain tried to reason with them "upon the impropriety of that measure [leaving the ship], when the only reply I heard, was, 'we are in duty bound to take care of ourselves, and not stay here and drown.'" The captain lost this round and the crew headed for shore.[41]

Captain Nathaniel Uring (1726) experienced such a problem. When shipwrecked off modern-day Honduras, most of his crew decided to take off down the coast, without regard to their injured captain. "There being no Remedy but to comply with them, or be left there to starve, I consented to go." They attempted to take a canoe out past the breakers and paddle their way to the nearest settlement. Once in the canoe, Uring again took control and coordinated efforts to steer the canoe over a high surf. However, the waves proved too much and they returned to the beach where Uring once again lost his authority and the sailors attempted several times to abandon him.[42]

Not surprisingly, Uring had few positive remarks about his crew. His observations fit well with common perceptions of sailors that often depicted them as the "dregs" of society. For example, Edward Ward described sailors as: "loving short voyages, as he does short prayers . . . His whole trust is on the wind and sea, that are as inconsistent and treacherous as a woman; and he knows it. Nothing makes him droop, like an empty Brandy-Bottle."[43] In the early nineteenth century, George Watson described his fellow crew as "highwaymen, burglars, pickpockets, debauchers, adulterers, gamesters, lampooners, bastard-getters, imposters, panders, parasites, ruffians, hypocrites, and threadworn beaux jack-a-dandies."[44] It was not surprising that reform movements worked to cure sailors and other laborers of drinking, cussing, and other forms of reckless passion that supposedly threatened American social order, and the perceived need to uplift American society made such "unsavory" individuals a favorite target.[45]

A common factor in these challenges to status came from the sailors' inclination to drink. Paul Gilje pointed out that both ashore and at sea, drinking was central to a sailor's liberty.[46] Aboard the *General Arnold* (1778), the crew attempted to cut down the masts in hope of keeping the ship upright. However, some sailors refused to do their duty and became intoxicated. In the bitter cold with no hope for survival "the authority of the officers had ceased—each one sought, as best as he could, his own safety."[47] Well before nineteenth-century reform, the narratives provided behavioral lessons that stressed the need to avoid liquor and of the results of drunkenness.

Losing control, especially when intoxicated, often led to death. While adrift on a small boat, Joseph Bailey, master of the *Alida and Catherine* (1749) of New York, remained collected and encouraged others to fast and to protect limited provisions. After several days in this condition they spied a ship and "our people fell to and eat and drank heartily, not considering that though we saw the vessel, she might not see us, or at least might not discover our Distress, and so pass by."[48] The captain maintained the ideal quality of moderation and strength, and refused to give in to his hunger. In effect he, as the leader, kept his responsibility to the common good rather than only to himself. Carroll Smith-Rosenberg suggested that by the late eighteenth century, society equated manhood with self-control, productivity, virtue, and independence.[49] Throughout many narratives, captains and officers remained cool and strong, while the crew despaired.[50] Audiences read favorable accounts of how officers reacted in a crisis situation as opposed to that of the crew.[51]

According to the narratives, common sailors experienced shipwreck in a much different manner than officers. Some lost control of their emotions; others rose to meet the new demands; a few took advantage of their situation; many continued as if nothing had happened. Men sometimes gave in to fear or drank and refused to work for the ship's common good. Rather than follow the captain's orders, these men wallowed in self-pity or formed their own course for survival. Numerous accounts suggested that occupying a low social standing, sailors lacked refinement and morals. Instead, they often behaved in ways that contrasted with the upper-class, genteel ideal. Drinking was a quintessential behavior that created brotherhood and an opportunity for honor and trust between men. On the other hand, it tested self-control and led to the loss of rationality appropriate to male gender.[52] Intoxicated sailors on the *General Arnold* (1778) from Boston refused to follow their officers and continued to drink rather than help save the ship. Not only did these men no longer work as a team, but they also exhibited "unmanly" qualities. According to Downs, "some of the sailors had not only drunk to excess, but to keep their feet from freezing, had filled their boots with rum, and they were the first to yield to dispair."[53] On the *Peggy* (1765) the crew broke open the supply of liquor and remained intoxicated until the time of their rescue. "What gave me concern was, the continual excess to which they drank—and the continued course of execration and blasphemy, which was occasioned by that excess."[54] The fact they broke into the cargo of wine and brandy did not upset the captain as much as the amount they drank, and the problems that arose from handling intoxicated sailors.

Of course, the *Peggy*'s captain claimed that he never imbibed. He continued his censure of alcohol throughout the narrative, and his fears proved well-founded. He added: "The next day my inconsiderate mate, Mr. Archibald Nicolson, who had so long wallowed, as I may say, in every mire of excess, having reduced himself, by a continued intoxication, to such a state, that no proper sustenance would stay on his stomach, fell a martyr to his inebriety."[55] Such statements demonstrated that moderate behavior increased chances for survival, and those who failed often died. Indeed, since the captain of the *Peggy* persevered, it was his reward to the write the story and to portray his first mate in such a light.[56]

Despite this overwhelming message of self-control, some sailors looked to self-preservation. For example, the survivors aboard the *General Arnold* had little regard for the safety of others; rather, "there was such a crowd upon the quarter deck we could not stand up without treading upon one another." As the author of this narrative explained: "Being in a struggle I was thrown down and trampled upon as if the breath would be crouded out of my body: However, I soon recovered my feet and trampled upon others in my turn; for the immediate regard which every man had to his own life prevented him from attending to the distress of others." In this melee the captain slipped on the deck and died. It was every man for himself with no sense of order. The officers lost control and most perished before the light of day.[57] For some mariners, the survival instinct won out and social expectations failed in the face of disaster. The narratives taught that when these norms no longer remained, survival expectations diminished.

In another instance, the *St. George* caught on fire while anchored at Spithead (1640s). According to Edward Coxere, "everyone shift[ed] for themselves; the captain was then no more regarded than the cook."[58] In situations of fire and potential cataclysmic destruction, a temporary leveling occurred. The narratives promoted an ideal that kept men in line and preserved the public good over the private.[59] Such reactions agreed with Paul Gilje's argument that sailors looked to the short term first and only secondarily thought beyond immediate gratification.[60]

Margarette Lincoln wrote that shipwreck "taught that the best chance of safety is secured by prompt obedience to captain's orders and attention to duty in moments of crisis."[61] Conservative by nature, the accounts revealed a sense of social order that readers and participants both recognized as necessary. Despite the language of egalitarianism and independence, whether a part of God's design, or from natural order, respect for rank and place remained important in Anglo-American culture.[62] The narratives detailed the importance of knowing one's place in society. However, sailors did question the master and subverted hierarchy, though such measures rarely approached mutiny or taking over the ship.[63]

In shipwreck, captains and crew needed one another to stay alive. Although someone with navigation skills proved necessary, especially when in an open boat, this knowledge did not always translate into survival.[64] Captains required sailors to man longboats, cut down trees, or perform necessary manual labor.[65] Good captains learned to balance authority with understanding.[66] Especially on ships where differences in social standing might not differ widely between officers and crew, authority depended on malleable features of respect and experience. Sailors constantly renegotiated a flexible chain of command.[67] The captain and crew had to strike a balance that regarded personal rights and necessary order.

Shipwreck narratives were essentially conservative, insisting that obedience, sobriety, and self-control were necessary for survival. Common sailors protected their own interests, which, however, centered on saving their lives. As long as the captain appeared to pursue a like end, sailors followed him. If not, they gave little thought to taking matters into their own hands. Social order was not always solid; yet, according to the narratives, class and power relationships did persevere in the face of the sea's ultimate challenge. And, once safe old hierarchies fell into place, social order again ruled the waves.

# NOTES

[1] See Amy Mitchell-Cook, "When God, the Devil, and a Friendly Cannibal Met at Sea" (PhD. Diss., Pennsylvania State University, 2004).

[2] David D. Hall, *Worlds of Wonder, Days of Judgment: Popular Religious Belief in Early New England* (Cambridge, Mass.: Harvard University Press, 1990), 81; Philip F. Gura, "The Literature of Colonial English Puritanism," in *Teaching the Literatures of Early America*, ed. Carla Mulford (New York: Modern Language Association of America, 1999), 145.

[3] The frontispiece for the 1700 edition states: "Printed in Philadelphia, re-printed in London, and sold by T. Sowle, in White-Hart-Court in Gracious-Street, 1700." John Carter Brown Library, Brown University, Providence, Rhode Island.

[4] Keith Huntress, *Checklist of Narratives of Shipwrecks and Disasters at Sea to 1860* (Ames: Iowa State University Press, 1979), 107.

[5] Archibald Duncan, *The Mariner's Chronicle* (London: J. & J. Cundee, Ivy-Lane, Paternoster Row, 1804-1808). Huntress suggested Duncan's compilation "was probably the most popular source for other compilers of later years," and that American authors "probably stole material from this set," Huntress, *Checklist*, 47-48.

[6] See Huntress, *Checklist*, for a more complete listing.

[7] Captivity narratives were some of the most popular literature in the seventeenth and eightcenth centuries, James Hartman, *Providence Tales and the Birth of American Literature* (Baltimore: Johns Hopkins University Press, 1999), 16.

[8] Richard Bushman, *The Refinement of America: Persons, Houses, Cities* (New York: Vintage Books, 1993), 38-39.

[9] Daniel Vickers and Vince Walsh, "Young Men and the Sea: The Sociology of Seafaring in Eighteenth-Century Salem, Massachusetts," *Social History* 24 (1999): 17-38, esp. 17-18. Historians such as Frederick Wallace and Samuel Eliot Morison found harsh class relationships, while Nicholas Rule argued they never existed. In the 1960s, Jesse Lemisch and Ralph Davis viewed authority on ships as a social construction.

[10] Kenneth Andrews, *Ships, Money and Politics: Seafaring and Naval Enterprise in the Reign of Charles I* (Cambridge: Cambridge University Press, 1991), 71; Paul A. Gilje, *Liberty on the Waterfront: American Maritime Culture in the Age of Revolution* (Philadelphia: University of Pennsylvania Press, 2004), 70-71.

11 Gary Nash, *Urban Crucible: Social Change, Political Consciousness, and the Origins of the American Revolution* (Cambridge, Mass.: Harvard University Press, 1979), 10-11; many of the "merchant princes" had ties to maritime endeavors, coming into contact with sea captains who traveled in the same circles, Samuel Eliot Morison, *The Maritime History of Massachusetts* 1783 to 1860 (1921; Boston: Houghton Mifflin, 1961), 122.

12 Allan Kulikoff, "The Progress of Inequality," in *New American Nation, Volume 11, American Society 1776-1812*, ed. Peter Onuf (New York: Garland Press, 1991), 385-86; Sean Wilentz, *Chants Democratic: New York City and the Rise of the American Working Class, 1788-1850* (New York: Oxford University Press, 1984), 27. Once they became rich enough, society accepted owners and captains in the highest circles, John Williams McElroy, "Seafaring in Seventeenth-Century New England," *New England Quarterly* 8 (1935): 364.

13 Edward Ward, *Wooden-World Dissected, in the Characters of a Ship of War* . . . (London: H. Meere, 1708), 6-8. However, when the captain's wife is around, he "truly fears her more than a storm but he makes no tiresome stay with her; for after the honeymoon is over, he pretends pressing order from the board," 10.

14 Richard Henry Dana Jr., *The Seaman's Friend: Containing a Treatise on Practical Seamanship* (Boston: Thomas Groom and Co., 1851), 133-36, 183.

15 Alfred Conkling, *Jurisdiction, Law, and Practice of the Courts of the United States in Admiralty and Maritime Cases*, vol. 1 (Albany: W. C. Little and Company, 1848), 314-15. In addition, seamen were not "bound to obey any unlawful command," 318. When the fear of desertion ran high, so was the threat of discipline. Christopher Lloyd, *The British Seaman, 1260-1860* (Cranbury, NJ: Associated University Presses, 1970), 87.

16 Marcus Rediker, *Between the Devil and the Deep Blue Sea* (Cambridge: Cambridge University Press, 1987), 212, 217, 222; threats, brutality and terror were longstanding means of keeping lower classes in order, Marcus Rediker and Peter Linebaugh, *Many-Headed Hydra: The Hidden History of the Revolutionary Atlantic*, (Boston: Beacon Press, 2000), 50-51.

17 Dr. Moses Adams to Moses Adams, May 1, 1817, cited in, Alan Rogers, "A Sailor by Necessity: The Life of Moses Adams, 1803-1837," *Journal of the Early Republic* 11 (1991): 29-30.

18 Rediker, *Between the Devil and the Deep Blue Sea*, 95-97; Andrews, *Ships, Money and Politics*, 74; Rediker, "A Motley Crew of Rebels: Sailors, Slaves, and the Coming of the American Revolution," in *The Transforming Hand of Revolution: Reconsidering the American Revolution as a Social Movement*, eds. Ronald Hoffman and Peter J. Albert (Charlottesville: University Press of Virginia, 1995), 158.

[19] R. Reynell Bellamy, ed., *Ramblin' Jack: The Journal of Captain John Cremer (1700-1774)* (London: Jonathan Cape Ltd., 1936), 225. Obviously, this was before he made captain. At the end of a voyage he was paid and "set free" to wander till out of money and then had to find another berth.

[20] See Rediker, *Between the Devil and the Deep Blue Sea*, 134, 138. See Gilje, *Liberty on the Waterfront*, for a discussion of sailors' abilities to assert their liberty.

[21] Rediker, *Between the Devil and the Deep Blue Sea*, 104-105; Rediker, "Motley Crew," 183.

[22] Olaudah Equiano, *The Life of Olaudah Equiano or Gustavus Vassa, the African* (1789; New York: New University Press, 1969), 177, 180. He later added that everyone was so grateful for his exertions that he was "a kind of chieftan amongst them."

[23] Letter transcribed for Mr. Brooks from the Log of the *Boston*, by Capt. Mckay's daughter, 1897, microfilm at Peabody Essex Museum, Salem, MA. According to Mckay's daughter, the passengers and crew presented Mckay with a silver pitcher embossed: "To Captain H. C. Mackay from his friends the passengers of the ship *Boston* on her first passage May 1828." "Loss of the *Boston*," in Thomas, *Interesting and Authentic Narratives*, 322-23. For his efforts, captain Mackay received a check for $500 and a gold watch from Admiral Isaac Coffin, a passenger aboard the Boston. Also, see Rediker's *Between the Devil and the Deep Blue Sea* for a labor analysis of the maritime world.

[24] James Riley, *An Authentic Narrative of the loss of the American Brig Commerce, wrecked on the Western Coast of Africa, in the Month of August, 1815* (New York: author, 1818), 27-28.

[25] C. F. Swift, *Genealogical Notes of Barnstable Families* (Barnstable, Mass.: F.B. & F.P. Goss, 1888-90), 352-54. Of the 105 who sailed from Boston, only 33 lived and of those only 16 recovered due to the bitter cold and ice. Barnabas Downs, *A Brief and Remarkable Narrative of the Life and Extreme Sufferings of Barnabas Downs. . .* (Boston: E. Russel, 1786).

[26] David Woodward, *Narrative of Captain David Woodward and Four Seamen, Who Lost Their Ship While in a Boat at Sea*, ed. David Vaughn (London: S. Hamilton, 1804), xxiii.

[27] *Narrative of Captain David Woodard*, 234, from a two-volume piece printed for J. Sewall, Cornwall.

[28] Judah Paddock, *Narrative of the Shipwreck of the Oswego on the Coast of South Barbary* (New York: J. Seymour, 1818). After much arguing, the crew, afraid the ship would sink during the night, insisted on going ashore.

²⁹ Ibid.

³⁰ Loss of the *Tyrrel*, Thomas, *Authentic and Interesting Narratives*, 132.

³¹ Loss of the *Betsy*, Thomas, *Authentic and Interesting Narratives*, 124.

³² Sir John Barrow, *The Mutiny and Piratical Seizure of HMS Bounty* (1831; Oxford University Press, 1928), 124. Bligh brought the carpenter to court upon their arrival in England, he was found guilty in some of the charges, and reprimanded. He was said to be in a mad-house at the time of publishing, 142. According to Greg Dening, Bligh was sensitive to any possibility of a person subverting his authority. That to question "any order was a sign of their relationship to him [Bligh], challenging his authority and changing the landscape of power on his quarterdeck," Dening, *Mr. Bligh's Bad Language: Passion, Power and Theatre on the Bounty* (Cambridge: Cambridge University Press, 1992), 60-61.

³³ Burning of the *Kent*, Thomas, *Authentic and Interesting Narratives*, 318.

³⁴ Ibid.

³⁵ Loss of the *Halsewell*, Thomas, *Authentic and Interesting Narratives*, 197.

³⁶ Loss of the *Margaret*, Thomas, *Authentic and Interesting Narratives*, 310.

³⁷ Loss of the Ship *Phoenix*, Thomas, *Authentic and Interesting Narratives*, 166. The proper English gentleman provided a good heroic example for male readers. Though the vessel was part of the British Royal Navy it is included because the story became appropriated by American authors and included in many collections.

³⁸ Burning of the *Kent*, Thomas, *Authentic and Interesting Narratives*, 320.

³⁹ Toby Ditz, "Shipwrecked; or Masculinity Imperiled: Mercantile Representations of Failure and the Gendered Self in Eighteenth-Century Philadelphia," *Journal of American History* 81 (1994): 53.

⁴⁰ Rediker, *Between the Devil and the Deep Blue Sea*, 298. See also Gilje's *Liberty on the Waterfront* for a discussion of sailors' liberty and rights.

⁴¹ The narrative failed to relate what happened to the ship, whether it stayed together or not. Paddock, *Narrative of the Shipwreck of the Oswego*, 30. On the *Mentor*, the captain wanted to abandon ship while the crew insisted on staying with the ship, *Narrative of the Mentor*, 22.

[42] According to his account, "the sea rose so high, and broke so terribly, they were frighted and confounded, and stared like Men amaz'd without obeying my orders." They made it back to shore only by the captain's quick thinking, and "When the seamen were got Safety, they swore the most bitter oaths, that they would not go to sea in the Canow anymore," Nathaniel Uring, *Voyages and Travels of Captain Nathaniel Uring*, ed. Alfred Dewar (1726; London: Cassell & Company, 1926), 130-31.

[43] Ward, *Wooden-World Dissected*, 96-98.

[44] Henry Gaynham, *From the Lower Deck: The Old Navy, 1780-1840* (Barre, Mass.: Barre Publishers, 1970), 116. For the opposite interpretation, look at E. Keble Chatterton's *Brotherhood of the Sea* (New York: Longman, Greene and Co., 1927).

[45] Rainer Baehre, ed., *Outrageous Seas: Shipwreck and Survival in the Waters off Newfoundland, 1583-1893* (Montreal: Carlton University Press, 1999), 30, 34.

[46] Gilje, *Liberty on the Waterfront*, 6, 92.

[47] Swift, *Genealogical Notes of Barnstable Families*, 353. The drunken sailors had earlier caused a "disturbances" but Downs provided specific details regarding the incident. It was these men who poured rum in their boots. See also, Downs, *A Brief and Remarkable Narrative*.

[48] Which was the case, and they were not rescued, except by accident the next day, Joseph Bailey, *God's Wonders in the Great Deep: or a Narrative of the Shipwreck of the Brigantine, Alida and Catherine, Joseph Bailey, Master, on the 27th of December, 1749, Bound from New York to Antigua* (New York: James Parker, 1750) 20.

[49] Carroll Smith-Rosenberg, in Linda Kerber, et al., "Forum: Beyond Roles, Beyond Spheres; Thinking About Gender in the Early Republic," *William and Mary Quarterly* 3rd Ser., 64 (1989): 573; cited in Mark E. Kann, *Republic of Men: the American Founders, Gendered Language, and Patriarchal Politics* (New York: New York University Press, 1998), 17.

[50] Anthony Fletcher, *Gender, Sex and Subordination in England, 1500-1800* (New Haven: Yale University Press, 1995), 323-25; Creighton, "Davy Jones' Locker Room: Gender and the American Whaleman, 1830-1870," in Margaret Creighton and Lisa Norling, eds., *Iron Men, Wooden Women: Gender and Seafaring in the Atlantic World 1700-1920*, (Baltimore: Johns Hopkins University Press, 1996), 126-27; Elizabeth Foyster, *Manhood in Early Modern England: Honor, Sex, and Marriage* (New York: Addison Wesley Longman, 1999), 212.

[51] Joyce Appleby, M. Jacob and J. Jacob, "Introduction," in Margaret Jacob and James Jacob, eds. *Origins of Anglo-American Radicalism* (London: Allen & Unwin, 1984), 7;

Ken Plummer, *Telling Sexual Stories: Power, Change and Social Worlds* (London: Routledge, 1995), 176.

[52] Foyster, *Manhood in Early Modern England*, 40-41; Philip Carter, *Men and the Emergence of Polite Society, 1660-1800* (Harlow, England: Pearson Education, 2001), 64-65. Rediker, *Between the Devil and the Deep Blue Sea*, 196. As Rediker pointed out, drinking may have acted as an opiate against the everyday harshness at sea.

[53] Swift, *Genealogical Notes of Barnstable Families*, 353.

[54] David Harrison, *The Melancholy Narrative of the Distressful Voyage and Miraculous Deliverance of Captain David Harrison, of the Sloop Peggy, of New York, on his Voyage from Fyal, one of the Western Islands, to New-York* (London: James Harrison, 1766), 10; in the *Providence Gazette* this scene was described thus: "During all this time the poor wretches were drunk, and a sense of their condition seemed to evaporate in execration and blasphemy. While they were continually heating wine in the steerage, the Captain subsisted upon the dirty water at the bottom of the case . . . with a few drops of Turlington's Balsam," *Providence Gazette*, September 20, 1766, taken from the *London Magazine* for June 1766.

[55] Harrison, *Melancholy Narrative of the Peggy*, 44.

[56] Kann, *A Republic of Men*, 113; Robert Shoemaker, "Reforming Male Manners: Public Insult and the Decline of Violence in London, 1660-1740," in Tim Hitchcock and Michèle Cohen, eds. *English Masculinities, 1600-1800* (London: Longman Press, 1999), 139.

[57] Swift, *Genealogical Notes*, 353; Downs, *A Brief and Remarkable Narrative*, 10-11.

[58] E. Meyerstein, ed., *Adventures by Sea of Edward Coxere; A Relation of the Several Adventures by Sea with the Danger, Difficulties and Hardships met for Several Years* (New York: Oxford University Press, 1946), 7-8.

[59] Kann, *A Republic of Men*, 31.

[60] Gilje, *Liberty on the Waterfront*, 129.

[61] Margarette Lincoln, "Shipwreck Narratives of the Eighteenth and Nineteenth Century: Indicators of Culture and Identity," *British Journal for Eighteenth Century Studies* 20 (1997): 160.

[62] Bushman, *Refinement of America*, 39.

[63] Jane Kamensky, "Talk Like a Man: Speech, Power, and Masculinity in Early New England," in Laura McCall and Donald Yacovone, eds., *A Shared Experience: Men, Women, and the History of Gender* (New York: New York University Press, 1998), 34.

[64] Edmund Fuller, *Mutiny! Being Accounts of Insurrections, Famous and Infamous, on Land and Sea, From the Days of Caesar to Modern Times* (New York: Crown Publishers, 1953), xi.

[65] Allen A. Arnold, "All Hands Drunk and Rioting: Disobedience in the Old Merchant Marine," in Timothy J. Runyon, ed., *Ships, Seafaring, and Society: Essays in Maritime History* (Detroit: Wayne State University Press, 1987), 234.

[66] Christopher McKee, "Fantasies of Mutiny and Murder: A Suggested Psycho-History of the Seamen of the United States Navy, 1798-1815," *Armed Forces and Society*, 4 (1978): 301; Andrews, *Ships, Money and Politics*, 71.

[67] Gilje, *Liberty on the Waterfront*, 83.

# IX

## DISCIPLINE BUT NOT PUNISH

Legality and Labor Control at Sea, 1790-1861

MATTHEW RAFFETY

"For liability purposes,
it is the sea that will
kill you."[1]

Captains and mates on American merchant vessels have always had an authority problem. In addition to often "saucy" and sometimes mutinous men, officers faced growing legislative and judicial limits on their authority from the creation of the federal judiciary to the beginning of the Civil War. As they found themselves increasingly proscribed in an expanding body of regulation and convention, officers responded by both arguing against outside legal encroachment on their authority, and by adapting their methods of labor control to conform to the letter of the law but the spirit of their sense of themselves as the source of all authority at sea. At the same time, the judicial system sought to bring order and coherence to the application of the law at sea. What resulted was a dialogue between seafarers, their officers, and the court that shaped the rights of all on board, and represented an early incursion by the federal government into labor law.

This essay seeks to explore the discourse that shifted from the decks of American vessels, to the federal courts and back, which sought to bring coherence to the meanings of authority at sea. In practical terms, it examines primarily criminal cases heard in the federal district court in New York City, stemming from incidents on board American merchant vessels before the Civil War. Although New York provides the main focus, other cases from the Boston legal practice of Richard Henry Dana Jr., and reported cases from other federal jurisdictions, as well as the work of memoirists and legal and maritime guidebook writers, are examined.

Most authors concerned with discipline and labor control at sea have quite reasonably focused primarily on what occurred on the ships themselves. In particular, flogging and other forms of corporal punishment were topics of interest among nineteenth-century reformers and remain important to recent historians. Myra C. Glenn has explored the anti-corporal punishment movement of the antebellum period that sought to change both the methods and the meanings of shipboard punishment.[2] Glenn's excellent work examines the social pressure brought to bear on the law from reformers. My focus, however, lies in the way the law came to understand, operate, and force adjustment in both the legal conception and the practical application of punishment on American merchant vessels before the Civil War.

What happened on the decks of American merchant vessels before the Civil War was shaped by an expanding legal discourse that served to legitimate and proscribe the ability of officers to "correct" the men before the mast. Officers, the courts, and "outside" observers, ranging from guidebook writers to anti-corporal punishment reformers, worked to define the legal status of discipline at sea. In addition to articulating the legality or criminality of a given form of punishment, these writers, jurors, and the officers and seamen on American ships struggled with complex and competing conceptions of the very nature and source of shipboard officers' authority.

Although there was a great deal of overlap in techniques, conditions, and personnel between the naval and merchant maritime services, here I am primarily interested in the nonmilitary seafaring world. The law draws distinct lines where real world experience does not. Despite their great similarities, U.S. law came to treat naval and merchant services as two entirely distinct legal worlds. In the merchant marine, the early federal courts found themselves forced to adjudicate cases that spoke to the core issues of the meanings of citizenship and the delineation of rights for American seafarers.[3]

Beginning with little code and a contradictory mélange of colonial and English precedents, American jurists confronted the difficult task of bringing coherence to disputes on the water at the beginning of the federal period. For labor relationships ashore, the individual states adopted British common law, as interpreted by Blackstone, to bridge the legal gap between colonial status and independence.[4] Admiralty law, however, had long been a distinct set of rules and, though men at sea could still claim some protections under common-law dictates, independence left a substantial legal void in the governance and regulation of the sea. The Articles of Confederation granted, and the Constitution reasserted and clarified, that jurisdiction over all maritime issues rested with the new federal government. Thus, an entirely new national system of laws and procedures had to be developed to govern American vessels. Legislation regulating life, labor, and *punishment* at sea marked an important early attempt at the creation of a single, coherent national legal system.

Indeed, one of the justifications put forward for a new Constitution was that it would bring legal and jurisdictional coherence to interstate and international commerce, most of which went by sea.[5] Moreover, because of the haphazard manner in which the British had operated their colonial courts of vice-admiralty, at the dawn of the constitutional era, the newly created federal court system faced a confusing patchwork of conflicting and non-authoritative precedent.[6]

As the number of American vessels expanded after the War of 1812, the courts, and in particular those for the Southern District of New York, faced an explosion of civil and criminal cases arising from disciplinary disputes on the decks of merchant ships.[7] Incidents at sea prompted increasing attention from judges and justices sitting for the nation's main port cities and led to a rapidly expanding body of case law on questions of maritime discipline and the rights and responsibilities of ships' officers.

With New York's Southern District as the most important maritime court, the federal judicial system slowly developed a nuanced set of rules about how American ships were to be governed.[8] Although New York could hardly be described as a "typical" American port, the sheer number of ships and seafarers passing through it (and through its federal district court) make this court a focal site in the legal debates and developments over the meanings, legalities, and application of officers' authority at sea. In addition to the volume of cases brought before the S.D.N.Y., the intelligence of its District Judge, Samuel Betts, and the longevity of his tenure made him an important figure in guiding the development and application of maritime justice.[9]

Although the captain of a merchant vessel believed (and regularly reminded his crew) that he ruled the decks by the strength of his will and, when necessary, the sting of the lash, the law both reinforced and limited that authority. Despite the autonomy that officers claimed, they were subject to an ever-increasing set of rules, regulations, and interpretations that sought to define, how, when, and to what end they might correct the seamen under their authority. In two 1790 acts, Congress required the registration of ships, set the basic terms of governance on American vessels, and defined what constituted crime at sea.[10] Although the federal government regularly added to or amended this maritime law, two main pieces of legislation had a significant impact on labor and discipline at sea. An 1835 act further defined what constituted criminal behavior for both seamen and officers, and spurred the growth of cases in federal courts.[11] By creating the categories of "revolt," "confining the master," and "endeavor to make a revolt," it allowed for a form of shipboard rebellion that was less severe than the older capital crime of "mutiny." The act also afforded substantial new protections for seamen and defined several new crimes that changed the way officers conducted discipline. The act made explicit that officers could not commit "assault," "assault with a dangerous weapon," "murder," or "cruel and unusual punishment" against seamen without risk of prosecution. In addition to the limitations placed on officers by the 1835 act, growing public scrutiny on the conditions of sea life led to increasing pressure for officers to move away from corporal punishment into other disciplinary methods. In 1850, a new law pushed through by reformers banned flogging, the traditional mainstay of ship's discipline, and again forced changes in how officers handled the men in their charge.[12]

Physical force underlay discipline and social order at sea. Officers used force, whether explicit or threatened, to motivate and intimidate the crew into submission to their authority. Just as officers understood that the threat of violent mutiny lay just beneath any conflict with the crew, seamen understood that all officers, even those of the most gentle temperaments, backed up their authority with the right to resort to physical force when the situation demanded. However, from the beginning of the constitutional era (and, indeed, even before), legal restraints governed how and when ships' officers could punish.

The use of force in labor control at sea was further complicated because each rank of officer had specific rights and responsibilities in both law and customary practice. The legality and acceptability of force differed depending on an officer's rank. While the captain bore absolute legal responsibility for all punishment on board, the lesser officers frequently handled the actual application of punishment. The lash in the hands of the ship's master meant something different than it did in the hands of a second mate, and a casual angry blow from the mate might have varying repercussions, whether among the men or in court, than a similar strike from the captain.

Violence was central to forming and maintaining the structure of life at sea. Regular seamen policed their own forecastle society with physical force and in dramatic cases, resorted to violence (or the threat of it) to stay the hand of excessive or brutal officers. Like the men's, the officers' actions ranged from subtle to brutal and from legal to illegal. Unlike the men, however, officers enjoyed, in both the letter and the application of the law, substantial leeway in how and when they might resort to force. Presiding over the District Court for South Carolina in the early years of the nineteenth century, Judge Thomas Bee borrowed from English jurist Sir James Marriott to explain the proper role of violence at sea. Mariott believed that "the preservation of ships and lives depends often upon some act of severe, but necessary, discipline." Without physical coercion "no commerce, no navigation, no defense of the kingdom can be maintained." Since sailors were "the most ferocious," men working "upon an ungovernable element," a captain was "placed every moment in danger of the loss of character and life." In short, "a ship is a little government, compressed into a narrow compass, in which there can be no hope of security for any man on board without a rapid and strong exertion of absolute power placed in one man."[13]

Bee and other American jurists agreed with Marriott. Maritime labor was legally distinct from land-based labor because it possessed a different ancestry from the "laws of master and servant" on land.[14] Additionally, after 1789, federal jurisdiction over the seas meant a different legal structure handled maritime issues.

If Bee can be taken as at all representative of jurists of his period with respect to maritime labor, then, as late as 1800, officers found in the courts a strong advocate for an expansive view of their authority in the courts. However, beginning after 1800 and increasingly after the 1835 law, both jurists and Congress backed away from this earlier, more expansive view, much to the chagrin of officers.

Officers adapted the way they approached discipline and control in order to stay within the new rules presented by Congress and interpreted by the federal courts. The constructive dialogue between the practice of discipline at sea and the law that interpreted that practice determined how, when, and why officers used force against seamen. Though force remained the bedrock of shipboard authority in the years before the Civil War, officers had to grow more mindful of the law, and they adjusted their approach, developing an increasingly nuanced, careful, and subtle approach to securing the necessary control over seamen. Officers moved from direct forms of punishment, like the lash, to more indirect (though hardly more pleasant) forms of punishment including harsh, dangerous, and taxing work assignments and deprivation of food or rest. Additionally, officers opted to rely on financial punishments (such as withholding the wages of upstart seamen) when possible, to avoid the legal hazards associated with physical discipline.

[187]

Between 1790 and 1861, officers found increasing resistance to their use of corporal punishment and other means of physical force in their attempts to govern the crew. From the earliest federal statutes on the subject, Congress showed a desire to limit and regulate the behavior of officers on American vessels for the protection of seamen. In the act of 1790 that first laid out the basics of ship governance and registration, Congress afforded some core protections to seamen and described criminal penalties for both hands and officers who went beyond their legal authority. Even Judge Bee himself warned, in a decision from 1790, that "the act of congress for the regulation of merchant seamen must be strictly followed, it being penal."[15] The legislature sought to clarify the rules for ships in 1803, further curtailing officers' authority.[16] In 1835, a substantial revision of these statutes was necessary to try to bring greater order to a shipping industry that was rapidly expanding, as well as to the growing list of cases from ships federal courts had to hear. Though this new law held additional restrictions for both seamen and their officers, it was the officers who found their range of action most reduced.

In 1850, after a sustained campaign by reformers, a new act criminalized flogging, the traditional linchpin of a captain's power at sea for both commercial and military vessels.[17] Although flogging was outlawed, the courts were quick to note that the proscription barred only flogging and left other forms of corporal punishment intact. Supreme Court Justice Benjamin Curtis noted: "The [1850] law does not abolish all corporal punishment. It is plainly restricted to one particular mode of inflicting corporal punishment."[18] In fact, no act wholly barred a ship's officers from using corporal punishment until 1915.[19] In his 1841 work *A Treatise on the Rights and Duties of Merchant Seamen*, attorney and guidebook author George Curits noted: "In our law it is well settled that moderate corporal punishment may be inflicted."[20] Curtis also warned his reader that while "no particular mode or instrument of punishment is prescribed by maritime law," considerable "latitude of discretion is here also confided to the master."[21]

The creation of new legal protections meant that seamen on merchant vessels came to enjoy broader rights at sea, and an expanding legal system where they might seek redress for shipboard outrages once they returned to shore. Nevertheless, the balance of authority continued to rest squarely with the officers, and the expanded theoretical rights created by Congress and the courts had little if any direct ameliorating affect on the conditions most faced at sea. Judges remained mindful that too much ex post facto interference from the courts could undercut the authority of captains and prove dangerous or even deadly at sea. Jurists were careful to insist that, for safety considerations alone, officers needed broad leeway to deal with miscreants before the mast.

From the beginning, the 1850 act had limited teeth. Though it outlawed the lash, it did not create or define any new behavior as criminal. Charges brought against officers who used the banned punishment still had to be formed under the 1835 act for "cruel and unusual punishment" and/or "assault with a deadly weapon."[22] However, with the most iconic and fearsome punishment forbidden, and no clear distinction as to what else might be considered legal corporal punishment and what could be constituted as an assault, officers found themselves increasingly unclear about how they could and could not punish the men in their charge.

Though their authority remained substantial, with each act the regulatory thicket surrounding officers expanded. As a result, a considerable literature developed to help both officers and seamen make sense of the tangle of rights and responsibilities at sea. In touting his *Merchant's and Shipmaster's Guide*, Frederic Sawyer noted that shipmasters, "more than any other class [of employer], have been made the subjects of special enactments. To very many of their acts and omissions, which, in themselves considered, are light and unimportant, very grave penalties have been affixed."[23] Moreover, as seamen became savvier about the law, and as a growing number of attorneys like Richard Henry Dana Jr. saw profit in representing seamen's claims, officers found their ability to enforce control circumscribed by the threat of legal action once the ship returned home.

Despite these legislative setbacks, the mounting resistance of seamen to corporal punishment, and the willingness of seamen to bring charges or a claim for damages against their officers once ashore, officers maintained broad powers at sea throughout the antebellum period. Officers stressed the need to have violent or even deadly force at their command as a way of keeping order among desperate and dangerous men. In his guide, *Sea Life*, William Sullivan, taking on the character of a "bad captain," explained: "some captains talk of treating sailors as though they are human beings and as though they were capable of being won by kindness and gentleness. I know better; the worse they are treated, the better they obey."[24] Though Sullivan described the attitude of a fictional master, he lamented that such ideas were all too common on the quarterdeck. Without a doubt, officers saw force as the single most important tool at their disposal to ensure the safety and efficiency of the vessel. Officers insisted that the only thing the undesirables before the mast would understand was the lash.

Just how much violent punishment officers doled out at sea, however, remains debatable. Most accounts, often modeled after Dana's narrative of his own youthful journey to the California coast, contain at least one story of the captain resorting to the lash, whether from brutality or necessity, and almost all describe menace (or worse) coming from the lesser officers. Herman Melville makes the brutality of the lash central in several of his nautical tales, including *Billy Budd, Benito Cereno,* and *White Jacket.*[25] Nevertheless, the men increasingly sought to block floggings, commenting frequently in court testimony that, at least in the merchant service, floggings were rare, and that masters who punished in this way were to be avoided.

In a deposition taken by Dana, one mate admitted that flogging, "is regarded" as a sign of "bad usage, and a bad ship."[26] The lash's primary value was not in its actual use (though many captains wore out their leather on the backs of the men), but rather as a fearsome last resort that remained always in the back of men's minds. Even captains who balked at brutality, or feared the effect a flogging would have on morale, relied to some measure on the security that the idea of the lash provided.

However, the lash was not the only form of physical punishment available to officers. With flogging on the wane on merchant ships, if not in the navy even before 1850, captains and other officers resorted to a variety of punishments to fill the void. A crewman who drew the ire of his officers still risked a number of strenuous punishments, including being placed in irons, confined below decks in cramped and dirty conditions, "bound up," or tied to the rigging, often suspended painfully. Seaman Brister Lewis described receiving such punishment on board the *J. U. Brookman* in 1859: "I was then suspended by my wrists with my toes just touching the deck. I was kept there about half an hour." Lewis was then transferred to the hold, where, resting on a "cargo of oats," he remained four days, manacled in a space that "would not permit me to sit up straight. I had to lie down most of the time." Lewis's captain, Charles Brookman, was found not guilty for his punishment of Lewis, who had bitten him in a scuffle before being bound up.[27]

Officers also punished seamen by withholding food or water. Although below certain limits such punishment was illegal, on many ships officers gave the men a choice much like that succinctly put to a seaman on board the *L. & W. Armstrong* in 1849. When one of the crew indicated that "he had a good mind to knock off duty & not do another hand's stroke aboard her. Capt told him as soon as he knocked off duty he would have to knock off eating."[28]

Finally, officers frequently turned "normal" shipboard tasks into punishments, extending the time men were to be on duty or forcing them to perform arduous and dangerous tasks that, nevertheless, could be construed as within the normal work of the ship. In 1858, Captain Ferdinand Crocker of the *Esther Francis* used work as punishment for seamen he saw as unmotivated. According to the complaint, Crocker "did maliciously force, oblige, and compel [seaman William Brown] to work continuously for an unreasonable time, to wit, the space of four consecutive hours," even though Brown had said he was ill and that later Crocker had "neglected to supply him with proper nourishment and medicine."[29]

The law presented confusing and often contradictory rules to both officers and seamen. Seamen had to follow officers' orders without question, but could be found liable if they participated under orders in some illegal activities.[30] Additionally, seamen could be charged with revolt or mutiny for disobeying even bizarre, dangerous, or counterproductive orders, leading to the saying in the forecastle, "obey orders, though you break owners,"[31] as well as to the occasional harrowing tale of a crew held hostage to a drunken or insane captain not unlike Melville's famous Ahab.[32]

The officers (and masters in particular) were liable under the law if they endangered the property of the ship and its cargo by being lax disciplinarians, but risked both civil and criminal prosecution if they went too far in disciplining the crew. Captains bore final responsibility for the outcome of a voyage, and their actions and inactions could be scrutinized for wrongdoing by the courts.[33]

Precisely because the line between acceptable and unacceptable punishment was both blurry and shifting, many argued that officers should have the benefit of the doubt in close cases. Judge Bee explained that the officers needed leeway in both the scope and method of inflicting punishment. "Moderate correction on board a ship is justifiable," insisted Bee, including the use of the fist, "but deadly weapons, such as a cutlass should only be used when a mutiny exists, or is threatened."[34] According to guidebook writer I. R. Butts, excessive punishment made a captain liable for both civil and criminal penalties, "but where punishment is merited, it must be clearly excessive to entitle the seaman to damages. It cannot be expected that masters can mete out with nice discrimination the exact amount of punishment which each case requires."[35]

Both judges and juries granted officers considerable latitude in prosecutions for abuse of seamen. Based on a survey of verdicts in federal courts in New

York from 1835 to 1861, officers were much less likely to be convicted of crimes against the men than the men were for crimes against their officers. In the Circuit Court for New York, which heard the most severe cases, in thirty-one cases brought against officers where the court recorded an outcome, the officer faced conviction only 16 percent of the time.[36] In the lower District Court, of twenty-seven cases with known officer defendants, the court records only three convictions. In contrast, seamen faced conviction at least 53 percent of the time in District Court.[37]

Though some attorneys defending officers from charges of abuse tried to claim that "the officers of the ship are clothed, not merely with a civil, but with a military power, over the seamen on board,"[38] the courts supported a more narrow definition of officers' power. Of course, distinctions between corrective and judicial punishment are impossible to make in any clear way, and most officers paid little attention to the distinction. Only when brought to court would an officer have to justify the punishment as corrective. In an 1849 case, Captain Simmons of the whaleship *St. Peter* was charged with abusing members of his crew because of a three-day interval between their alleged mutiny and his meting out of punishment with the lash. Though he was within his rights to use the lash, argued the U.S. Attorney, Captain Simmons had applied an illegal punishment by waiting so long to do so.[39]

Force was all the more complicated when used by officers precisely because it could be both legal and illegal, and the line between the two often blurred in the heat of the moment. Particularly in ordering men to perform punitive duties, or in the application of humiliating but not directly corporal punishments (such as shaving the head or stripping a man of warm clothes), officers found ways to let the weather or the ship perform the corporal punishment to insulate themselves from liability, and to enhance the sting of that punishment through the use of public shame.

Although punishments predicated on humiliation held legal advantages for officers in that they involved no direct person-to-person violence for the courts to reexamine and reinterpret later, they embraced crews and officers into what Greg Dening has described as "a dangerous kind of theatre."[40] By raising the emotional and symbolic stakes of punishment in their move to escape new legal encroachments through creative punishments, officers risked even greater disobedience and danger by overstepping what the men would tolerate. As officers lost some of their traditional methods of punishment to legal encroachment, they had to face crews resistant to new and unfamiliar punishments, and many officers found themselves in an untenable position, bound on the one side by federal law and on the other by the conventions of shipboard behaviors—the so-called "forecastle law" that set traditional limits on both men and officers.[41]

Of course, the end of the lash did not mean the end of brutal treatment of seamen, since many of these indirect punishments could be even more painful and dangerous than a flogging. In an 1854 civil proceeding in which Dana appeared for the defense, Captain Hotchkiss of the ship *Harvard* was accused of excessive punishment against a sixteen-year-old cabin boy, Stephen Whatley. Whatley, who took his first (and in all likelihood last) voyage on the *Harvard*, complained that Hotchkiss "kept him at the wheel much longer that the regular and accustomed time" and "that he kept him aloft much more than the necessities of the ship required." As a result Whatley was "uncomfortable & wretched on board" and "was frozen in hands and feet, and suffered greatly in his health, so that he is now disabled for duty, and he fears permanently injured in his health."[42]

Fearing either criminal or civil prosecution, officers like Hotchkiss sought to avoid legal problems by using tasks and duties that, though onerous, were indisputably a part of regular life at sea as a way to let work and weather do their punishing for them. Though, as in the case of poor Whatley, an officer could be held responsible for permanent injury or unjust cruelty from excessive duties and deprivations, these forms of punishment found increasing vogue as seamen became more litigious about punishment. Even when brought to trial, the ambiguity of such punishments made conviction difficult. Conviction became all the harder when the courts ruled that the punishment must be both cruel *and* unusual to fulfill the indictment.[43] Thus, use of the lash could be excessive and illegal as an "assault," but could never be considered an "unusual" punishment at sea.

The number of officers charged with "cruel and unusual punishment," which usually meant deprivation and/or overwork as opposed to "assault," suggests this trend.[44] In 1853 Justice Curtis noted that the 1835 statute protecting seamen from "cruel and unusual punishment" appeared "more frequently perhaps than any other criminal law . . . [in] the courts of the United States."[45] In one such case, Paul Oliver, master of the *Tybex*, was found guilty of cruel and unusual punishment after forcing seaman John Gaspar to strip down and go aloft in the rigging as punishment. Though Oliver furthered Gaspar's punishment with an old-fashioned beating (which lead to a conviction for assault), "passive" punishments like Gaspar's frigid trip aloft became more popular as the legal restraints on more straightforward corporal punishment became more complex.[46]

In contrast to developments in the merchant marine, naval officers maintained a claim to judicial authority. As was affirmed in the 1843 *Somers* case, a naval commander had the right to serve quite literally as judge, jury, and executioner. Although in the popular consciousness the *Somers* incident remained controversial, and became a rallying point for those who sought to reform the treatment of men at sea, the courts upheld a broad definition of naval officers' powers.

On merchant ships, in contrast, the federal courts increasingly ruled that captains had paternal but not judicial authority over the men. In other words, they had authority to "correct" the men, but not to exact justice or "punish" them for misdeeds.[47] An 1857 guide for shipmasters tried to parse these distinctions, explaining: "when the punishment is for past offences, the reference to them must be clear and distinct. This punishment, however, is not judicial, but parental in its character. It is not to vindicate the claims of justice, but to produce reformation in the offender, and to maintain discipline in the ship."[48] Thus, punishment had to be nearly immediate and related directly to the correction of a wrong and the reestablishment of discipline, proper respect, and subjugation. However, as reformers began to pressure captains to adopt more humane methods, captains were urged not to strike while tempers flared but wait for cooler passions of a later time. Paradoxically, an officer courted danger either way. If he acted immediately, it might be claimed he acted from the excesses of his passion; yet, if he delayed punishment, it could be ruled illegal because it failed to be corrective in nature. "As the law now stands, a parent may correct moderately his child, and the master his apprentice; and the case of the shipmaster has been placed upon the same principle," reflected Dana in his memoir; however, "if the punishment is excessive, or the cause not sufficient to justify it, he is answerable."[49] Precisely where the line stood between "moderate correction" and "excessive punishment" was a matter constantly before the courts for clarification and revision, and thus remained a thorny issue for officers while at sea.

Though the officers might use force—even deadly force—to quell a rebellion or threat to themselves, passengers, or the ship, as soon as the threat had passed, any such force would be criminal. Justice Curtis noted that the law made a "distinction between punishment and the use of force to compel obedience to a lawful order . . . In all such cases, the master, or other officer in command has the right to compel obedience by the use of necessary force. He also has the right, and it is his duty to interpose to quell all affrays between the officers and men, and especially all forcible resistance to his lawful commands."[50] In other words, no hard limits existed on the use of force by an officer who acted in defense of ship, self, or fellow officers. However, the officer "should use that degree of force in doing so, which the occasion renders apparently necessary."[51] Yet it was often difficult for officers (and, later for juries) to determine just when an action drifted from quelling insurrection to unjust punishment.

Captains insisted they needed a free hand to govern their ships as they saw fit. In a revolt case from 1842, the defense attorney, seeking to prove that excessive punishment had made his clients' resistance necessary, asked Captain Charles Stoddard if it seemed an appropriate punishment for sleeping while on watch to be ordered aloft to drain water caught in the main sail without assistance, a difficult and potentially dangerous task. Stoddard answered, summing up many captains' attitude, that "it depends very much upon the offence . . . different captains have different ways of punishment."[52] Captains used work, particularly dangerous or physically demanding work, as a way to punish men without running afoul of the law.

Though the lash—the ultimate form of legal physical force at a captain's disposal—undergirded all shipboard authority until (and, on some ships, even beyond) its outlawing in 1850, it was only the most extreme and perhaps most desperate way for a captain to assert his power.[53] For a captain to need to resort to the lash meant that his authority had already become dubious. Had the captain been the powerful figure he should have been, no man who was not drunk or deranged would have dared step so far out of line as to need such extreme physical chastisement. Thus, flogging undermined the captain's authority even as it served to assert it, for the very necessity of that reassertion belied his ability to command successfully. Additionally, because masters had been facing increasing resistance to the lash both on and off the decks, merchant captains began moving away from the lash even before 1850. In the naval service, which had always been freer with the lash, its abolition set off a near-disastrous disciplinary crisis throughout the fleet.[54]

As the ranks of attorneys like Dana and Alanson Nash (his closest Manhattan counterpart) focused on prosecuting brutal or cheapskate officers and owners on behalf of seamen grew, officers, and in particular captains, found themselves in a bind between a need to maintain order and increasing legal limits on their ability to do so. One guide lamented that "without authority in the master to enforce obedience by correction, the whole adventure may by abandoned to the mercy of the wind and waves."[55]

As a result, officers made decidedly different assertions about their intent and the extent of their authority from the quarterdeck than those they made before the bar. In court, officers carefully asserted that any violence was merely the result of "acting in his lawful capacity," as was the case with Captain John Farland of the *Leonidas* when he sought to restrain a belligerent seaman.[56] At sea, however, the officers expressed a far more expansive assessment of their powers. Faced with a disgruntled crew, Captain Lyon of the *Fairfield* inquired, hyperbolically, "Do you know that I am authorized to shoot all hands one by one?"[57] Though Captain Lyon overstated his authority from a legal perspective, his view was that of many a master.

Officers faced a growing array of forces limiting their authority in the wake of the 1835 law. In addition to the broader delineation of seamen's rights and officers' limits in both the text and later judicial interpretation of the law, growing public pressure in the wake of exposés of shipboard cruelty, like Dana's 1840 *Two Years Before the Mast*, meant that a concerted reform effort sought to educate seamen about their rights in order to curb officer excesses. Finally, shortages of able-bodied seamen in many busy ports meant seafarers had more leverage in their dealings with officers. Captains and mates feared the erosion of their power.

Officers chafed at the inroads made on their authority, arguing that the latitude needed to deal with the dangerous characters who sailed before the mast was now denied them. In some cases, officers complained that they were being charged for merely doing their duty, while seamen seemed to get away with violent and mutinous behavior. Captains explained that, because of shortages of able and skilled American seamen, they were forced to bring aboard an ever more violent and dangerous element to serve before the mast. At the same time, the outside influence undercut their ability to maintain proper discipline. John Proctor, master of the *Congress* in 1835, found himself convicted of assault and cruel and unusual punishment for an incident with a hand named Nicholas Demeter. Before sentencing, Proctor sent a petulant affidavit to the court, insisting that although "the Jury have imputed to him malice, hatred or revenge in the affray with said Demeter," he acted "solely with the desire and intention to enforce proper subordination of the ship." He went on to insist that he was as much a victim as Demeter, and that Demeter gave as good as he got in the altercations, save for the last time, "when Demeter was tied up."[58]

How could the ship be governed, argued captains like Proctor, if the officers could not resort to force to curb a belligerent hand like Demeter? The theme of an officer frustrated with the imposition of the law on his authority appears regularly in the testimony of cases wherein officers found themselves as defendants. In another case, a captain frustrated by the threats of both mutinous violence and legal assaults by his crew complained to them "that if they supposed a master of a ship would be hanged ashore for shooting pirates, he, for one, would as soon be hanged at San Francisco *for that* as murdered at sea by a bunch of rascally mutineers."[59]

U.S. District Court Judge Peleg Sprague of Massachusetts tried to describe when a merchant captain might and might not use deadly force. In his charge to the jury, he explained that "the master not only has the right, which every man has, of self-defense against impending danger, but it is also his right and his duty to defend his authority." However, "the law requires that he shall use only such force as is necessary to accomplish the end," and the jury's task was to ascertain whether the captain acted within these parameters. Sprague did warn jurors that, while "in the abstract" they could parse such subtle distinctions between necessary and excessive force, some latitude had to be given to captains to account for the confusing, dangerous, and decidedly unsubtle situation of a captain facing an unruly and possibly mutinous crew. To Sprague, the most important aspect was whether or not a mate "has knowingly violated his duty" and willfully stepped beyond what the situation warranted. The question is, whether there was an apparent necessity for the use of the weapon; whether the master might reasonably think so, acting in good faith, as well as could be reasonably expected given the circumstances. Sprague placed considerable responsibility on the shoulders of the master, explaining that the captain's "discretion and control" was to guide his behavior. In short, the difference between a legal correction and a criminal beating came down to whether or not the master acted in "good faith."[60]

Although Sprague himself did not make a direct comparison between the captain's responsibilities and that of a parent, he essentially argued that the master was legally required to be as a good father to his crew. Both legal and moral pundits made the comparison between ship's masters and fathers more explicit, and promoted an image of the ship's master as a benevolent but firm-handed patriarch for his crew. William Sullivan warned the captain to remind himself that "it is true that I am clothed with a high authority by the law, but that same law supposes, will be a friend and father to the family which it has entrusted to my care."[61]

"The trust given to a master of a ship is a much more serious one than is commonly supposed," explained William Sullivan in *Sea Life*.[62] The law identified the captain as the "master" of the vessel, and this mastery was expected to extend over everything on board. Captains often presented themselves as absolute rulers on the waves, and the law did indeed grant them sweeping powers. Sawyer explained how important the captain's control was to the safety and security of the voyage: "The necessities of the sea service have given to the ship master, when at sea, great authority over the officers and crew under his command. A prompt and cheerful obedience of orders, on the part of seamen, is of the utmost importance."[63] Even the most ardent reformers insisted that the captain needed tremendous powers to secure the safety of all on board. Sullivan, who wrote his guide at the behest (and expense) of the Reverend Edward Taylor of Boston's Mariner's Church, insisted that the captain needed broad powers in order for the ship to function properly.[64] Dana, in his *Seaman's Friend*, which was designed both to serve as a guide for seamen and as an advertisement for his Boston legal practice, insisted that "the shipmaster is a person in whom, by both the general maritime law of all commercial nations and by the special statutes of the United States, great powers are confided, and upon whom heavy responsibilities rest."[65]

All officers on antebellum American merchant vessels faced a maze of ever-increasing and ever-changing regulation as to how, when, and why they might punish the misdeeds of the tars before the mast. Pressure from men at sea and reformers on land led both Congress and the federal courts to tighten restrictions on officers as they sought to protect and make coherent the rights of seamen. Although it could hardly be argued that seamen found a steady friend in the legal system, even minor interferences in shipboard discipline meant that authority rested increasingly in the hands of land-based authority, at the expense of officers at sea. Even when the courts upheld officers' authority, the mere fact that an external body was called upon to legitimate their position weakened it.

Nevertheless, officers did not simply accept their diminishing authority. Instead, they sought to find new methods of labor control within the law, so that they could continue to control the ship as they saw fit. With the increasing threat of both civil and criminal prosecution for their actions after 1835, and the legislature removing the lash from their hands, officers were forced to become creative in the ways they could continue to get their "corrective" message through to recalcitrant tars. As a result—and despite the best efforts of the

Federal judiciary—the legality of force in labor control continued to be an open and contested legal issue until into the twentieth century. The discourse that began on the decks, was revisited in the courtrooms, reinterpreted in the work of Dana, Sullivan and other guidebook writers, and then re-deployed onto the decks of American ships developed into an active, vibrant, and often violent debate about the position of seafarers as men and as citizens, and marked an early attempt to delineate the rights and responsibilities of both labor (seafarers) and management (officers) at the federal level.

## Acknowledgements

This paper is an outgrowth of my doctoral project completed in 2003 under the supervision of Eric Foner at Columbia University. A number of scholars and friends have been kind enough to assist me at various stages of its creation, including Betsy Blackmar, Herbert Sloan, Robert McCaughey, Robert Ferguson, George Steckley, Pam Kelly, L. K. Neck, Joshua Waxman, Anne Polland, and Jennifer Fronc. Additionally, this paper would not have been possible without the assistance of the National Archives and Records Administration's New York branch, the American Antiquarian Society in Worcester, Massachusetts, and the support of Knox College in Galesburg, Illinois.

## NOTES

[1] Pirate Captain, "The Mansion Family," *The Simpsons*, Episode #1112 BABF08, original airdate: January 23, 2000.

[2] Myra C. Glenn, *Campaigns against Corporal Punishment: Prisoners, Sailors, Women, and Children in Antebellum America* (Albany: State University of New York Press, 1984); see also Glenn, "The Naval Reform Campaign against Flogging: A Case Study in Changing Attitudes Toward Corporal Punishment, 1830-1850." *American Quarterly*, 35 (1983): 408-25.

[3] The history of punishment in the American naval service during this period is the subject of James E. Valle's *Rocks and Shoals: Naval Discipline in the Age of Fighting Sail* (Annapolis: Naval Institute Press, 1980); see also Harold Langley, *Social Reform in the United States Navy, 1978-1862* (Urbana: University of Illinois Press, 1967).

[4] A considerable literature exists on the effect of Blackstone on the Revolutionary generation. For example, see Morton J. Horwitz, *The Transformation of American Law 1780-1860* (Cambridge, Mass.: Harvard University Press, 1977), 16; Beverly Zweiben, *How Blackstone Lost the Colonies, English Law, Colonial Lawyers, and the American Revolution* (New York: Garland, 1990); Shannon C. Stimson, *The American Revolution in the Law: Anglo-American Jurisprudence before John Marshall*, (London: Macmillian, 1990); Richard B. Morris, *Studies in the History of American Law*, (New York: Octagon, 1964), 11-13; and Akhil Reed Amar, "Jurisdictional Stripping and the Judiciary Act of 1789," in Maeva Marcus, ed. *Origins of the Federal Judiciary*, (New York: Oxford, 1992), 40-65.

[5] Alexander Hamilton, *Federalist* 80.

[6] Richard B. Morris, *Government and Labor in Early America* (New York: Harper, 1946), 225-61.

[7] Robert G. Albion, *Square Riggers on Schedule: The New York Sailing Packets to England, France, and the Cotton Ports* (Princeton: Princeton University Press, 1938), Appendix 1; Jeffrey B. Morris, *Federal Justice in the Second Circuit: A History of the United States Courts in New York, Connecticut & Vermont 1787 to 1987* (New York: Second Circuit Historical Committee, 1987), 51.

[8] The bulk of primary research for this paper comes from the records of the U.S Circuit and U.S. District Courts for the Southern District of New York (hereafter D.C.S.D.N.Y and C.C.S.D.N.Y.) The unreported cases are found in the collection of

the National Archives and Records Administration's New York City Branch, Record Group 21. Cases from the records of Richard Henry Dana Jr.'s Boston legal practice come from the Dana Manuscript Collection at the American Antiquarian Society in Worcester, Massachusetts. Other cases are identified by the reporter in which they appear. For more on the place of the U.S. Southern District of New York and its jurists, and in particular, Samuel Betts in the development of admiralty law, see Morris, *Federal Justice in the Second Circuit*, 63-65.

[9] Georgina Betts Wells, *Life and Career of Samuel Rossiter Betts* (New York: Maurice Sloog, 1934), 27, 35.

[10] *An Act for the Punishment of Certain Crimes against the United States*, 1st Cong., 2nd sess., ch, 9, April 30, 1790, §8-13; 16.; *An Act for the government and regulation of Seamen in the Merchant Service*, 1st Cong. 2nd sess., ch. 29, July 20, 1790, §1-2.

[11] *An Act in Amendment of the Acts for the punishment of offences against the United States*. 23rd Cong., 2nd sess., ch. 40, March 3, 1835.

[12] *An Act to provide for Recording the Conveyances of Vessels, and for Other Purposes*. 31st Cong., 1st sess., ch. 27, July 29, 1850.

[13] Cited in *Aertsen v. Ship Aurora and James Brady*, Dist Ct. S.C (1800), Bee, 161.

[14] Morris, *Government and Labor In Early America*, 227.

[15] *Ellenson et al. v. Ship Bellona*, Bee, 48.

[16] *An Act in Amendment of the Acts for the punishment of Offences against the United States*, 23rd Cong., 2nd sess., ch. 40, March 3, 1835.

[17] *An act making Appropriations for the Naval Service for the Year ending the thirtieth of June, one thousand eight hundred and fifty-one*, 31st Cong., 1st sess., ch 80, September 28, 1850.

[18] Charge to Grand Jury, Circuit Court, D. Rhode Island (November 15, 1853), 30 F. Cas. 981; 1853 U.S. App. LEXIS 583; 1 Curt. 590.

[19] *An Act to Promote the Welfare of American Seamen in the Merchant Marine of the United States; to Abolish Arrest and Imprisonment as a Penalty for Desertion and to Secure the Abrogation of Treaty Provisions in Relation thereto; and to Promote Safety at Sea*, 63rd Cong., 3d sess., ch. 153, March 4, 1915.

[20] George Ticknor Curtis, *A Treatise on the Rights and Duties of Merchant Seamen, According to the General Maritime Law, and the Statutes of the United States* (Boston: Charles Little and James Brown, 1841), 89.

[21] Ibid., 88.

[22] Ibid.

[23] Frederic Sawyer, *The Merchant's and Shipmaster's Guide, In Relation to Rights, Duties, and Liabilities* (Boston: Benjamin Loring & Co., 1840), v.

[24] William Sullivan, *Sea Life; or, What May or May Not Be Done by Ship-Owners, Ship-Masters, Mates and Seamen* (Boston: James B. Dow, 1837), 54

[25] Herman Melville, *White Jacket* (New York: 1850); "Benito Cereno," in *The Piazza Tales* (New York: 1856); and *Billy Budd, Sailor* (New York: 1924).

[26] Last v. Porter et al. (1847), Dana Case File #730, Box 1, Deposition of Charles James (2nd Mate), Dana Manuscript Collection, American Antiquarian Society, Worcester, Mass. (hereafter cited as AAS/Dana).

[27] U.S. v. Charles B. Brookman, C.C.S.D.N.Y. (1859), Criminal Case #1-195, Deposition of Brister Lewis.

[28] U.S. v. Justus Marshall, D.C.S.D.N.Y. (1849), Criminal Case #1-189, Deposition of James Jones.

[29] U.S. v. Ferdinand Crocker, C.C.S.D.N.Y. (1858), Criminal Case 1-147/8, Complaint.

[30] See, for example, U.S. v. Thomas Lewis, C.C.S.D.N.Y. (1806).

[31] Herman Melville, *Redburn, His First Voyage. . .* (New York: Harper, 1849), 74.

[32] Herman Melville, *Moby Dick; or, the Whale* (New York: 1851). For accounts of real-life Ahabs, see Margaret S. Creighton, *Dogwatch and Liberty Days: Seafaring Life in the Nineteenth Century* (Salem, Mass.: Peabody Essex Museum, 1982); 39; Joan Druett, *In the Wake of Madness: The Murderous Voyage of the Whaleship Sharon* (New York: Algonquin Books, 2003).

[33] Hunt v. Colburn et al. District Court, D. Massachusetts 1853 Case No. 6,886, U.S. Dist. LEXIS 40; 12 F. Cas. 905; 1 Sprague 215

[34] *John Jarvis v. Captain and Mate of the Ship Clairborne*, Dist Ct. S.C. (1808), Bee 248.

[35] I. R. Butts, *Laws of the Sea: The Seaman's Assistant: Coaster's and Fisherman's Guide, and Master's and Mate's Manual* (Boston: I. R. Butts, 1849), 56.

[36] Five of thirty-one convictions, fourteen acquittals, twelve *nolle prosequi*. These numbers may be skewed by the large number of cases where the defendant's rank is indeterminate. Of thirty-eight such cases, twenty-five resulted in conviction. If it may be assumed that a number of these cases were officers, 16 percent would seem low; however, for cases where the defendant can be identified as a regular seaman or cook, the jury convicted in twenty-seven of thirty-four cases.

[37] Again, the numbers for officers are likely to be artificially low. In fifty-one cases, mostly for an assault of one kind or another (the most frequent charge brought against officers) for which the status of the defendant(s) cannot be determined, the court recorded twenty-seven men convicted, many of whom were in all likelihood officers. Additionally, a large number of criminal cases against officers were brought concurrently with, and in support of, civil charges. Often, if the civil proceeding either settled or was decided favorably for the seaman, the criminal charges would be dropped.

[38] *U.S. v. Hunt*, C.C.D. Mass. (1841), Case No. 15,423, 25 F. Cas. 432; 1841 U.S. App. LEXIS 324; Additionally, in *Gifford v. Kollock*, a suit to recover wages from a whaling journey, Judge Ware noted that, while in earlier times officers' punishment in the merchant service may have had a military character, that usage had fallen out of practice by the time of the U.S. service. (*Gifford v. Kollock*, District Court, D. Massachusetts 1856, Case No. 5,409 U.S. Dist. LEXIS 111; 10 F. Cas. 341; 3 Ware 45; 19 Law Rep. 21.)

[39] U.S. v. Simmons (1849), Dana Case File #887, AAS/Dana.

[40] Greg Dening, *Mr. Bligh's Bad Language: Passion, Power and Theatre on the Bounty* (Cambridge: Cambridge University Press, 1992), 99.

[41] Eldridge S. Brooks, *The Story of the American Sailor in Active Service on Merchant Vessel and in Man-of-War* (Boston: D. Lothrop Co., 1888), 189-90.

[42] Whatley v. Hotchkiss (1854), Dana Case File #1365, folder 1, Box 9, Complaint, AAS/Dana.

[43] *U.S. v. Collins*, C.C. D. Rhode Island (1854); Case No. 14,836; 25 F. Cas. 545; 1845 US App. LEXIS 518; 2 Curt. 194.

[44] Cruel and Unusual Punishment was criminalized in 1835. The New York Federal Courts heard eight such cases before 1839, twenty-eight during the period 1840-1844, thirty, 1845-1849, forty-one, 1850-1854, and thirty-one, 1855-1861.

[45] Charge to Grand Jury, C.C., D. Rhode Island (November 15, 1853), 30 F. Cas. 981; 1853 U.S. App. LEXIS 583; 1 Curt. 590.

46 U.S. v. Paul Oliver C.C.S.D.N.Y., 1835.

47 Richard Henry Dana Jr., *The Seaman's Friend: Containing a Treatise on Practical Seamanship* (1841; Delmar: Scholars' Facsimiles, 1979), 193.

48 Joseph Blunt, *The Shipmaster's Assistant and Commercial Digest*, 9th ed. (New York: E. & G. W. Blunt, 1857), 14.

49 Richard Henry Dana Jr. , *Two Years Before the Mast: A Personal Narrative of Life at Sea* (New York: Harper & Brothers, 1840), 471.

50 Charge to Grand Jury, C.C., D. Rhode Island (November 15, 1853), 30 F. Cas. 981; 1853 U.S. App. LEXIS 583; 1 Curt. 590.

51 Ibid.

52 U.S. v. Henry Schriever and William Harding, C.C.S.D.N.Y. (1842), Deposition of Charles Stoddard.

53 Even after the 1850 law, floggings continued on ships governed by stubborn or ignorant masters. Whalers, in particular, sought to claim that the ships in the fisheries should be exempted because they were not "vessels of commerce," the terminology used in the 1850 act. Additionally, whalers insisted that flogging remained necessary because, paid in shares, whalemen could not be controlled with threats of lost wages on unsuccessful journeys, Charge to Grand Jury, C.C., D. Rhode Island (November 15, 1853), 30 F. Cas. 981; 1853 U.S. App. LEXIS 583; 1 Curt. 590. Whaleships had previously claimed (unsuccessfully) that, because they were "licensed" rather than "registered," the 1835 law did not apply to them, U.S. v. Charles Jenkins et al, C.C.S.D.N.Y. (1838), Draft of Special Verdict.

54 James E. Valle, *Rocks and Shoals: Naval Discipline in the Age of Fighting Sail* (Annapolis: Naval Insitute Press, 1980), 2.

55 Sawyer, *Merchant and Shipmaster's Guide*, 89-90.

56 U.S. v. Henry Sackett C.C.S.D.N.Y. (1831), Deposition of John Farland.

57 U.S. v. William Read et al., C.C.S.D.N.Y. (1840), Deposition of Robert Richards.

58 U.S. v. John Proctor, C.C.S.D.N.Y. (1835), Affidavit of John Proctor.

59 *The Spirit of the Times* 21, March 1, 1851, 20.

[60] U.S. v. Lunt (1855), Dana Case File #1510, Box 12, undated clipping from the *Boston Daily Advertiser*, AAS/Dana.

[61] Sullivan, *Sea Life*, 50.

[62] Sullivan, *Sea Life*, 47.

[63] Sawyer, *Merchant and Shipmaster's Guide*, 89-90.

[64] Sullivan, *Sea Life*, 47-56.

[65] Dana, *Seaman's Friend*, 131.

# CONTRIBUTORS

HESTER BLUM is Assistant Professor of English at the Pennsylvania State University; she received her Ph.D. from the University of Pennsylvania. In revised form, "Before and After the Mast: James Fenimore Cooper and the Production of the Sea Narrative" will appear in her forthcoming book *The View from the Masthead: Maritime Imagination and Antebellum American Sea Narratives*, University of North Carolina Press, 2008. She is currently editing William Ray's Barbary captivity narrative, *Horrors of Slavery*, for Rutgers University Press.

AMY TURNER BUSHNELL is a comparative colonialist with a special interest in frontiers. She received her Ph.D. from the University of Florida in 1978 and is the author of *The King's Coffer: Proprietors of the Spanish Florida Treasury, 1565-1702* (1981) and *Situado and Sabana: Spain's Support System for the Presidio and Mission Provinces of Florida* (1994). Retired from the College of Charleston, Professor Bushnell holds courtesy appointments at the John Carter Brown Library and the Department of History, Brown University. Her article in this collection is a revised version of "How to Fight a Pirate: Provincials, Royalists, and the Defense of Minor Ports During the Age of Buccaneers," which appeared in the *Gulf Coast Historical Review* 5 (Spring 1990): 18-35, and is reprinted here with the kind permission of the journal.

FRANCIS D. COGLIANO is Professor in American History at the University of Edinburgh. He received his Ph.D. from Boston University. The author of *Thomas Jefferson: Reputation and Legacy* (2006); *American Maritime Prisoners in the Revolutionary War* (2001); and *Revolutionary America, 1763-1815: A Political History* (2000), he is currently writing a book on American foreign policy during the early nineteenth century.

PAUL A. GILJE is Professor of History at the University of Oklahoma. He has published *The Road to Mobocracy: Popular Disorder in New York City* (1987); *Rioting in America* (1996); *Liberty on the Waterfront: American Maritime Culture in the Age of Revolution* (2004); *The Making of the American Republic* (2006) and edited or co-edited five other books.

DAN HICKS received his bachelor's degree from the College of William and Mary in 1996. In 2007 he completed his dissertation, "True Born Columbians: The Promises and Perils of National Identity for American Seafarers of the Early Republican Period" at the Pennsylvania State University.

MICHAEL JARVIS is Assistant Professor of History at the University of Rochester. He received his Ph.D. from the College of William and Mary in 1998. He is currently working on two books on the Atlantic World maritime connections of Bermuda in the 17th and 18th centuries.

AMY MITCHELL-COOK, a professional underwater archaeologist, received her Ph.D. from the Pennsylvania State University in 2004 for her dissertation, "When God, the Devil, and a Friendly Cannibal Met at Sea: A Study of Early American Shipwrecks." She is Assistant Professor of History at the University of West Florida.

WILLIAM PENCAK is Professor of History at the Pennsylvania State University. His latest book, *Jews and Gentiles in Early America: 1654-1800* (2005) was runner-up for the National Book Award in American Jewish History. He is working on a biography of William White, first bishop of the Episcopal diocese of Pennsylvania, and a collective study of the Jay family.

SARAH J. PURCELL teaches history at Grinnell College in Grinnell, Iowa. She is the author or co-author of four books, including *Sealed with Blood: War, Sacrifice, and Memory in Revolutionary America* (2002) and *The Early American Republic: An Eyewitness History* (2004). She is at work on a new project on "The Politics of Mourning and the U.S. Civil War."

MATTHEW TAYLOR RAFFETY is Assistant Professor of History at Gonzaga University in Spokane, Washington. He received his Ph.D. from Columbia University in 2003. His current book project, *The Republic Afloat: Labor, Manhood, and the Law at Sea, 1789-1861*, is forthcoming from the University of Chicago Press.

CRYSTAL WILLIAMS is Associate Professor of History at Kaplan University. Ms. Williams has BA and MA degrees in History from the University of Oklahoma. She is currently writing a Ph.D dissertation entitled "Saving the Tribe Zebulon: Religion and Sailors in Early America."

# INDEX

*Index*